Liam Houlihan is an award-winning News Ltd journalist, a former lawyer, and author. He has reported from New York (for the *New York Post*), done a brief stint in the White House press pool in Washington, DC, reported from Sri Lanka after the Boxing Day Tsunami, and has trailed Mick Gatto's pursuit of missing Opes Prime money in Singapore. He is also the author of *Badlands*.

BIGWIG

THE REMARKABLE RISE AND FALL OF **TONY MOKBEL**

LIAM HOULIHAN

HarperCollinsPublishers
www.harpercollins.com.au

HarperCollins*Publishers*
First published in Australia in 2012
by HarperCollins*Publishers* Australia Pty Limited
ABN 36 009 913 517
harpercollins.com.au

Copyright © Liam Houlihan 2012

The right of Liam Houlihan to be identified as the author of this work
has been asserted by him under the *Copyright Amendment (Moral Rights) Act 2000*.

This work is copyright. Apart from any use as permitted under the *Copyright Act 1968*, no part may be reproduced, copied, scanned, stored in a retrieval system, recorded, or transmitted, in any form or by any means, without the prior written permission of the publisher.

HarperCollins*Publishers*
Level 13, 201 Elizabeth Street, Sydney NSW 2000, Australia
Unit D, 63 Apollo Drive, Rosedale, Auckland 0632, New Zealand
A 53, Sector 57 Noida, UP, India
77–85 Fulham Palace Road, London, W6 8JB, United Kingdom
2 Bloor Street East, 20th floor, Toronto, Ontario M4W 1A8, Canada
10 East 53rd Street, New York NY 10022, USA

National Library of Australia cataloguing-in-publication entry:

Houlihan, Liam.
  Bigwig : the remarkable rise and fall of Tony Mokbel / Liam Houlihan.
  ISBN 978 0 7322 9002 3 (pbk.)
  Mokbel, Tony.
  Drug dealers – Australia – Biography.
363.45092

Cover design by Brendon Cook
Front cover photograph of Tony Mokbel by AFP/Getty Images
Back cover image by Getty Images
Typeset in Adobe Caslon by Kirby Jones

Tonymonials

'The Mokbels were the ringleaders. They didn't like to lose.'
— Team-mate, East Brunswick Magpies

'A fat fucking obnoxious little wog.'
— Brian 'the Skull' Murphy

'People say he's a gentleman in a suit and tie. Whether he's in a monkey suit he's still a pig. He came across as being arrogant, short and fat. A bald-headed fat arrogant person.'
— Wendy Peirce

'You can't help who you fall in love with ... I'd rather Tony out there somewhere than sitting in a cell.'
— Danielle McGuire

'You, as members of that squad in particular, see criminals such as Tony Mokbel living what could be described as the "high life", splashing out hundreds of thousands of dollars on gambling, restaurants, fast cars and a party lifestyle.'
— Judge Betty King

'A very, very excellent bloke, top bloke, one of the best blokes you could ever meet ... He's the best dad you could ask for, the best uncle, brother. You can't fault him.'
— Roberta Williams

'This one feeds others, he does not kill.'
— Tony's mum, Lora Mokbel

'We're not whistling Dixie here. Everyone else is dead.'
— Lawyer for scared and absent witness against Mokbel

'I'm a drug dealer not a killer.'

– Tony Mokbel

'Even when frigging Saddam Hussein got caught and everything, you put my brother before him [in the newspapers].'

– Kabalan Mokbel

'When you talk about Tony Mokbel, to me Tony Mokbel isn't just a person. Tony Mokbel is a group. He had a company running for him.'

– Detective Sergeant Jim Coghlan

'As a result of his business and property ventures Mr Mokbel is making a significant contribution to the community and employing a substantial number of people.'

– Kelvin Thomson, MP

'As we all know, he had people in every high-up place. It's mindboggling. He was a person who infiltrated so many dimensions of everything.'

– Judy Moran

'He used to be a friend of mine but he's no friend of mine anymore.'

– Mick Gatto

'I don't think he really, really looks at drug trafficking as if "I'm killing all these people, I'm going to stuff the health system". He just knows it's lucrative.'

– Former Head of Purana taskforce Detective Inspector Bernie Edwards

For Queenie.
For Filthy.
For hacks.

Contents

Author's note		*xi*
Gang and slang glossary		*xiii*
	Prologue	1
1	From Lebanon with love	3
2	Brunswick boy	12
3	Small business	17
4	Risky business	24
5	The fix is in	36
6	Off and racing	42
7	Big business	50
8	Boomtown rat	60
9	Mokbel's elephant	67
10	Cocaine	73
11	Bent	85
12	Dirty deeds	96
13	Nabbed	102
14	Snitches get stitches	109
15	Tony on the town	120
16	Fat Tony and the gangland war	138
17	Into thin air	162
18	The Company	169
19	Escape	176
20	Bruvvers	194
21	Greek unorthodox	208

22	Paradise and porridge	216
23	Manhunt	223
24	House wins	244
25	Homecoming	262
26	Bigwigs	270
27	Dead cat bounce	293
	Epilogue	316
	Acknowledgements	*319*

Author's note

In some instances ongoing court hearings, legal appeals and similar events have been crunched together to stop the reader dying of boredom. Similarly, time between chapters and within chapters jumps around a bit to keep thematically similar events together, but hopefully this is still flagged for those keen to follow the chronology. Where I felt I had to choose between forensic and potboiler I opted for potboiler.

On dates of birth and spelling of names, multiple variations on official documents have meant I have had to go with best guess. Based on Tony's age on Sajih's death certificate I have gone with the 1965 birth date, despite reports by his lawyer saying he turned sixteen on the day his father died, not fifteen (and other different birth dates given on Tony's company records). Names are spelt differently between Sajih's tombstone and his death certificate. Tony's mother's name is variously referred to as Lora, Lord, Laura and Lorde on documents. His dad is recorded in various places as Sagit, Sajih and even more distant variations.

Relatives saying Tony was born in Kuwait have been chosen over Tony putting Achache and Tripoli on company documents as his place of birth. The words 'amphetamines' and 'methamphetamines' are used interchangeably here although experts tell me there is very little if any of the former in Australia.

Other disclaimers: Please don't try anything contained herein at home. No animals were hurt during the writing of this book although James Campbell did try to eat three chickens.

Gang and slang glossary

back-dooring: having an affair with a person's partner behind that person's back

beak: judge

bent: corrupt

clams: money

coffeehousing: poker term for talking in an attempt to mislead other players about the strength of a hand

crispy: burnt

dead cat bounce: financial term for a slight recovery enjoyed by a plummeting stock during its continual demise

dockethead: known criminal with a long list of prior convictions or 'dockets'

dog: police informant/witness (particularly a criminal)

fizz: informant

fuzz: police

gopher: errand boy as in 'go for'

'hood: neighbourhood

ice: smokable methamphetamine

in boob: in jail

jacks: police

London to a brick: gambling parlance for absolute certainty; would bet London to win a brick

lumps: as in 'take your lumps' – to suffer or endure your bad fortune or punishment for actions

meth: methamphetamine (or methylamphetamine)

mouthpiece: lawyer

on the lam: on the run/at large

plastics: derogatory police term for the Australian Federal Police; shortened from plastic fantastics, also sometimes fantastic plastics

plebs: plebeians; low-level, unimportant operators; see *skrotes*

pseudo: pseudoephedrine

silk: senior barrister, such as Queen's counsel (QC), now senior counsel (SC)

skrotes: derogatory shortening of scrotum, similar to plebs

Soggies: Special Operations Group police

speed: amphetamine/methamphetamine

squarehead: non-criminal; straight person

staunch: reliable, trustworthy, won't sing to police

stooks: hidden places to store cash away from scrutiny

tinny: lucky

supergrass: special police informant

toe-cutters: police-speak for internal affairs bodies such as the Ethical Standards Department (ESD) who police police, based on brutal methods used by robbers who rob robbers

trannies: transsexuals/transvestites

walk and talk: method of discussing sensitive matters while avoiding fixed bugs

wifebeater: blue singlet

Prologue

It was an appropriately large homecoming for the Mr Big who had boasted before disappearing, 'I don't do small things.' The nation's most wanted man was very reluctantly being delivered back to the country he fled and on his own luxurious private jet funded by the public.

On the ground Australia's biggest drug criminal and one of the country's most senior lawmen came face to face.

The inspector discharged his legal duty and told the captured fugitive that while he was on the run a jury had found him guilty of drug offences. The inspector also detailed to the prisoner the crimes for which he was wanted and further offences now alleged against him.

It was a Saturday and the courts were closed. The inspector explained a bail justice would come out to the prison. The seriousness of the moment hung in the air as the two men – each respectively the personification of law and lawlessness – went through the motions. It was the formal procedure that could pave the way to a lifetime, and even death, in jail.

'Because of these offences and the fact you breached bail when you fled, you will not be granted bail,' the inspector said.

A thought registered on the prisoner's face. Then the man who had rocked and embarrassed the legal establishment broke into a broad, toothy grin. 'Won't stop me applying though,' he said.

When it was all over, when the last skerrick of his legendary luck had dried up, Tony Mokbel was still backing himself at long odds, still grinning, still believing he could take on the system and win.

1
From Lebanon with love

Throw a Lebanese to the sea and he will come out of it with a fish.

– Lebanese adage

Fawkner Cemetery in Melbourne's north is so large a train runs through its grounds. The fields of dead are so vast that visitors tend to drive around their mini-roundabouts and signposted streets rather than walking. It is mostly row after row of low-to-the-ground headstones poking out of green lawns.

When visitors reach the Roman Catholic vaults section the real estate becomes conspicuously high-rise. Mediterranean surnames have a near monopoly on the gilded, ornate vaults, making it a kind of posthumous Little Italy. Everywhere are Italian family names that, in the generations since arrival, have risen to prominence in food, hospitality, fashion, the law, and crime.

There among the tall headstones thrusting skyward and crowned with dozens of mini-Madonnas is a grave decorated with a cedar tree – the symbol of Lebanon. Under fresh flowers, laid for the anniversary of the occupant's death, a golden scrawl chipped into its stone spells 'Mokbel'. A pair of piercing tough black eyes peers out from a black-and-white photograph mounted behind glass. They belong to a man with a serious, even severe, look on his face. His head is round and balding and his moustache is small and pointy. The resemblance is strong enough that a passer-by might remark how similar the man staring out from the tombstone looks to the notorious criminal of the same name.

This decorated patch of ground marks a place one Mokbel story ended and another altogether different one began. It is where one man's journey across the planet to seek exile from entropy and chaos ended. And it is where his son's opposite journey, one that would take him back across the world as a pilgrim of disorder, was forged. This is where Sajih Mokbel came to rest, half a world away from where he started.

In a sleepy village in the top end of Lebanon not too far from Tripoli, the mayor is a Mokbel. The local Maronite priest is Father Mokbel and about a quarter of the 1200 villagers are Mokbels. In the house that belonged to Tony Mokbel's paternal grandfather and was boyhood home to his late father, Sajih, Mokbels still meet for meals.

While the name Mokbel conjures one particular type of image in Australia, in Lebanon it has multiple, altogether more pedestrian associations. The criminal adventures of 'Fat Tony' Mokbel have successfully monopolised the family name in his adopted country, but in his family's homeland, 'Aussie Antonios' is simply yet another of a multitude of Mokbels. The Mokbels were one of the founding families of the sunbaked rural community of Achache, but it was the Mokbels leaving Achache and the land of the cedars, not arriving, that launched the remarkable globetrotting criminal life of Tony Mokbel.

Half a century ago Sajih Mokbel, thirty-four, married Lora Naffaa in Lebanon. Children followed soon after. Lora gave birth to five children over six years during the 1960s. The first two were boys: Kabalan and then Horty. The pair played together and joined the boy scouts. But Sajih soon left his ancestral village and home nation, with Lora, to work as a truck driver in Kuwait. Kabalan and Horty remained in Lebanon and were reared by their grandparents.

'They had a normal life the same as any family,' said Tony's cousin Wajih Mokbel, who still lives in the village. 'When they went to work they left the children with their grandparents.'

The tubby little bundle of joy they named Antonios Sajih arrived in 1965 in the oppressive summer heat of the oil-rich desert nation of Kuwait. Antonios – who not long after he started talking would be calling himself Tony – was born in August. The Kuwaiti summer, which lasts from May to September, is extremely hot and dry with temperatures easily exceeding 45°C during the day, rising to around 52°C at midday. After Tony the only girl was born, Gawy, named after Sajih's mother, and finally another baby boy: Milad.

'Part of the time the children were with their parents in Kuwait, part of the time with grandparents in Achache,' Wajih Mokbel said, speaking through an interpreter. 'They used to go backwards and forwards because Kuwait is very close to Lebanon,' he said.

Wajih Mokbel said Tony and his siblings had an uncle who was a monk, an aunt who was a nun, another uncle who was a schoolteacher for forty-five years, and an uncle in charge of the fire brigade for the whole of northern Lebanon.

'The family were well known, well liked and well respected by everyone, and those kids were brought up in a very positive disciplinary environment. They weren't brought up with hooligans, I can assure you, and not as ratbags.'

By the early seventies sectarian tensions were threatening to tear Lebanon apart. The republic had maintained an uneasy power-sharing arrangement between Maronite Christians, Sunni Muslims and Shiite Muslims since gaining independence from France after World War II. The Palestinian Liberation Organisation (PLO), involved in an ongoing fight with Israel, had set up base in Lebanon and by the early seventies was launching military skirmishes across the border into northern Israel. The PLO had been driven out of Jordan and again it found itself unwanted by its host. The predominantly Christian Lebanese government sought to crack down on its activities on Lebanese soil (which were also unpopular among some groups of Lebanese Muslims). But the move simply prompted the PLO to open a second front in its military campaigning, the Palestinians forming an alliance with Lebanese Muslims in their fight with Lebanese Christians.

In the early seventies Sajih returned to his homeland from Kuwait with his family. He had earnt some money but the future in Lebanon did not bode well.

'They all went together. They all came to Lebanon and then they all left Lebanon together to go to Australia,' Wajih Mokbel said.

The Mokbels, Maronite Christians, flew halfway across the world, arriving Down Under in the mid-seventies. Sajih, listed on legal documents as a mechanic, got a job in Victoria with Ford.

The family would make a permanent home in Canberra Street in the inner-north Melbourne suburb of Brunswick. Tony was no older than ten and the oldest of his four siblings was just thirteen when they landed in their bizarrely different adopted nation.

By 1975 the Lebanese conflict had erupted into a full-blown civil war which raged for two years, killed thousands and reduced much of the country to rubble. Syria, Israel, Saudi Arabia and the UN would become involved before a fragile ceasefire succeeded over still-simmering tensions. The Mokbels' home village of Achache was devastated in the fighting. The local school, founded by Maronite monks, was reduced to cinders, and more than half of the villagers fled to start new lives abroad, many in Melbourne and Sydney.

Rolling waves of post-war migration from Europe had enlivened and changed the face of Melbourne and in particular its inner-north. The Mokbels arrived almost at the ebbing of a mass tide of Greek and Italian migrants. The paddocks at Tullamarine had opened as an airport just four years before the Mokbels arrived and the West Gate Bridge would not be completed until four years later. The 'New Australians' would pile out of ocean liners at Port Melbourne into brick homes predominantly in the city's inner-north.

The Mokbels were part of the Lebanese wave but got the jump on many of their countrymen who left as the civil war worsened. Ten thousand Lebanese arrived in Australia in 1976 and 17,000 five years later. Lebanese bakeries and sweets became increasingly common in the city's north and Lebanese-born residents went on to make up three per cent of the population of neighbouring inner-north suburbs Brunswick and Coburg by the early nineties.

Brunswick in the seventies was a flat, strange suburbia for the refugees from the mountainous republic. The northern suburbs had been mined voraciously for stone that had gone into countless buildings, including the imposing prison up the road. Once spent, the quarries had been filled in and turned into the area's parks and football ovals. The area's last blacksmith had just closed his doors and supermarkets were opening all over.

The Mokbels settled there at a time when Brunswick and the inner-north were rapidly changing. The city's work was becoming cleaner, more white-collar and less backbreaking. While the suburb's tough working-class roots were still not a relic of the past, a slow gentrification had begun, although it would be some time before Brunswick became a playground for bohemians, yuppies and artists, where a shoebox apartment could sell for a million dollars. Quarrymen and brickmakers had given way to a vibrant local textiles and manufacturing industry. Migrant women flocked to these jobs. And Lora Mokbel described herself on property documents as a machinist. But those industries too would slip into Brunswick's past in the decades after the seventies.

The 1970s Lebanese migrants had some teething problems. They had escaped a war-torn homeland but in their new nation unemployment was rising. To many of the new inhabitants, Brunswick's houses seemed ugly and its streets too quiet. Tony's mum, Lora, maintained the Lebanese custom of sitting out the front of the house watching the passing foot traffic. But there was less opportunity to call out to passers-by she knew. Despite a strong diaspora of Achache villagers in nearby Carlton, there was a serious cultural clash for Lora. She said she could not sleep from boredom in the new country.

Sajih was by all accounts a hard worker who earnt an honest living. No one I interviewed knew of him having any links to crime or any dealings with police. Others, like Achache mayor, Georges Mokbel, a distant cousin, described him as a giving man who would always try to help others: 'He had a bit of money when he went to Australia. He could have stayed here easily, but he wanted to make a better life over there,' he said.

The Mokbels set up a temporary home, renting in Third Avenue, Brunswick, but within a year had bought a house just minutes away in Canberra Street in the same suburb. It would remain the family home and centre of Mokbel operations, with Lora sitting out the front, for more than the next three decades.

The Mokbel children were sent to local northern suburbs state schools where they were neither academic superstars nor complete social misfits. However, the aggression of some of the Mokbel boys in the schoolyard was noted, and one source recalled that teachers occasionally found them 'scary'. There might have been eyebrows raised or even outright complaints about the boys but none of them could do any wrong in the eyes of their adoring mother. For a religious woman taken with blessing herself during conversation, Lora would be strangely quiet when her boys strayed from the path of righteousness.

Tony, with fewer ties to Lebanon, quickly ditched the family traditions and embraced the Australian way of life. A cousin still in Achache later recalled: 'His mother and elder brother are closer to this village. I was staying at our uncle's house and you feel that the uncles and brothers had this Lebanese way of life, but Tony didn't.' Tony's uncle in Achache agreed: 'Tony always said, "I left Lebanon as a kid, I'm Australian, I can't go back there, my life is here."'

Despite disliking school and not being brilliant academically, Tony had more street smarts than nearly anyone at Moreland High in Coburg in the late seventies. But he was nevertheless a moody teenager with a bad attitude and a short fuse. Then, on 11 August 1980, Tony's father, Sajih, who had been in the country just six years, suddenly and prematurely dropped dead from a heart attack. He apparently had few signs of illness before his surprise demise which the death certificate listed as 'Coronary sclerosis and thrombosis. Myocardial fibrosis' – a heart attack from hardening of the arteries and heart tissue damage from a blockage.

Sajih Mokbel died aged fifty-four, just two decades after marrying Lora. The death occurred on Tony's fifteenth birthday. A requiem notice appeared in the *Sun* on the eve of Sajih's funeral. Three days after his death the requiem was held at Our Lady of Lebanon church in Carlton at 10 am. Ninety minutes later the funeral procession travelled up Sydney Road and Sajih was interred at Fawkner Cemetery in a tomb with a second space reserved for Lora for when she passed. It was a harrowing winter day as the close migrant family buried their patriarch in their new country. The eldest of Sajih's surviving children, Kabalan, was just eighteen, Horty was seventeen, Gawy fourteen and Milad just twelve. Lora Mokbel was left a widow in a strange land with a brood of aggressive young pups.

Sajih's brother Antonios, a Maronite priest, came to Australia for the first time after the death. Tony acted the dutiful nephew, he said. But the death deeply affected teenage Tony and left him with an even bigger chip on his shoulder; according to one of his later defence barristers, it sent him off the rails.

It was a grim occasion for Tony, his world rocked on the eve of becoming a man. He was a fatherless migrant in a country founded by convicts at the arse end of the world. And he had just learnt it can all be taken from you in a heartbeat. Tony would later recall: 'In August 1980, I thought that was the saddest day of my life and not a day has passed that I have not thought of my father.'

2

Brunswick boy

When I was a child I spoke as a child, I understood as a child, I thought as a child. But when I became a man I put away childish things.

– Corinthians

It was a bittersweet passage to manhood for Tony. There was the melancholy and vacuum left by Sajih's death. But he also had the fraternity of two tough older brothers, his younger brother Milad who looked up to him, and a caring sister. He had the unswerving love and devotion of his mother, albeit a woman already life-weary and seemingly over it all while still in her thirties. But for the naturally curious Tony during the seventies and eighties, his home 'hood of Brunswick was a hive of activity, legal and illegal.

Melbourne had a thriving criminal scene in those decades. Some of the most serious crims, like notorious hitman Christopher Dale Flannery, aka Mr Rent-a-Kill, got banged up in Coburg's Pentridge prison. The infamous 'bluestone college' was just two kilometres up Sydney Road from the Mokbel family home.

As Tony was growing up, war was breaking out up the road behind the cold walls of that gladiator academy. The prison gang of a member of a multi-generational Melbourne crime family clashed with Mark 'Chopper' Read's overcoat gang. The jail battle that raged over years of bombings, bashings and stabbings apparently had its origins in Chopper eating all the sausages promised to H Division for Christmas one year.

In 1987 smoke was visible from the Mokbel home as a quieter Pentridge war between inmates and guards saw five prisoners die, caught in a fire they had started themselves. Wharf enemies the Kanes and Coles were also tearing around the area, and Tony, seventeen at the time, was likely to have heard how two gunmen in balaclavas stormed the nearby Quarry Hotel in Brunswick and gunned down Brian Kane. One of the gunmen was thought to be 'the Duke', a figure who would loom large in Tony's future.

The raw feelings from the death of their dad combined with the Mokbel boys' already existing machismo to form something like rocket fuel. In a still tough pre-gentrification suburb the Mokbel boys more than held their own. The teenage Mokbels' intimidating presence on the football field is remembered still with some fear and trembling by their old team-mates who are now middle-aged. In the early 1980s the brothers – particularly Milad – cut a violent swathe through teams visiting Fleming Park. What Horty, Tony and Milad lacked in finesse playing for the East Brunswick Magpies they made up for in grit, strength and determination.

'They were hard bastards back then,' a team-mate, now in his forties, recalled. 'They were muscly-big. It was their bulk that got them by and made them useful on the team. Milad was solid like a tank. Milad was that bloody psycho that even as your team-mate you thought he could attack you at any second.'

Some of the Mokbels' pigskin peers on the Brunswick paddock went on to fame, some to infamy. Mil Hanna lost his youthful locks and became the AFL's bald bombardier, helping Carlton to their 1995 premiership. Jed Houghton became a career crim and was shot dead by police during a raid in Bendigo in the wake of the Walsh Street cop killings. Horty, Milad and Tony played during the same period but in different divisions at East Brunswick, and made a distinct and lasting impression. Club officials and other players were often left wondering just what was in the water at their Canberra Street home.

When Milad was fifteen he knocked down an adult umpire – taking him down by either punching or jumper punching the official. A former team-mate said, 'They were adults, the umpires. But once Milad got violent towards one. He took the umpire down and the umpire fell to the ground. And that umpire would have been considerably older. You just knew he would snap at any time. You just knew there was going to be an incident whenever he played. It didn't take much to set him off. He had the shortest fuse of anybody I played with. You're meant to feel a bit safe and secure that you're on the same team with him. But you got a feeling he could turn on his own team-mates at any time.'

One day East Brunswick were defeated by East Reservoir in a hotly contested game. In the cramped change rooms, the Mokbels and other Magpies suffered the ignominy of the victors singing their club song on the other side of a flimsy partition. 'You can hear the other team singing the song. It did not go down well. They smashed through the partition and attacked them. The Mokbels were the ringleaders. They didn't like to lose,' the player said.

Antonios went to Coburg's Moreland High but quit in Year 11.

'He was just another kid. In between quiet and a larrikin,' a classmate recalled. 'He was a lovely bloke. If you knew the bloke from when we were kids to now – it's all been blown out of proportion.'

Mokbel was already making friends that would stick with him when he entered his prime as an adult criminal. From school he knocked around with Jack Doumani and from the local streets he ran with Willie Thompson and Paul Howden. For Mokbel the three men would become a crony, a corpse and a cook respectively. Doumani and Howden later got involved with race-loving Mokbel's horse ownership, and Doumani had his crimes collide with his cafe career. Doumani's chic but wild Toorak Cafe lost its liquor licence in the early nineties following breaches and after it emerged that Doumani had been convicted of nine counts of receiving stolen goods.

A year after his father's death Antonios came to the attention of the police. As the eighties progressed he was constantly involved in minor infractions and run-ins with the law. His barrister, Con Heliotis, QC, later explained to a court: 'The prior convictions ... start in 1983 and thereafter, in quick succession, three in 1983, one in '84, five in 1985, one in '86, one in '87.' There were assaults and minor offences among them. In one case Tony went down for punching a parking inspector. But none of the early charges related to drugs.

Police from the area remember him as Antonios. Hardboiled ex-copper Brian 'the Skull' Murphy had come across a teenage Mokbel playing up and given him a kick in the arse as a warning. He described Tony as: 'A fat fucking obnoxious little wog.'

He might have been a high-school dropout disliked by the local constabulary, but Antonios was no unemployed teen waster. Rather he was finding time for trouble on top of a busy working life and a regular girlfriend. On leaving school Mokbel worked as a bouncer and got a job washing pots out the back of now defunct Carlton pasta and pizza restaurant, Spaghetti Graffiti.

Though short and stumpy, teenage Tony still had sufficient moxy to back himself with his fists in the club scene and out of it. But through his troubled teens Tony discovered instinctual charm and less aggressive ways to get what he wanted. Not that he wanted much. Just fame, fortune, fast horses, faster cars, and the fastest women, payola, power, prestige … and pizza.

3
Small business

To him nine to five was odds on a horse.

– Archie Bunker

In 1984, at the age of nineteen, Tony had found a vivacious young Melbourne girl called Carmel. Not only did they share an amorous relationship, Tony and Carmel went into business together. The pair bought a failing suburban milk-bar business in Melbourne's north-east. It was a 'squarehead' path for ambitious Tony, albeit one taken at a precocious pace.

Tony and Carmel, who would later marry, poured their hearts into the Rosanna business, working seven-day weeks. But after two years of hard slog and milk deliveries they sold the business for the same price they had paid for it. The young lovers were left exhausted and disheartened at just breaking even after twenty-four months' solid grind. For Tony, in particular, it was a hard knock to a determined young man.

Mokbel already had petty criminal acquaintances in his network of family and friends in and around Brunswick. During the eighties, a hirsute Tony played cards in Carlton backrooms before the Crown Casino behemoth landed and crushed them out of existence. At the illegal card games Tony, often accompanied by brother Horty, met characters like rising Carlton crime figure Mick Gatto for a few hands of Russian poker. Like Gatto, Mokbel had a virulent strain of the gambling bug and developed a love of what poets have called the holy game of poker.

'We had a few games and he used to frequent. More so his brother Horty – he's an absolute gentleman. Horty's a mate of mine, he's a really good bloke. Tony's no friend of mine. Simple as that,' the Carlton Crew figure said.

Cards can teach skills for life. They can reveal a person's real character. They can hone one's ability to detect coffeehousing in the real world. And they can diagnose human frailties. In poker a player is 'on tilt' if they let their emotions disrupt their play. Tilting is what you do when annoyance or disappointment pushes you to do what you would not normally do. The milk-bar experience put Tony on tilt. If he was ever in any doubt that virtue is not its own reward, the failed business made concrete his scepticism. He walked away from milk crates and chocolate bars resolved that the only way to insure against failure was to diversify into revenue streams with huge and guaranteed returns. Tony took his lumps on the milk-bar misadventure but would bounce back to invest in pizzas and a trade of an entirely different sort.

Mokbel's troubled decade of the 1980s had started with the horrible harbinger of his father's death. But as the eighties gave way to the nineties Tony's ambitions bloomed as he diversified his income streams to pills and powders. The times would perfectly suit his most successful business endeavour. The power ballads, hair bands, wine coolers and leather pants of the previous decade were giving way to a completely different music and recreational scene. Techno music, sometimes called 'doof doof' for its bass-heavy repetitive beats, and its associated party drug use, was creeping out of gay venues into mainstream clubs and raves.

The Mokbel boys grew up, married (none of them to Lebanese girls, relatives lamented), reproduced and got their own houses in or near the family nucleus of Brunswick. Meanwhile, a network of family, friends and local petty criminal acquaintances had grown around Tony. Tony and Carmel were living in Grandview Avenue, Pascoe Vale, just a seven-kilometre dogleg from Brunswick on gridlocked roads heading north-west.

Mokbel had set about establishing himself as a player in Melbourne's drug scene, using his innate charm to woo hostile crime figures into friends and friends into accomplices. In the process he notched up a few more criminal convictions including receiving stolen goods, possessing an unlicensed pistol and hindering police. Then in the nineties he set up an amphetamine lab in a suburban Brunswick house using a plumber friend, Paul Howden, and another lab churning out the lucrative white powder in Coburg.

Amphetamine labs are volatile endeavours that often betray their location to police by exploding. Their high risk also makes them high yield, and the money Mokbel brought in from his drug initiatives made his profits from selling capricciosas look like loose change.

But in his efforts to network, look after friends, earn favours and generally empire-build, Mokbel the new player landed for the first time in some serious trouble that would cause ructions in his family and thrust him further into a life of crime.

* * *

In 1988 two Mokbel associates, Marcel Karim Nassour and Trevor Douglas Young, were arrested on charges of drug trafficking. Young was willing to plead guilty but was petrified of going to jail. So with Mokbel's help the criminal duo hatched a double-or-nothing plan to pay off a judge in return for a soft sentence for Young with no jail time. Nassour approached a former associate to a judge at the Accident Compensation Tribunal and asked for ideas on a bent beak who might be a good candidate for a brown paper parcel. The authorities were alerted to the scheme and a police operation was launched to nab the brazen criminals in their bribery attempt.

A drug squad detective posed as a bent court staffer and met Nassour at North Melbourne watering hole the Arden Hotel. As the two stood on the sticky carpet Nassour told the detective he was acting as an agent for Young who was very hesitant about meeting anybody. 'We're frightened of someone taking us for a ride,' Nassour confided to the undercover cop.

The detective said bribing a County Court judge would cost more than $30,000. But the high asking price was no problem – the men were willing to pay up to $53,000 for the right result. 'We're willing to supply whatever it takes as long as the results are there,' Nassour said. Mokbel, ostensibly an aspirational small-businessman, stepped in as the influence-peddling bagman of the scheme to rescue his drug associates. He attended a second meeting with the undercover cop, this time at the President Motel in South Melbourne. There Mokbel handed over $2000, stating there was plenty more to come in cocaine and cash. He thought he had bought the law but, ultimately, the law won. After a third meeting, which connected the nervous Young to the scheme, the trio were arrested and, with Tony also nicked, the original two defendants became three. The men were charged with conspiring to pervert the course of justice. And, in a decision that must have induced a profound feeling of regret in the plotters, a magistrate dismissed the initial drug charges against Young and Nassour – the reason for the botched bribe scheme – due to lack of evidence.

Had he done nothing, Young's fears of going inside would never have been realised, but his attempt to change his destiny had created the very real prospect of a future in the slammer. Seemingly exhausted and resigned to his fate Young, unlike Mokbel and Nassour, did not bother applying for bail.

Mokbel was found guilty over the bungled bribe in 1992 and copped his first jail sentence – a year inside with a six-month minimum.

There is more to be learnt from defeat than victory and though smarting from misadventures in crime and milk bars, it was a slightly more learned Mokbel who, in the mid-nineties, bought an Italian restaurant in Boronia specialising in pizza. The residents of Boronia (sometimes referred to by its neighbours as Bosnia for its rougher elements) proved partial to Tony's quick and greasy carbohydrate-laden dishes, and business boomed. The menu's No 15 pizza – with tomato, cheese, bacon, beef, onion and egg – was dubbed Tony's Special. Mokbel bought next door and expanded the restaurant to include a takeaway counter as well as the dining room. The business was promoted on the awning by a cartoon of a short, portly Tony-like pizza chef.

Tony and Carmel ran the pizza parlour from November 1995 to July 1998. Tony was then still green enough, or sufficiently well meaning, to have his name down as an owner of the business – a practice he would soon ditch. Later Mokbel sold the business while keeping ownership of the building, using it as a springboard to a more leisurely life as landlord, not workhorse.

One of the employees at Mokbel's pizza house was a young man who we cannot name but will call 'Pizzaboy', and who was ripe for Tony's picking. Pizzaboy's parents had split when he was sixteen and he had enjoyed scant contact with his father since. He had dropped out of high school and started a chef's apprenticeship. Pizzaboy worked in several commercial and business kitchens before landing among the pots and pans of Tony's Boronia lair. The food-loving boss took an interest in him and eventually moved him to Brunswick to be chef at his next restaurant. Pizzaboy still lived with his beloved grandmother and when she died he was left distressed and disturbed. Around that time he started seeing more of Mokbel and his conspicuous displays of wealth, position and influence.

According to a forensic psychologist who later analysed Pizzaboy, the chef was dazzled by Mokbel's charisma and his seeming aura of immunity to the mundane trappings of society. So impressed was Pizzaboy by Mokbel's flashy ways, he ditched working as a chef for the more ambiguous role of 'Mokbel associate'. Life as an associate was much more instantly gratifying than humping potato sacks and slicing and dicing in overheated kitchens. It involved expensive cars and lavish VIP rooms. Pizzaboy started hitting the nightclubs and using amphetamines. 'It was exciting and rewarding, although it totally contradicted the values with which he had been raised,' psychologist Ian Joblin found. Pizzaboy's corruption would be complete when Mokbel made him his speed gopher and pill runner – the drug world equivalent of potwash in his old hierarchy. Pizzaboy was not to be Mokbel's last corruption. And the pizza parlour would become just the first of many pies Mokbel would get his stubby fingers into across the quasi-respectable fields of real estate, fashion, horseracing, bars and clubs. But those ventures were all far from his most lucrative earner.

Over the coming years Tony would go from small business suburban dad to the flash king of Sydney Road. It would be a seductive transformation but one made at the cost of a lot of things, not least his young love who helped lay the first foundations of empire. The marriage was not destined to last as Mokbel's business got larger, less respectable and less legal.

4
Risky business

*I always keep a supply of stimulant handy in case
I see a snake, which I also keep handy.*

– W C Fields

While in custody during the bribery trial Mokbel's investments began to struggle and he missed the birth of his first child (a boy named Sajih, who would be followed by a little sister). Carmel, a new mum with an absent husband stuck behind bars, was shaken by the experience. She was now married to a jailbird, an accused associate of drug criminals and a deadbeat hubby and dad. She became, in the words of Tony's sentencing judge, 'psychologically disturbed'.

Tony, on the other hand, seized the opportunity prison life provided for an up and coming player who wanted to win friends and influence people, particularly if they had the right criminal skill set. But he still resented the chaos the jail term had wrought on his private life. His own father had been taken from him while he was still a youth and now he was stuck behind bars when his first child had emerged screaming into the world. Getting locked up in these circumstances was completely his own doing, but according to some, the incident simply turned Mokbel more defiantly anti-authority.

As well as a stretch, Mokbel had attracted another must-have underworld accessory – a criminal nickname, albeit a slightly second-hand one that had already done a bit of mileage. Portly New York mob boss Anthony Salerno had been dubbed 'Fat Tony'. *The Simpsons* lifted Salerno's moniker for Springfield's head mobster. The husky-voiced cartoon character gave the nickname global cachet and soon Mokbel's associates and Brunswick locals had started using it for him. Given the hours he spent in gyms trying to battle his natural barrel build, Mokbel was quite sporting in his embrace of the tubby tag. He apparently took it as an affectionate Mafiosi-style title rather than an insult.

The media first got wind of the moniker when Greg Domaszewicz, a Carl Williams associate acquitted of child killing, let it slip in an interview about Lewis Moran. 'Lewis, he's with, like, Fat Tony and them,' he told a reporter in May 2004. The rest was history. Headline writers and news scribes have since rarely resisted enlivening any copy about Mokbel with the Fat Tony tag.

While in jail Fat Tony made friends with Phillip O'Reilly, a drug criminal who had been making amphetamines for the Bandidos outlaw motorcycle gang in Sydney. Once released, Mokbel cosied up to another major drug figure with links to the bikie world – 'Kiwi Joe' Moran. Not related to the Melbourne gangland Morans, Kiwi Joe had been supplying Black Uhlans bikie gang founder John William Samuel Higgs with the precursor chemicals for amphetamine production. Higgs was then presiding over the nation's biggest amphetamine ring – a position that Mokbel, in time, would wrench from him. When Higgs and Kiwi Joe fell out,

Mokbel sensed only opportunity and pulled off a brazen switch. He seized the initiative to sell amphetamine to Higgs's syndicate while buying precursor chemicals from Kiwi Joe.

In April 1993 Mokbel popped in on Kiwi Joe for a business meeting at his inner-city Lonsdale Street unit. Tony was not long out of his first prison stint and the visit was to pave the way for his second. Mokbel and Moran spoke about bad speed yields and cook-ups gone wrong with a trainspotter-like intensity for their subject matter.

Kiwi Joe was still dirty that bikie boss Higgs had left him copping a half-million-dollar loss on a previous deal gone bad. He bemoaned the fact that he had shown Higgs his way around the kitchen before getting burnt by him and was now seeking to switch cooks. 'He couldn't cook before he come to see me,' Kiwi Joe complained to Mokbel in a comment eavesdropping police suspected was not about duck à l'orange.

Mokbel made his application for the vacant position in the standard cryptic criminal patois designed to cheat any listening devices out of meaningful evidence. He made himself clear when he said he was keen to 'have a go' at cooking. But once some trade terms were thrown in, the stunted crim staccato became basically impenetrable.

Touting for business, Tony told Kiwi Joe: 'I have got plenty of the red. I have got plenty ... Yeah, I have got plenty of everything, it is just a matter of ... No just a matter of ... No I have got a fair bit of the HI, I have got three-quarters of it.'

It was all quite cryptic except to speed experts who knew that pseudoephedrine, an ingredient in some flu tablets, when heated for hours with hydriotic acid – or HI – and red phosphorous can make methamphetamine. Mokbel sometimes coded his conversations further by calling pseudoephedrine 'Suzy' or, by extension, 'the girls'. It meant shady business could be done under the noses of spies with inconspicuous statements like 'Why don't you pick up the girls tonight?'

As Kiwi Joe got more comfortable with Mokbel, the supply deal grew from one 25-kilogram barrel of pseudoephedrine to as many as ten. 'If you don't get this one you'll get the other one that comes through ... cos I'll get ten on the way and you are going to get half of them,' Kiwi Joe said.

Despite their cautious lingo neither of the two crims knew police bugs had been set up to cover Kiwi Joe Moran's apartment. For the detectives monitoring Moran's activities, Mokbel wandering into their net on his opportunistic visit had been an unexpected bonus.

Kiwi Joe: 'Yeah, I'm still debating whether to give you that run or not. Cos when can I get it done if I give it to you?'

Mokbel: 'Yeah, I can pretty well straightaway ... It would be good to have that extra.'

Kiwi Joe: 'Well, I could give it to ya.'

Mokbel: 'Thanks, Joe'

One of Mokbel's more colourful lifelong contacts was a crook called 'the Grifter' (his real name cannot be used). It was rare for Mokbel to come across anyone who worked the angles as emphatically as himself, but the Grifter was a kindred spirit. An energetic and audacious crim of Middle Eastern ancestry, often seen with beautiful women, the Grifter must have reminded Mokbel more than a little of himself. In fact the two would lead strangely parallel, echoing lives. The Grifter subscribed to the view that it was morally wrong to let a sucker keep his money. And, to borrow from the song lyric, he stole from the rich, and the poor, and the not-very-rich and the very poor. No con was too elaborate for the ex-private-school boy who, like Mokbel, had spent a stint as a bouncer.

In one hustle the Grifter created a fake position vacant, advertised it in newspapers and requested that applicants send copies of their licences with their resumes. He then used the details to open a swathe of bank accounts with multiple credit cards. In eleven years he received about 400 convictions for fraud offences – and they were the ones he was caught for.

The Grifter once got wind that the *Herald Sun* newspaper was working on an article involving him. He confidently represented himself at the Supreme Court hearing to prevent the story being published wearing sandals, shorts, a T-shirt, and with hair halfway down his back. But the Grifter really made his mark as a talented speed cook at a time when the world of major crime was experiencing a quantum leap from armed robberies, cannabis and heroin to methamphetamine pills and powders.

'He is a very accomplished cook,' a police officer said of the Grifter. 'Tony is a very good cook as well. He's on tape telling a guy how to change it to get more out of it and make it better.'

Mokbel was also in close contact with Melbourne's Moran clan, and between Tony, the Grifter and the Morans, most of the state's flourishing meth trade ended up being spoken for.

Moran family patriarch Lewis was a shockingly tight-fisted crim who had raised his boys – son, Jason, and stepson, Mark – to be his brutal enforcers earning their pa fear and respect on the street. The old-school crim had got involved in the new drug scene through Jason and Mark. Lewis Moran was of a different criminal era to Mokbel. Tony started his life of crime with drugs and developed his trade in the city's nightclubs. Lewis was an ex-pickpocket and SP bookie. For entertainment when he was younger, Moran and colourful friends like Graham 'the Munster' Kinniburgh would suit up to go to Sunday night dances with girls in bobbysocks. If Lewis didn't like the meals his partner, Judy, made him, he would brutally bash her with a stick.

Lewis's boys, half-brothers Jason and Mark, had a strong villainous heritage through marriage and bloodlines to the Kanes and Coles – the serious gunmen of the city's last major shoot-'em-up criminal stoush. But the Morans would have struggled to break out in the new drug scene without the smarts and expertise of the Grifter.

The Grifter had been an interloper in the Moran family for years. In the Moran photo albums he looks out smiling at the birthday parties of Mark's and Jason's kids. Moran matriarch Judy recalled the Grifter in her autobiography: 'There is a boy who befriended my sons and ate so many family meals at my kitchen table. He was at the funeral of Mum and Dad and later Mark … there was always something about this boy that didn't quite gel.'

The Grifter, as intelligent as he was amoral, was the brains behind the Moran drug operation. He educated himself in the burgeoning criminal industries of methamphetamine creation and pill production. This made him a pioneer at a time few in Melbourne or Australia had the necessary specialised knowledge. The gifted cook would arrange chemical deliveries, manufacture the drugs and sometimes even handle the supply end to VIP clients.

Mokbel groomed the Grifter as a friend and colleague after learning he had a reputation as a cook par excellence and was one of the best pill makers in the country.

As well as drugs, crime and Aussie Rules football, Mokbel, the Grifter and the Morans all had the track in common. Mokbel had horses stabled near Lewis's brother Tuppence's Ascot Vale house on the edges of Flemington racecourse. Matriarch Judy Moran told the author, shortly before being thrown in the clink for organising a gangland hit on her brother-in-law Tuppence Moran, how she met Mokbel at the track: 'Mark first met Tony through racing and the only time I ever met Tony I was introduced to him at the races during the Spring Racing Carnival back in the nineties,' she said. 'I only met him for five minutes – just hello goodbye sort of thing and I never saw him again. So that was the only time I ever had anything to do with him. I wouldn't have known him again if I fell over him – only for all that happened.

'This was in the members at Flemington. He was dressed up. He just said, "Oh yes, I know your boys." It was just a mutual friend introduced us and I didn't take any notice of it. When I saw Mark later in the day, when he was in one of the marquees, I said, "Oh, there was this guy I met today, Tony Mokbel." He said, "Oh yeah, he's a big punter, Mum," and that was as much as he said to me.'

In the succeeding years Mokbel made the change from Brunswick boy to the powerful millionaire property magnate he had longed to be. Smart decisions and the rampant 1990s property market buoyed his rapid financial growth and success, but the wheels of Tony's remarkable commercial rise were being lubricated by his secret businesses. Always with one eye on the future, Tony had made contacts in the nightclub world during his first job. And his easy charm attracted an array of friends he would ruthlessly assess in terms of their usefulness to him as either helpers or stooges, or both.

One such friend since childhood was the plumber Paul Howden. Mokbel was godfather to one of Howden's children and had lured Howden into his plans with the promise of quick, easy riches. Mokbel had created a productive speed lab in a suburban house, nominally owned by Howden, on quiet Downs Street in Brunswick, and got Howden to run it. There are few signs to distinguish a regular house from a speed den. Some telltale clues are perpetually closed curtains, occupants keeping irregular hours and a persistent smell like cat urine from the cooking process. Behind the Brunswick den's closed curtains was a goldmine operation that produced more than forty kilograms of pure methamphetamine over the life of the lab, with a potential street value of $78 million.

Mokbel's licence to print money was revoked one day in February 1997 when Howden accidentally knocked over a container of solvents, starting a fire in the house. As speed labs often do, the volatile operation exploded in a fireball consuming the house. Police followed the smoke to a residential street, discovered the largest speed lab in Victorian history, and made one of the biggest and easiest busts on record. Howden had been burnt in the inferno but by the time the authorities arrived he had fled the crime scene. He was found in hospital and eventually moved from the burns ward to a small jail cell.

Investigators could not fail to notice that the house next door to the smoking remains was owned by a Mokbel. But as it turned out, they could not prove beyond reasonable doubt that Tony was linked to the lab. The Mokbels knocked down the burnt remains of the neighbouring drug house nominally owned by Howden, extended their backyard and put in a pool.

Howden refused to sing about his boss to police and a grateful Mokbel made regular visits to the loyal plumber in prison. On one visit Tony even persuaded the guards to let him take Howden out to a nearby McDonald's for a respite from prison food, later dropping his mate back off at the prison.

The Big Mac might have been a nice break from the prison's shredded lettuce and pressed meat but it was cold consolation for the risks Howden had taken in Mokbel's employ. The jailed plumber soon died of heart disease at just thirty-six – twenty years younger than even Sajih Mokbel had been when he suffered his premature coronary demise.

Howden's ill-health was possibly caused by his toxic work environment. A kilogram of meth produces about six kilograms of toxic waste, and exposure to lab chemicals in cooking can be fatal. Sampling the produce can be equally lethal. Amphetamine use had offed Melbourne gangster Denis 'Mr Death' Allen, whose speed-addled heart actually broke into bits. At the age of thirty-six also, Allen joined an estimated dozen of his murder victims below ground.

Mokbel put a heart-on-sleeve tribute in the newspaper for his dead lab rat. He drew a comparison with his father's death but conspicuously failed to see his role in the demise of his professed friend. 'My dearest friend. I just cannot believe this. I'm thinking of you and your family,' Mokbel wrote. He recalled his sadness at his father's passing in August 1980. 'In December 2001 it has rehaunted me again and this is thought to be the saddest day since my father passed away. You'll always be in my prayers and I will never, ever forget you. I promise to you my friend to be there for your family till the day I die. Your true friend Tony Mokbel.'

Dodging heat over the lab explosion was one of a string of lucky breaks for Mokbel. Authorities were flabbergasted by the Brunswick lab's lucrative and lethal output. They could not lock Mokbel up over the lab – although he was being brought to court in the nineties over simmering small-time offences of possessing a pistol without a licence, driving while disqualified, failure to show P-plates, entering a building with intent and receiving stolen goods – but the inferno removed any illusions about the scale of the Brunswick boy's criminal ambitions.

A few months later police busted Mokbel's Coburg lab but again could not categorically connect 'Teflon' Tony. It was an enviable lucky streak but with each close call Mokbel was losing perhaps his most valuable asset – his anonymity.

A year after his lab went up in smoke Mokbel faced court over his incriminating chat about barrels of pseudoephedrine with Kiwi Joe years earlier. In April 1998 a jury found Mokbel and Kiwi Joe guilty of conspiring to traffic in a drug of dependence – methamphetamine. Both men were far from cleanskins. Mokbel had nineteen prior convictions in nine years and Moran had thirty-two over nearly three decades committed to crime. More time in the big house was inevitable. For Mokbel the judge ordered three more years, but Tony had a plan which would see him serve only months.

While Mokbel was locked up, Carmel, struggling to keep the home fires burning, came a cropper over another of her husband's dodgy indulgences – his criminal love of fast horses. When she was questioned by racing officials over horses Tony had put in her name to avoid scrutiny, she clearly knew little about the steeds. Tony had been in jail when Carmel gave birth to their first child and now with the authorities pursuing her over her husband's schemes, he was again behind bars, nowhere to be seen. Fortunately for Mokbel he was not like most of the other poor saps stuck in the penitentiary. He had the funds to buy back his freedom by hiring top lawyers to find holes in the prosecution case.

'Tony's usual form in court is to exhaust every potential avenue no matter what,' said a federal policeman who came to know him well, Agent Jarrod Ragg. 'Tony's MO is if there is the slightest chance, he'll go for it. He'll be told, "This will not succeed at court but there is a slight chance it will succeed." He'll say, "Just do it." If there's a one per cent chance, he'll do it.'

Mokbel would drive his barristers to distraction, sometimes calling ten times a day with new ideas for his cases – some legal, some just bizarre. He would also pass their phone numbers on to friends with legal queries that would range from large-scale problems to fencing disputes.

The case Team Tony mounted to appeal the conspiracy to traffic conviction involved the sort of mental gymnastics that make perfect sense to lawyers but leave police and many in the community aghast. Their argument had three parts. One: the police evidence showed only an agreement that Kiwi Joe would supply Mokbel with pseudoephedrine. Two: pseudoephedrine was not the same as the drug they were charged over – amphetamine. And three: even though the pair discussed recipes for turning the one into the other, the most that could be proved was that Kiwi Joe *expected* Mokbel to manufacture the amphetamine. This fell short, Mokbel's mouthpiece argued, of establishing that the pair had committed the crime of plotting to traffic amphetamine. The Court of Appeal of the Supreme Court agreed with the defence argument and quashed the jury's guilty verdict.

In the meantime Kiwi Joe, who was also acquitted of the traffic charge, had pled guilty to an amended count – conspiracy to possess a drug of dependence. But for Mokbel the legal win meant a key in the latch, civilian clothes and a walk from prison to freedom. The racetrack beckoned and it would not be hard to ditch prison porridge for ponies.

5

The fix is in

The race is not always to the swift, nor the battle to the strong, but that's the way to bet.

– Damon Runyan

Antonios Mokbel had a passion for the track rivalled only by his love of food, women and filthy lucre. At about five foot six, or 167 centimetres, he was eleven centimetres shorter than some of the taller jockeys. That made him the right height to get on the back of a horse and channel his racing passion in a constructive, legal way. Of course for Tony to become a jockey a substantial slimming of the girth would have been required, as would have an increase in discipline and a reduction in la dolce vita. So instead, Mokbel opted to keep his danger, thrills and spills off-track. And rather than a jockey he became something else entirely – the scourge of the racecourse.

In making his choice Mokbel was following in an ignoble but strong national tradition of criminals exploiting legal and ethical blind spots at the track. The Mr Bigs of the drug world, like Griffith don Robert Trimbole, had used the punt to wash their money years earlier, and colourful racing figures like George Freeman had made fortunes fixing races with jockeys. Sometimes the fix has come at a deadly cost. In the 1980s the body of trainer George Brown was found broken and burnt in a torched car south of Sydney. He had been got at and was meant to secretly swap one horse – not expected to win and attracting good odds – for a much faster horse. But Brown got an attack of morals and put the original horse in the race. His eleventh-hour decision to play it straight attracted the chagrin of the would-be fixers and cost Brown his life.

In another incident dubbed the Fine Cotton affair, linked to Robbie Waterhouse, a member of the Waterhouse racing dynasty, the switch actually went through. A horse called Bold Personality was brought in to play the role of slower steed Fine Cotton. The two animals were far from doppelgangers in either appearance or form. Bold Personality had white feet. The horse it was impersonating, Fine Cotton, did not. The fixers tried to conceal the anomaly with brown paint. But word of the plot spread. The horse's feet came out a strange red colour from the paint job, and the fix descended into farce. Odds on Fine Cotton shortened from 33-1 to 7-2 and even as the equine impostor tore past the post, punters in the stands shouted 'wrong horse' and 'ring-in'.

Not even the horses themselves have been safe from standover tactics when money has been on the line. There were attempts to shoot Beau Vite and Phar Lap. And the conventional wisdom now is that Phar Lap's sudden demise was a deliberate killing.

In 1969 Bart Cummings-trained Melbourne Cup favourite Big Philou was snuck a debilitating dose of laxatives on the eve of the race. A strapper to Cup king Cummings, Les Lewis, who later came clean on being behind the sabotage, was candid about the power of the almighty dollar to corrupt the integrity of racing: 'Money was speaking all languages, which it always has. And you get a thousand dollars waved in front of you when you're only working for a dollar an hour,' Lewis said. 'It's a lot of money to have put in your hand, a lot, and you're willing to take that risk for it.'

To Mokbel the sport of kings, with its thin veneer of respectability, fitted well with his own delusions of grandeur and nobility. The thunder of racehorse hooves coming down the straight provided him with a soundtrack to a thousand dodgy deals stretching from the stables to the bookies' enclosure. Then on race day beautiful women would appear dressed up in heels, flesh on show, with feathers sticking out of fascinators like rare exotic birds. It was heaven. But the track and its characters were more than cause for a punt to Mokbel. They provided the insidious charmer with a smorgasbord of lucrative illegal schemes.

Mokbel was a big fan of Scorsese gangster flick *Casino* and felt an affinity with Joe Pesci's pint-sized psychopath character Nicky Santoro. The mobster narration in *Casino* is about another type of quasi-legitimate gambling – the slots and tables of Vegas. But it perfectly sums up the attraction the track held for a crim with a creeping record like Mokbel. 'For guys like me Las Vegas washes away your sins. It's like a morality car wash. It does for us what Lourdes does for humpbacks and cripples,' a mobster recounts in the film. 'And along with making us legit comes cash. Tons of it.'

In the nineties Mokbel created a corporate vehicle he wanted to use to build a ten-storey tower in Brunswick and named the company for his passion – Trackside Pty Ltd. His actual trackside ventures, while similarly ambitious, were much less respectable. And it seemed Mokbel's passion for the horses was surpassed only by his love of arranging the order in which they arrived past the post.

Mokbel made his first major appearance on the scene during the nineties as the leader of an unorthodox group of punters called 'the tracksuit gang'. Tony and the designer tracksuit-wearing group had an uncanny knack for picking winners and would simultaneously unload thousands on the same bet at the last minute. The scheme allowed uncapped wagers while protecting the group from shortened odds and too much attention. It was no new trick. Commission agents who place bets for punters who value their privacy are an accepted part of the food chain at the track. A variety of people have adopted the tactic of using a team of helpers and agents for last-minute cash drops on multiple bookies to maintain the best possible odds. But Tony's cartel of tracksuited terrors brought it to a new level of organisation and combined the synchronised plunges with improperly obtained inside information. They struck up and down the east coast for years, troubling the sleep of the nation's bookmakers. If Mokbel and his casually attired associates were plunging heavily on a horse, London to a brick it would run well.

In 1997 at Flemington the group put $100,000 on Swords Drawn at $3.50, making a quarter-of-a-million-dollar profit. They also reportedly won half a million after a national punting swoop on Timeless Winds, a winner at Queensland's Doomben racetrack. On some swoops Mokbel also took the opportunity for a criminal double dip, money-laundering the payout by insisting bookies pay in fresh $100 green notes after the bets were placed with the older 'grey ghost' $100 notes.

The tracksuit gang would also buy winning tickets from punters, paying them handsomely for paperwork seemingly showing legitimate track profits. The one certainty in gambling is, no matter how smart or tinny the gambler, the house always ultimately wins. But after much hard work buying win tickets and arranging bent paperwork, Tony's financial records said different.

The tracksuit gang's picks did not always come in but wins were frequent enough to rattle the bagmen. One rails bookie lamented during the tracksuit gang's reign that the members threw money on regardless of the odds, and as they shortened they did not stop punting. 'They had bundles of tickets and a bigger bundle of cash,' the bookmaker said. 'They've been around for a while now. They've just got an unlimited supply – a truckload of money. And when they bet they rarely miss.'

Over time Mokbel became one of the biggest racetrack punters the nation had seen since late media mogul and 'Prince of Whales' mega-gambler Kerry Packer. Mokbel would openly brag of bets in the thousands and wins in the hundreds of thousands. But tactics as much as ego were behind the boasts. Mokbel would pretend to some he had made his small fortune through property. But his self-perpetuated image as a professional punter meant that whenever authorities inquired how an unemployed Brunswick boy had garnered a fortune in assets, Mokbel, with more credibility than most, could answer with three words: monster winning streak.

6

Off and racing

Listen, I think that horse got scratched.

– Hitman to Carl Williams minutes after
Michael Marshall was shot dead

Over time Mokbel expanded his influence at the track from terrorising outsider to that of a corrupting insider. With older brother Horty by his side, Tony set about establishing himself as a dapper doyen of the industry. Both brothers established their own stables. In the early nineties Tony bought a large Kilmore farm and started filling it with promising horses, initially paying up to $28,000 for some, but later the brothers would pay closer to half a million for a good steed. A stream of notable trainers and jockeys passed through their doors as the brothers dreamed of etching the Mokbel family name in racing's pantheon, alongside Cummings, Waterhouse, Freedman and Hayes. Or if that didn't happen, at least they would fix enough races and clean enough cash to justify the adventure. Some passed through, sniffed the wind, smelled something fishy about their employers and moved on. More than half a dozen jockeys and trainers, including Damien Oliver, were warned off getting too close to Mokbel.

Tony's racing scams were not always well-kept secrets. On one occasion a private inquiry agent partnered to former colourful cop the Skull was drinking at a Middle Park hotel where jockey Damien Oliver was also imbibing. The agent, after a few too many, fired a round into the ceiling and shouted at Oliver: 'You're pulling horses for Tony Mokbel!'

Oliver and another jockey present were not impressed. Oliver denied the account, stating, 'I have no idea what you're talking about.' It was not long before the Skull got a call from a Mokbel contact. 'Damien called and Tony is very angry,' was the message.

A meeting was arranged between the Skull and Mokbel. When the Skull saw Tony he remembered the teen tearaway. 'You! You little fat cunt,' he said. 'I remember shining my shoes on your arse when you were fifteen.'

Tony reacted to quell the insubordination in front of his henchman. 'Shh. Turn it up,' Tony said, changing the subject to the agent Mokbel was unhappy with. 'He's going to cost me an absolute squillion!' Mokbel complained.

The Mokbels would stop at nothing to ensure their horse came in. A police officer once got a late-night tip-off about the brothers' plans. 'They're going to shoot Mahogany,' the tipster confided. The horse's owner – Lloyd Williams – was contacted and the beast was promptly moved out of harm's way to a secret location.

Some stuck around either oblivious to or unconcerned by Mokbel's gradually growing notoriety as the track became his mistress, laundromat, theatre and goldmine. Mokbel groomed jockeys and trainers for illegal tips and he paid bookies for inflated win receipts or even cheques showing wins he never won. Authorities suspect he corrupted jockeys to fix races on which he and associates would bet heavily. Helping him to this end was his secret ownership of at least nine racehorses, concealed behind the names of his wife, trainer and assorted trusted cronies.

Mokbel paid trainers an often lucrative cut of his winnings for helpful tips and he is believed to have made secret bets through an illegal unlicensed betting ring, later busted, run by Melbourne bookie Frank Hudson and two of Tony and Horty's main commission agents. But if Mokbel was happy to know the result of a race before it had run, he was less forgiving if the race did not go as he planned. In November 2003 the favourite at Sandown, Leone Chiara, failed to justify her short odds after beginning awkwardly and throwing her head in the air. Mokbel is believed to have dropped $80,000 on the mare and was among those contacting stewards and crying foul, prompting a probe that led to the disqualification of five people, including jockey Craig Newitt.

It was much more fun when the jockeys were on side, and two of the track's little people Mokbel got very close to were Sydney brothers Jim and Larry Cassidy. Jim, the older of the brothers and one of Australia's best jockeys, had won two Melbourne Cups, two Caulfield Cups, a Cox Plate and a Golden Slipper. But his career had been marred by the 'jockey tapes affair'. He had copped a lengthy suspension from riding in the mid-1990s after police involved in a major drug probe recorded him and others selling tips to criminals on the basis that they would fix their races. His form did not go unnoticed, and when he was back racing he was questioned by stewards over allegations that he had been paid more than $50,000 by Mokbel for tips.

Someone else who believed in the redistribution of wealth, Karl Marx, once said history repeats itself the first time as tragedy, the second time as farce. And in the late nineties Jim Cassidy, whose memory must have been as short as he was, got the starring role in the jockey tapes affair 2 – the sequel to his initial public disgrace.

Police targeting Mokbel's drug activities were surprised to hear Mokbel and the star jockey chatting amicably. The same police were also surprised to see another high-profile jockey zipping around town in Mokbel's Ferrari. Jim Cassidy did not back away from his Mokbel links, describing the drug criminal as a friend and saying that he had been to his mother's place and that their families were friends. Even later, when Mokbel's notoriety sharpened and he became Australia's most wanted man, the jockey said he had nothing but respect for him. But the closeness of the Mokbel and Cassidy clans would ultimately threaten Mokbel's racing ambitions.

While Mokbel was behind bars doing time for plotting to traffic speed, his wife, Carmel, got a nasty surprise in the form of a steward's inquiry into horses in her name. In 1998 New South Wales authorities queried the bona fides of racehorse Brief Promise, which was bought in the names of Tony's wife, Carmel, and Larry Cassidy's wife, Michelle, before Carmel handed over her half of the horse to Michelle as a 'gift'. Mokbel was doing time when Carmel's nominal horse ownership started to unravel. Larry and Michelle Cassidy were interviewed by stewards. Carmel was requested to appear at the inquiry but did not front. Brief Promise was sold after being refused approval to race. That sorted out the authorities' concerns over that one horse, but alarm bells were now ringing about the size of the web Mokbel had quietly spun through racing. And on closer scrutiny a number of areas of concern emerged.

Victorian stewards interviewed a cast of Mokbel cronies including Horty and Carmel, and Natalie Doumani – wife of Tony's childhood friend Jack – in relation to eight suspect horses. The owners of one horse, Scotch Gambit, were Carmel and crispy plumber turned jailbird Paul Howden (before his death). Carmel, whose name was involved with all the horses, took a lawyer to the inquiry and in a canny preemptive buckle (and an echo of the Mokbel solution to the heat over Brief Promise) said she wanted to relinquish ownership in all of them. The Mokbels were no longer invisible players in racing.

In April 1999 Tony's owner's ticket was torn up. The Victoria Racing Club announced both he and Carmel were banned from owning racehorses. The effort to shut the gate after the horse had bolted was by its very nature pointless. Ownership, after all, was always a fairly elastic concept for Mokbel and he was still free to mix at the track as a punter.

The law may require someone's name to be on a piece of land, on a corporation or on a racehorse, but the system of nominal ownership can sometimes bear little resemblance to who might really be pulling the strings through friendship, fear or favour. Aside from his wife, no other Mokbel cronies who had been used to acquire Tony's ponies received ownership bans. And in any case Mokbel, always a fan of the double-or-nothing approach, would not be so easily deterred.

There's an old gambling trick some punters swear is foolproof so long as you don't lose your nerve – or all your funds – before you hit paydirt. If you lose $10 on the first race you double your stake to $20 on your pick in the second. If that doesn't come in you bet $40 on your pick for the third, $80 on the fourth and so on. The theory is that when your horse eventually comes in, the size of the stake ensures the payout will recoup the losses of the earlier bets. The problem is that if none of your horses have won after your seventh bet, a bid of $1280 is required as an attempted recoup of the initial $10 bid. And most serious punters bet with stakes in the hundreds and thousands, not $10, and some losing streaks last for years, not just seven races. But to a certain kind of tragic gambler the never-say-die double down makes perfect sense.

When Mokbel got banned from owning horses he did not take it as a warning or a defeat but an invitation to push on despite the increasing heat and mounting stakes. Mokbel the owner reinvented himself as Mokbel the breeder. Records showed 'T Mokbel' as the breeder of two horses in 2000 and 2001. Audaciously, Mokbel was using for his brood mare one of the horses he had earlier been banned from owning. And with Tony now in breeding it was time for Horty's ownership scandal, which involved the family's most promising racehorse.

Horty had named his lightning steed Pillar of Hercules – a geographic reference to its father, Rock of Gibraltar. It was a clever tribute to the horse's lineage and allowed the Mokbel myth to mingle with the Greco-Roman warrior legend. But the mingling was more appropriate than intended, as Hercules, though a fearless soul, was not above cheating and using any unfair trick to his advantage. The colt had purportedly been seized by underworld finance adviser Tom Karas in lieu of a $100,000 debt owed by Horty. Majority ownership of the horse had then been transferred from Horty to Karas's wife.

In the spring of 2007 the horse was in fine form, zipping home at Caulfield and poised to take out the $1.5 million Victoria Derby. But Melbourne's celebrated Spring Racing Carnival was rocked when gangland detectives applied in court to seize the horse as an asset of Horty, who was then also an accused drug criminal. Police told the court that Karas, who had played the role of aggrieved creditor turned repo man, was actually behind a 'large scale money laundering operation' involving the horse.

Track officials announced a racing ban for the horse pending a steward's inquiry into whether it was still secretly owned by the Mokbels. Just weeks later Pillar of Hercules went under the hammer. The auctioneer told the gathering that vets had inspected the horse and his potential as a sire was good, as the genitals were in working order. A Melbourne businessman spent $1.8 million to snap up the horse originally bought as a yearling for $475,000. In the years following the 'trackside Tony' era, Mokbel would demonstrate multiple similarities to the family's estranged horse Pillar of Hercules. Not only would he, through his proclivities, cast aside any doubt that his genitals were in working order, his growing notoriety would belie a skyrocketing net worth.

The track had been a great college for Tony the high-school dropout (although it's unclear whether he took or dispensed more lessons). He would remain reliant on it to launder his drug riches. And he would continue to indulge in horse talk over mobile phones if only because race numbers proved a handy code for conversations that were really about drug deals. But as it came time to move on and up the criminal tree, powders and pills replaced ponies, and his personal appearances at racecourses became much rarer.

In 2001 the Victoria Racing Club held a trial at Flemington in which rails bookmakers were relocated to a different area. As part of the pilot reforms the body specifically banned access to punters wearing T-shirts, thongs or tracksuits. Tony would have been chuffed at leaving a lasting mark. But by the time of the trackie ban, Mokbel's tracksuit gang had retired into racing folklore undefeated. Mokbel himself had by then swapped FUBU sweats for pinstripes, the old gang for a new crew. And dead tracks for greener pastures.

7
Big business

Capitalism is the legitimate racket of the ruling class.

– Al Capone

After his 1998 conviction for conspiring to traffic drugs with Kiwi Joe was thrown out of court, Mokbel strutted out the prison gates with very big plans. His jail time seemed to invigorate rather than deter both his criminal activities and his particularly brazen way of pursuing them on a grandiose scale. Mokbel set about producing and importing drugs in audacious quantities and with missionary zeal. He built an empire on a druggie's smorgasbord of almost every illicit substance: cocaine, hashish, ecstasy, LSD and, most of all, amphetamines. Mokbel either had it made locally or imported it into Australia from all corners of the globe.

In the nineties the party drug scene had spread from the fringes to the mainstream, and opportunists like Mokbel, tuned into the booming, moneyed middle-class customer base, were riding the wave to their fortunes and becoming multimillionaires. A man on a mission, Mokbel was among the first to pioneer pressing home-made methamphetamine into pills for a hungry market of users.

Pill presses, traditionally the sole province of the legitimate pharmaceutical industry, were adjusted to imprint a logo so each batch of pills with its unique chemistry had its own identity based on colour and stamp. Word of mouth about the batch – whether the pills were pure or poison – could spread accordingly. Long after they had come down, pill-heads reminisced in their own language about pandas (pills imprinted with the World Wildlife Foundation logo), green apples (an Apple Mac logo), pink safe-sex pills (Durex logo), bats (Bacardi logo), and red Russians – sometimes attributed to Mokbel – which featured a hammer and sickle. On internet forums today drug users have mixed recollections – critical and sentimental – of Mokbel's products. Ironically, Melbourne's portly drug barons have always shown a predilection for stamping their supplies with sportswear logos like Puma, FILA or FUBU.

Mokbel would press his millions of fake ecstasy pills out of locally cooked amphetamine, throwing in any leftover detritus from the manufacturing process. Sometimes he would add ketamine, glucose or other mystery ingredients in an attempt to mimic the euphoric effect of the MDMA in real ecstasy.

A cop of three decades, Jim O'Brien worked in the homicide squad and the drug squad before being appointed officer in charge of the anti-gangland Purana taskforce. A large man with equally big attitude, ex-Inspector O'Brien believed even breast implants bankrolled by drug money should be seized as the proceeds of crime. O'Brien jokes that his phone monitors should be compensated for post-traumatic stress after having to listen to hundreds of hours of calls by intense gangland wife Roberta Williams.

Over the course of his career O'Brien saw the frontline of crime change from armed hold-ups to drugs. He watched the criminal kingpins go from tough wifebeater-wearing maddies wielding sawn-off shotguns to suited amoral Mr Bigs dealing in pills and powders. As he rose through police ranks so did Mokbel through the underworld. A collision was inevitable.

According to O'Brien: 'Criminals finally realised that the thing about dealing in drugs is that you never get to confront the victim. There's always someone there in between. Based on pure pyramid selling you never get to confront the victim. So the chances of being identified and prosecuted are somewhat less. And it's a whole lot less dangerous because you're not actually pointing a gun at someone where you're likely to get shot by the police. I think they learned that lesson in the eighties. Victoria Police were shooting straighter than anybody in those days.

'Even when we had 326 heroin deaths in the state in 1999 – which outstripped the road toll – amphetamine seizures were still outstripping heroin. What does that tell you? The drug of choice of Australians, and Victorians in particular, is methamphetamine. Ecstasy is just a methamphetamine tablet with a hallucinogen mixed in – most of the time ketamine. Australians are currently crunching in the order of 100,000 ecstasy tablets made per minute. Now if you took $15 to $23 as the wholesale price at a minimum, it will give you an idea of the money involved. No tax paid either.'

Mokbel was also shipping hundreds of thousands of real ecstasy pills, actually containing the euphoria-inducing ingredient MDMA, from Europe into Melbourne's docks on container vessels. The locally cooked and the globally smuggled drugs were then distributed down the chain to Mokbel's ring of sellers equipped with bumbags and giant early-model mobile phones.

One of the street dealers Mokbel used in the nineties was a baby-faced Broadmeadows boy called Carl Williams. Like many of Tony's younger charges, Carl looked up to him as a criminal mentor. As well as having drugs in common, both were fond of a feed. Mokbel went on to become a household name as 'Fat Tony' and the cops labelled Williams 'Fat Boy'. Neither of the big-boned boys could have known what a big and bloody future lay ahead of them when the underworld they led would combust in a brutal war over drugs, women, money and egos.

Mokbel baptised Broady boy Carl 'the Truth' after the nickname of Carl's namesake, the American boxer best known for losing to Mike Tyson. But police said the name was a bad fit. 'He never told the truth. He was always blaming someone else,' ex-Purana head Jim O'Brien said.

While Mokbel was an ex-jailbird up to his hips in illicit pills and powders, his growing profile was as a rapacious property tycoon buying up his childhood suburb of Brunswick, chunk by chunk. At the time of writing Mokbel's doting mum, Lora, still attributed her son's fortune to his real estate savvy. All the jail time and court dates were just a conspiracy by jealous police, she said. Antonios's millions were made from canny land deals – certainly not drugs.

There are many criminal fiefdoms in Melbourne, a city like Chicago before it, quietly proud of its distinctly colourful underworld. And there are different parading grounds for well-to-do office-less crims to broker kerbside deals, splash their cash, and ostentatiously display allegiances. Slain gangster Alphonse Gangitano, one of the earlier gangland war victims, was known as 'the black prince of Lygon Street' for lording it over the Italian inner-city strip of barbers, baristas and perfect coffees. For a while Carlton identity Mick Gatto became part of the footpath furniture outside his favourite restaurant in Bourke Street, a vibrant, bustling strip of bars, restaurants and cafes a stone's throw from Parliament. He would keep himself amused by getting passing pollies to sign their autograph with a trick exploding pen. Mokbel, on the other hand, copped the short straw when fate selected his Brunswick stamping ground.

Sydney Road is named for its now antiquated claim to fame of being the best way onto the Hume Highway – the main arterial between Australia's two biggest cities. Its modern incarnation is as a pointless, gridlocked, tram-clogged road to nowhere. The road's narrowness, measuring a 'chain' or 20.11 metres, is a relic of an 1839 survey completed before the route became a muddy pot-holed goldrush thoroughfare. Even the *Encyclopedia of Melbourne* has a go at the paved purgatory, stating: 'Sydney Road in Brunswick is 2.5km of straight, narrow, commercial and retail chaos.' If any more needs to be said, the official history of the road is titled *Almost Pretty*.

Sydney Road is festooned with dilapidated discount shops, vendors of ageing spinning kebab meat, dusty Muslim prayer rooms and cheaper-than-CBD-rent lawyers that locals disparagingly refer to as 'Sydney Road solicitors'. These were Mokbel's mean streets. They were streets whose criminal past almost emanated from the bitumen. In 1965 Ronald Ryan and Peter Walker had bolted to Sydney Road after breaking out of Pentridge and shooting dead a prison guard. Ryan swung for his effort, the last man hanged in Australia, in 1967.

But Mokbel would be the first of the non-Anglo-Celt crims, and the first with a corporate front, to make the street his own. And if Tony was based in the gutter he was looking at the stars. In the late nineties he bought a $200,000 flashy red Ferrari roadster. It would remain his most beloved chariot even after he added a Mercedes Benz (with personalised plates, RU DARE, aimed at any watching police) and an Audi to his fleet.

He used his Boronia pizza palace as a springboard to open a restaurant, TJ's Bar & Grill, on Sydney Road, just a quick No 19 tram ride from the bright lights of the inner city. His co-director in the venture was an equally colourful import, Jacobus 'Jack' Smit. Smit was born in the Dutch sex centre of Rotterdam but had made a life in Australia. For a period Tony and Jack lived in adjoining apartments overlooking the coast in Port Melbourne. Smit proved you can take the boy out of the red light district but not the reverse when he became pimp-in-chief at Melbourne's Top of the Town brothel.

Decorated with cherubic angels, the Top of the Town is considered one of the classiest of Melbourne's whorehouses. It boasts of being 'Melbourne's Longest Established Brothel & Escort Agency', although brothels were only legalised in the state in 1984. Just a few years before Tony and Jack built TJ's from a shelf company, the Top of the Town was involved in less classy moments, reflecting its generic status as a house of ill-repute. In 1992 the Brunswick Magistrates Court found charges proven that an underage girl was present on the premises; however, no one was convicted. And Mokbel's connection to the brothel was likely to have been stronger than just being mates with Jacobus Smit.

At least one prominent underworld figure has told authorities that Mokbel was the real owner of the Top of the Town – a puppeteer pimp working through Smit and using the bordello to launder his millions. The gangland informer said: 'Tony would place at least twenty-five per cent of his money through Jack Smit, who would put the money into business and properties. Jack also bought the Top of the Town with Tony's money and Tony told me that $2 million had gone through there under the table.'

Around the same time, the colourful Mr Smit – who at one point was involved in a venture with ex-PM Bob Hawke selling pokies to Madagascar – was named at a coronial hearing into the unsolved mafia execution of Alfonso Muratore. Muratore was gunned down with a 12-gauge in 1992, a fortnight after telling internal Coles investigators that fruiterers were bribing supermarket bosses to win lucrative contracts. The coroner was told that Muratore and his employer, Orlando Luciano, who liked to refer to himself as 'the Boss', were both present at the secret city hotel meeting when they blew the whistle on market corruption. As well as the Italians, two internal Coles investigators were also present and, mysteriously enough, Jacobus Smit.

So TJ's Bar & Grill was more than a meat and martini munch-house. For Jack and Tony – two slightly soiled but well-laundered suits – it was a tilt at a toehold in respectable industry. If that didn't work it still gave Tony an opportunity to launder while lunching. With its dark surfaces, garish bar, large windows and spotlighting, TJ's was like a before-its-time version of the now ubiquitous dimly lit lounges attached to pokies venues.

Mokbel's stake in the steakhouse gave him an office above the restaurant he could use as a base to organise his nefarious activities. There the crim on the make could admire the view from the upstairs window: the Brunswick police station directly across Sydney Road. A former Mokbel friend said Tony used the space more for 'blow and blowjobs' than paper shuffling and clerical work. In TJ's carpark Mokbel's drug-running foot soldiers were plying their trade just metres from the local cop shop. And at the end of a hard day at the office Mokbel could wander down from his business loft and wheel and deal with questionable characters over free grilled steak in his own den.

As he got richer, Mokbel's sphere of influence was expanding beyond blue-collar crims to respectable local community figures and small-time politicians. With the restaurant at his disposal Mokbel could present as a charismatic, hardworking, up-and-coming businessman. A simple entrepreneur who could use some help to keep the wheels of commerce moving against the tyranny of red tape, rule-obsessed bureaucrats and ratbag not-in-my-backyard residents.

In August 2000 fellow northern 'burbs boy and Federal Labor MP Kelvin Thomson responded to a request for a reference in support of Mokbel's application for a liquor licence (apparently for another Mokbel venue) on official letterhead. Mokbel would have been happy with the result.

The MP wrote: 'I understand that Mr Mokbell [sic] has been married for the past eight years and has two children. I further understand that over the past eight years he has been a responsible caring husband and father. Mr Mokbel has in partnership purchased a number of business properties in the Brunswick area. As a result of his business and property ventures Mr Mokbel is making a significant contribution to the community and employing a substantial number of people. I urge you to take into account Mr Mokbel's last years of unblemished conduct, his commitment to family and his successful establishment as a local businessman in making your decision concerning his application.'

At the time Thomson's wife, Marsha, was the Victorian consumer affairs minister – responsible for liquor licensing – but grog authorities still knocked back Tony's application on advice from police.

The controversial reference emerged seven years later in the course of a tooth-and-nail pre-election battle, by which time Mokbel's infamy was widespread. In the intervening years the member for Wills had scrabbled to the position of shadow attorney-general. Thomson said he did not think he had met Mokbel. He said he regularly gave out references, that he believed at the time Mokbel was reformed, and that he had been unaware of Mokbel's 1998 conviction for conspiring to traffic drugs. But the special pleading was pissing in the wind and ultimately there was no option for Thomson, the man most likely to become attorney-general, but to step down. His inappropriately kind words for Mokbel cost him that job in the same year the ALP was swept to victory after more than a decade in the wilderness of opposition.

Larceny was indeed among Mokbel's multitude of criminal tendencies but it's unlikely even he would have conceived his influence could rob a man from becoming the nation's most senior legal officer. The MP was not alone in finding good in what otherwise appeared to be a scofflaw's lengthy priors docket. Mokbel had also charmed a senior police officer – the licensing sergeant for the Brunswick sub-district – into providing a letter of reference supporting a doomed liquor application.

The letter, from Sergeant Ray Dole, which appeared in the Victorian Civil and Administrative Tribunal file, said Dole had known Mokbel for a decade and conceded his character 'back many years ago' was not good, but Dole was confident he was now 'worthy' and 'of reformed habits and is making a worthwhile contribution to society'.

8

Boomtown rat

The higher the building
the lower the morals.

– Noël Coward

In 1996 the economy was just starting to properly fire up after a debilitating recession. The median price for properties in Melbourne was $150,000 but the only way was up for speculators like Mokbel, who were getting in on the ground floor. Eleven years later the median Melbourne property price was $485,000 – an increase on investment of 223 per cent. In the interim those with enough money to throw around, and sufficient cajones to back their judgement that it would be a long time before property prices plateaued, were set to make a mint.

Melbourne was a boomtown. And Mokbel – an amphetamine czar and land pirate – was its rat. He started buying up properties around his restaurant on Sydney Road. He bought units in Templestowe, and real estate in nearby Coburg. He bought a property in Queensland and a hotel and farm in Kilmore. His brother Horty was linked to valuable properties in Coburg and Safety Beach and two each in Caulfield, near the track, and Preston. In conversations about importing drugs Mokbel would speak airily of property investment. 'I reckon if you can buy two or three million a year in ... fucking solid assets, you're laughing ... that's what I try ... and average,' he said.

Tony's family home with Carmel and the nippers was a high-tech camera-festooned haven in the relatively inner suburb of Pascoe Vale. Its proximity to the city meant Tony's purchase of a waterfront Port Melbourne penthouse – next door to Jack Smit – must have screamed 'love pad' rather than convenience even to Carmel.

Mokbel continued his unholy TJ's alliance with Smit, and the pair made ambitious plans to crown their Brunswick patch by erecting an $18-million winged-keel apartment tower on Sydney Road. The planned ten-storey avant garde edifice, dubbed 'the winged wonder', would contain 120 apartments, restaurants, a gym, a four-storey carpark, solar lighting and solar hot water. To residents it was a money-spinning monstrosity that could only jar with its low-rise urban village surrounds. But bombastic proponents touted Tony's tower as an architectural jewel with the potential 'to be a strong landmark in the sense of buildings like the Eiffel Tower and the Arc de Triomphe'.

Unhappy locals derided the comparisons, instead labelling it 'the Eye-Full Tower' and 'Bent Penis'. They compared the design's appearance to periscopes, Lego blocks, Rubik's cubes and exhaust stacks. And the riled residents formed a protest group to trump the tower before it permanently put them in the shade. Some argued that no one in their right mind would want to live in the design's outermost 'wing' apartments which were cantilevered eight metres out from the main structure, hovering twenty-three metres above the ground with no visible means of support.

Following seventy-four objections, the council's own planning unit rejected the proposal. But it seems some Moreland councillors were sufficiently charmed by the pimp and the man rapidly becoming Australia's biggest drug dealer to put those reservations to one side and give Tony's tower the green light. One of the councillors at the time was a Kelvin Thomson staffer, who later insisted he did not vote on the project. Whatever the case, Tony's towering aspirations were finally kyboshed seven months later when residents successfully appealed to a civil tribunal which ruled that the size of the project went beyond the council's planning guidelines.

Their phallic ambitions rendered flaccid, Jack and Tony must have pined for the absence of red tape and democratic process involved in their more lucrative fields of running whores and drugs. But another exotic business opportunity – a multimillion-dollar stake in a 460-hectare East Gippsland marina and resort – would ensure Mokbel and Smit's lifestyles of the rich and heinous would roll on. Smit and a lawyer and property developer, Douglas Harle, had planned to build a boat basin on the Nicholson River to provide dockage to watercraft on the Gippsland Lakes near Bairnsdale. Harle had acted for Tony before and Tony took an active interest in the marina development, even visiting the site.

Police feared their interest in the location was as a means of funnelling drugs into the country by sea. But the Mokbels' desired involvement and attempt to muscle in ended in tears. When an attempt to buy a half stake in the project by a Mokbel-linked company was rebuffed, the Mokbels defaulted to a traditional shakedown. Milad Mokbel met Mr Harle and his wife, Barbara, at Kew restaurant QPO and said he had lent Jack Smit the money for his stake and now he needed it back from the Harles. The squarehead couple patiently tried to explain that Smit was responsible for any debts he incurred, not them. They said if Smit wanted to be paid out what he had put in the project they would repay it to Smit directly.

Six weeks later the put-upon property developer, Douglas Harle, and his wife, Barbara, were out at dinner with two friends at another Kew restaurant, Di Palmas, when Douglas got a call on his mobile. According to Douglas, he recognised the voice as belonging to Tony's ostentatiously vicious little bro, Milad. 'We met a few weeks ago in the restaurant in Kew. You will be approached in the next few days by someone ... You will sign an agreement,' the menacing caller said. 'Tell your wife with the Luna Park mouth to shut up or the last thing both of you will see is my eyes at 4 am in the morning.'

The Harles were left in fear for their lives and the project fell over as Harle and Smit sued and counter-sued. Milad got his threat-to-kill charges dropped by pleading to attempting to blackmail. At the hearing Milad was flanked by three large security guards in the dock lest he decide to arc up over a point of law.

Tony had registered a company in the name of his father, Sajih, in the mid-nineties and dozens more followed. The registered names of the companies Mokbel was either a shareholder in, or director of, reveal the sweep of Tony's investments and influence. There were Trackside, Street Side, South Yarra Shopping, Apparel Shopping, Bridge Road Shopping, Chapel Street Shopping, Brunswick Market, Chadstone Store, Collins Street Shopping, Fashion Innovations and Brunswick Market Deli, to name a few. Carmel Mokbel was a director of the Half Glass Hotel, and Horty's wife, Roula, was a director of H & R Petroleum. Paul Howden was also a co-director in one venture. Mokbel had secret stakes in dozens of other businesses not directly linkable to him.

'How it operates is I go to someone and I'll say: this is my hotel but it's in your name. The profits will come to me. If I want to liquidate that hotel you'll sell it and give me the money. And if you ever step outside, I'll kill you,' ex-Purana chief Jim O'Brien said.

Mokbel bankrolled fashion designer Chris Chronis to launch a chain of LSD – Love, Style and Design – clothing stores. Mokbel and Jack Smit were also involved when Chronis, a one-time fight promoter and dab hand at poker, launched his own 'personal fragrance', Christos. Like a number of colourful characters, Chronis, who was also *Playboy*'s Australian licensee, later became embroiled in the Opes Prime corporate collapse.

Mokbel had a genuine love of corporate procedures, corporate language and the way company structures and protocols could be abused. His penchant for mimicking and sheltering under legitimate commercial structures even saw him label a later crime crew The Company. It is hard not to wonder whether Mokbel, had he finished school, might have had his ruthlessly sociopathic smart-alec capitalism and compulsive desire for status satisfied by becoming a stockbroker in the 1980s.

As things turned out it was a drug kingpin who wore the fine suits, made the attempted entrees into high society and drove the speedy red sports car that went from zero to 100 kph in four seconds. 'I am the kind of guy who drives the latest Ferrari,' Mokbel said.

His cousin Jamil Abou Baker had a more defensive position on the flash wheels and conspicuous wealth of the Mokbel boys, their friends and associates. 'A lot of people think that because we're young and drive nice cars that we're drug dealers. It's just that we work hard,' he explained.

Mokbel was not a blue-collar or white-collar crim but a particularly devastating mix of both. If his corporate interests expanded it was usually as a result of an expansion in his criminal endeavours. Sometimes the police quietly intercepted an imported Mokbel motherlode but Tony was so prolific that others simply slipped through the net. A massive Mokbel three-million-pill import worth $50 million was likely among the ones that got away.

Mokbel was behind the biggest haul of LSD police had nabbed in Victoria when in 1999 a drug dealer was caught with 50,000 acid tabs. The dealer confirmed to police he had obtained the booty from Mokbel but would not give evidence against him. In another deal Mokbel upped the ante and organised an even larger batch, this time of 80,000 LSD tablets. Despite the hauls being busted, Mokbel had still not been linked to the biggest speed lab and the biggest seizure of LSD in his state's history.

Mokbel would pay top dollar for precursor chemicals that could be spun into more lucrative products. But if he could steal drug ingredients for free that was even better. Packaging found in the lab explosion (which saw plumber Paul Howden jailed) was traced back to a 750-kilogram load of pseudoephedrine stolen from docks in New South Wales in late 1996. And in 2001 Mokbel was believed to have organised the theft of 175 kilograms of pseudoephedrine from a colourful former police officer who was taking the amphetamine-precursor chemicals to a drug company in Melbourne's eastern suburbs. But it was two of his most notorious drug schemes that would reveal just how far Antonios Mokbel had come. The twin schemes – international imports of hashish and cocaine – would also reveal just how a greedy but self-preserving Mr Big could become obscenely rich and remain free by getting a series of fall guys to take all the risks.

9
Mokbel's elephant

> Hey cats, it's four o'clock in the morning ... Here
> we are in Harlem. Everybody's here but the police,
> and they'll be here any minute. It's hiiiiigh time.
>
> – Fats Waller, 'The Reefer Song'

As a diminutive drug dealer Tony Mokbel knew that when it came to hard-to-get imports size mattered. Mokbel would tout 'I don't do small things' and reckoned he could smuggle an elephant past customs. He never actually pirated in a pachyderm but one of his bolder drug shipments came close.

In his busy August of 2001, Mokbel used two shipping containers to import 2930 kilograms – over 2.9 tonnes – of cannabis resin. The total weight of the drugs was just below that of a full size Asian elephant, which can grow to between three and five tonnes. The illegal hashish booty looked like thousands of dark brown oversized stock cubes and had been wrapped to look like a shipment of coffee.

Marijuana is a mix of flowers, leaves and small stems of cannabis. Hashish – or resin – by contrast comes from a sap-like substance stored in the flowers of the female plant. Hash can be four times as potent as marijuana and its superior strength is reflected in a much higher onsale value. Mokbel's motherlode would have been worth $147 million on the street.

He had arranged for the Afghan hashish to be smuggled from the Middle East to Melbourne using false shipping documents piggybacking on the name of a reputable importing company. His half-kilogram blocks of resin were wrapped in plastic then an outer layer of brown and gold foil stamped with a distinctive gold logo and Finnish coffee label markings. The documents stated the shipping containers held 27 tonnes of black marble tiles. While the description was technically true, the unmentioned elephant in the room was the 2.9 tonnes of hashish wrapped in coffee bags hidden away under false floors in the containers.

Mokbel's general on the job was Jessie Franco, thirty-seven, who had recruited four helpers of his own as an unloading crew. A middling crim, Franco had no gun licence when he was nabbed eleven years earlier with an unregistered .22-calibre handgun and bullets. The weapon and ammunition were found in his girlfriend's handbag and Franco maintained, though few believed him, that he was chivalrously taking the rap for his gun-toting girl.

The year before the hashish job Franco assaulted a cop who was playing for a rival team in the Essendon District Football League. After Senior-Constable Morris tried to break up an onfield scuffle involving Franco and others, Franco approached him, king-hit Morris, who did not see it coming, and said, 'Take that, you fuck.' Morris felt his jaw break. The assault charge that followed resulted in a twelve-month suspended sentence – no jail time.

For Mokbel's jumbo drop Franco had organised himself a pre-paid mobile phone in the fake – if not entirely incredible – name of Tony Fontano, and another for one of his crew. As the drugs travelled across the globe toward Melbourne Franco used the phones to call his crew and the scheme's shadowy organisers.

Helping Franco were a pizza cook, Paul Pratico, thirty-eight, Robert Cetrangolo, thirty-six, and David Ciampoli, forty-six, as well as Tony 'the Croat' Crnac, a thirty-nine-year-old shop steward in Victoria's colourful building and construction industry. The two shipping containers found their way to a workyard in the industrial suburb of Campbellfield where, under cover of night, the five rugged-up middle-aged European-Australians set to work on them like a colony of ants.

Crnac knew the owners of the yard from the largely Croatian Melbourne Knights soccer club, the Croatian Club in Footscray, and the building industry. He was the first to arrive at the yard, getting to the gates at 11 pm to meet the two trucks carrying the containers. He was familiar with the yard and knew the owners kept a spare set of keys hidden on the premises.

As Crnac signed for the delivery, detectives settled in for an action-packed night using cameras to secretly record the crew's movements. When midnight approached Franco and Cetrangolo arrived in borrowed utes and Ciampoli and Pratico in hired removalist trucks. For three hours the crew lugged crates full of tiles into the yard with the Croat driving a forklift to stack them. Rugged up in gloves and a beanie Franco used a spanner to unbolt the specially constructed false floor of the first container. He prised up the planks with a crowbar and passed them out to the other workers. As the boards came up the heady sweet stench of the cannabis resin dispersed into the cold early morning air.

Despite the illegality of their venture Pratico was taking no chances with occupational health and safety and wore an orange safety vest. To vary the look he wore a blue baseball cap and had a black balaclava in his pocket. He backed his truck up to the first container while the Croat set about dismantling the floor in the second. At 4 am, when half the first container's hashish had been loaded into Pratico's truck, the AFP officers swooped.

The federal agents moved through the yard loudly announcing who they were and informing the removalists they were under arrest. Cetrangolo did a runner, throwing off his work gloves as he went. He was grabbed by police as he reached the corner of the yard. Franco did a bolt too and was also grabbed by the feds. The Croat had just finished a casual cigarette and was in the second container using a crowbar to lever up the floorboards when the police landed, catching him red-handed and cornered. The other two hid but were soon uncovered. Ciampoli was found hiding between two stacks of metal and Pratico lying on the roof of a shipping container.

All five claimed they were just there to lug tiles in the cause of an honest middle-of-the-night's work. They said their virtuous plans went pear-shaped when cunning and cruel criminals stepped in and took advantage of their work ethic. The workers claimed the job went bad when Mokbel materialised waving his handgun around and threatening the men's families unless they lifted the boards and unloaded the dope.

'The instructions were very clear,' Franco said. 'This was a threat and I had no intentions of doing anything but cooperate from that point on.'

The Croat backed up Franco's story. 'He said "Things have changed, you are doing this now, and just do what we say,"' Crnac said.

The story opened the way for the workers to argue that they acted firstly in ignorance then under duress, and so were guilty of no crime. It is possible, as Franco claimed, he met with Mokbel in the carpark of a nearby McDonald's before unloading began. But it would have been out of character for Mokbel to have risked the direct involvement of going to the yard. The video or human surveillance of the federal agents also saw no 'sixth or seventh man' enter the yard at any stage.

Franco's crew fingered Mokbel and alleged crim Pasquale Barbaro as the organisers of the massive import. Police believed the scheme's shadowy financiers were Mokbel and the Morans. The closest authorities got to the senior organisers of the import was prosecuting a Mokbel mate we will call for legal reasons 'Lucky', who was acquitted.

Both vengeful and vain, Mokbel would not have forgiven Franco for implicating him but would have been relieved he forgot Tony's surname and flattered by his description. Franco told authorities Barbaro was at the yard that night as well as 'a well-built man of Turkish or Lebanese appearance' known to Franco only as 'Tony'.

Pratico's version was that he did some tile unloading for which he was to be paid in tiles but a football injury from the weekend flared up and he went to rest in a vehicle forcing him to miss all the floorboard-prising action. Pratico said that when police arrived, he hid on the top of a container at the front of the yard, because he felt that the tiles might have been stolen. But authorities couldn't help wondering why, if Franco's crew were just there for the tiles, they hadn't loaded any into their vehicles. Or why they had put the forklift away once the tiles were dumped on the ground.

Franco's crew had also left a few clues indicating this was not a legit job. They had been very keen, in the case of a bust, not to be linked to their hired vehicles or the phones inside them. Franco had parked away from the yard in a nearby Kmart carpark and after he was arrested police located his car key in his sock. Ciampoli ditched his truck key near his hidey-hole but it too was found by police.

Their precautions and stories of duress helped them little in the end. The court did not mollycoddle the five men, handing out stiff jail terms to the crew hired to shift tiles and transport the bags of hash. 'Organisers of criminal operations on a scale like this cannot succeed without underlings like you to perform their dirty work,' the judge said. Franco was ultimately sentenced to seven years with a minimum of four. His crew – Pratico, Crnac, Cetrangolo and Ciampoli – all copped five and half years with a minimum of three.

The five men were never the primary targets of the AFP's surveillance. The feds were much more interested in the scheme's puppeteer. Mokbel's drones had just wandered into the police gaze because they were working the high-risk end of the drug tycoon's game. And when dawn broke on their moonlit mischief, they realised they had ended up on the other side of the bars to Tony.

10

Cocaine

> Cocaine's for horses and it's not for men,
> Doctor said it kill you, but he didn't say when.
>
> – 'Cocaine Blues', traditional

Despite importing and manufacturing drugs on a gargantuan scale, Teflon Tony had enjoyed a lot of luck and dodged a lot of attention. But the scheme that eventually brought the heat down on Mokbel was a plan to import just a couple of kilograms of cocaine from Mexico. On any Australian street the cocaine import of about two kilograms pure and three kilograms cut was worth at least $733,000, but by Tony's measure the profits were puny. 'I don't know why I bothered risking it in the end because this is just small beer to me. I usually do bigger deals,' Mokbel said.

His very simple plan was to make some Mexican connections, buy the gear and smuggle the valuable white powder into Melbourne through the postal system. To bring the plan to fruition Mokbel would not need to sip tequila with deadly hombres in Tijuana, board a Mexico-bound plane or even leave Brunswick. Instead he would assemble a crew of dupes who would do the real work, take the real risks and, if necessary, take the fall and do the time for their benevolent boss.

By the time Mokbel's Mexican mission was launched his team of amoral amigos included a world champion strongman, a Mokbel sycophant, a Judas and members of Mexico's deadly organised crime syndicate Arellano-Felix. Despite their differences, when the deal eventually went bad the crew members would be united by a common profound regret for ever falling under Mokbel's spell. Among the plotters was a man with a wire who had planned all along to betray Mokbel, and another who only later decided he too was willing to sing like a mariachi. By the bitter end Mokbel too may have learnt a very specific lesson. Never work with bodybuilders, wire-wearing informers, angry snitches and brutal Mexican gangsters.

Mokbel had counted his mate the Grifter into the international plot, but he did so not knowing that something had fundamentally changed. Two months after his mate and colleague Mark Moran was gunned down in Melbourne's then embryonic gangland war, several of the Grifter's houses were raided by police still probing the Moran drug syndicate. The drug squad dragnet produced more than nine kilograms of ecstasy, two kilograms of cocaine, almost two kilograms of cannabis, a pill press and two guns. The Grifter already had a lengthy list of priors, having racked up hundreds of convictions including drug trafficking and gun offences.

When the Grifter looked across the table at his police captors it's likely he saw the prospect of a lengthy jail stint. Mark Moran had been just thirty-six when he was shot dead outside his Aberfeldie home in June 2000 by rival Carl Williams. With the killing of his boyhood mate still fresh in his mind, it is also possible that the Grifter realised he needed to find a circuit breaker to dodge an early death. To the police the Grifter was potentially a very handy informant. If they could turn the Grifter into the 'the Snitch' he could feed them vital intelligence while his street reputation would rebuff nearly all suspicion. They offered him a juicy cut on his prison sentence. In return police won a chance to get tape recordings that could reduce the rogue Mokbel empire to rubble. A deal was done and lifetime crim the Grifter went from dealing grass to grassing for police.

In poaching the pill-making Grifter, Mokbel was arguably stepping on the toes of the surviving Morans, including family patriarch Lewis, and Mark's violently deranged half-brother Jason. The Grifter told police that Mokbel planned to discount his drugs to corner the amphetamine and ecstasy market. A bloody falling out in the Mokbel–Moran drug duopoly could have been on the cards, but if offence was taken at Mokbel nicking one of the country's best pill-pressers, either Mokbel used some of his legendary charm to smooth things over or the Morans chose to bite their tongues. For a little while at least, Lewis Moran and Tony Mokbel would keep working together.

Also in the ranks for the Mexican mission was an eager-to-impress, not too bright vulnerable character of the sort Mokbel seemed to groom so easily. His real name also cannot be used so we will call him 'the Stooge'. His recollections of the events are inevitably self-serving but they still paint a dark picture of Mokbel as a canny and ruthless user and abuser.

The Stooge had known Mokbel since Tony was a young milk-bar owner but had not seen him in fifteen years. 'I heard Tony was doing well for himself from property and business deals and that he was driving a Ferrari,' the Stooge said. He had also heard that Mokbel drove a special Mercedes Benz that had a glovebox always filled with cash bundled in $5000 lots. 'From what I'd heard I formed the impression that Tony's business activities were not all legal,' the Stooge said.

Their paths crossed again among the dumbbells and treadmills of a Brunswick gym in 2000 at a time when the Stooge was depressed and disillusioned. Mokbel offered him a path of hope, glamour and the prospect of making money. 'Over a short period of time I became deeply impressed by Tony's empire and trappings,' the Stooge said. 'He owned a lot of commercial property, businesses and houses. He ate at the best restaurants. He drove a Ferrari ... he bet up to $50[000] to $60,000 on a race. He encouraged me and became my mentor, and as a result I trusted him.'

The Stooge was dazzled by how Mokbel attended a lot of high-profile functions. Mokbel wooed him by involving him in some of his more respectable ventures. 'Tony offered me the path to financial success and security by inviting me to join him in several property and business deals,' he said.

Mokbel had confided in the Stooge that he wanted more overseas drug contacts to expand his global network. He already had people in England and Amsterdam but what he really needed was a new contact on the other side of the world. 'I knew I had to impress Tony in order to get close to him and become worthy of his attention,' the Stooge said. So when a strongman friend told the Stooge he knew a cocaine exporter in Mexico the Stooge saw an instant opportunity to further bask in the warm glow of Mokbel's affection.

Edmond 'Sonny' Schmidt was a moustachioed man-mountain who had won the coveted Mr Olympia title. Like Lou Ferrigno, who played the Hulk on television, and Arnold Schwarzenegger, the world-champion bodybuilder had made it to the highest levels of the competition. Friends and bodybuilding fans described 'Samoan Sonny' as a sweet-natured gentle giant. But somewhere along the line the strongman with a heart of gold had made some not so sweet friends. One of them was a Mexican called Gino who was looking to export cocaine.

Sonny told this to the Stooge who in turn boasted to Mokbel of his link to an overseas contact who could supply unlimited quantities of cocaine. 'I decided to try and put Sonny and Tony together, because I wanted to get into Tony's good books and stay close to him,' the Stooge said.

Sonny's contact, Gino Brunetti, was a senior officer in the vicious Arellano-Felix drug cartel. The family-based gang delivers up to a quarter of the US's illegal drugs and is a major cause of Mexico's thousands of drug-related homicides every year. Its victims include wives and children and its members recently dropped three heads on the floor of a disco as a sign of the gang's dominance.

Soon the 100-kilogram strongman and the eager-to-impress Stooge were on a free flight to Mexico to arrange for Mokbel to be sent a free sample so he could test the quality of the drugs. Mokbel was happy with the result of the dress rehearsal and told the Stooge the quality was excellent. Sonny was redeployed to Mexico with $37,000 in American greenbacks (roughly A$70,000 at the time) plus a $5000 sweetener for himself, to arrange the first full-scale cocaine import. Sonny and the Stooge had arranged the Mexico end of the scheme but Mokbel had his own local contacts to usher the drugs into Australia.

Ron Cassar, a stumpy, balding man with a sheepish disposition and the unfortunate nickname 'Buddha', was nothing special to look at. To most people Buddha's job as second in charge at the United Parcel Service (UPS) in Melbourne would also have seemed particularly unglamorous. But to Mokbel the university dropout and career freight worker was the golden goose – a perfect inside man, who, with a little charm and some appeals to greed and vanity, would do whatever Mokbel wanted.

In Mexico Sonny paid the cartel and arranged for the cocaine to be sent to fictitious people at addresses in Footscray and Carlton. The cocaine was hidden in Mexican handicrafts, candles and decorative ornaments, including a miniature unicorn, before being parcelled up. In early November 2000 the two parcels were sent out of Mexico City using the UPS system and the game was afoot.

The Grifter's role in the Mexican mission was to buy and on-sell the drugs once they arrived. That way Mokbel had no risk of actual possession. One day, as Mokbel was on the street telling the Grifter of his ambitions to regularly import cocaine, a stumpy, balding man in a maroon Ford pulled up and honked. Mokbel walked over and chatted with Buddha Cassar for a minute then returned to his candid conversation with the Grifter – and his wire.

'He's got the keys. He's the boss and he goes in and gets it for me,' Mokbel said on tape.

The Grifter did not know the man in the maroon Ford. But unfortunately for Mokbel he had the nous to record the vehicle's number plate, which he passed on to his police handlers. Once they had an identity for the insider, authorities were able to map and follow the plot much more closely. From that moment there were many more eyes and ears paying close attention to the movement of the Mexican cocaine than just Mokbel and his merry band of amigos.

En route to Australia the cocaine parcels containing three kilograms of white powder travelled first from Mexico to the American UPS hub in Kentucky. It had been impressed on Sonny that he should immediately relay the parcels' tracking numbers. This would mean Mokbel's inside man could trace their journey to Melbourne and sneak them out of the warehouse before they were inspected by customs. But there was a delay in getting the packages' numbers and at a vital time Sonny could not be contacted. Without the numbers the cocaine would be lost in a sea of freight and would end up before customs officers.

In Kentucky, US customs, alerted by the Australian Federal Police, grabbed the parcels just as Mokbel was finally able to pass on the vital numbers to his inside man. US customs drilled one of the artefacts, X-rayed the other parcel and ran tests that showed cocaine was present. Equipped with the numbers, Buddha Cassar tracked the parcels on his work computer and found they were stuck in America.

Police accompanied the drugs on a flight from the US to Sydney where, upon arrival, federal agents removed most of the cocaine. Mokbel ascribed the delays to quarantine holding up the cocaine because some of it was in wood. 'Fucking idiots, they put it under wood ... won't let you in wood ... still in LA,' Mokbel told a friend. But his criminal instinct was functioning enough to smell a rat and he contemplated walking away from the deal. 'I reckon it's off ... don't go near it,' Mokbel said, but later changed his mind.

The plan was reaching its end in spring and despite the import's high stakes the season meant one thing to horse-mad Mokbel – the Spring Racing Carnival. The Grifter told him if the drugs came in on a particular day, 'I'll just come and see you.'

But Mokbel had other plans: 'I'll be at the Oaks, mate. Forget it.' And it would be a very large carnival indeed for Mokbel. At Derby Day that year undercover police tailing the drug lord were shocked at the brazen way he distributed cocaine samples and how flagrantly TV, modelling and society celebs indulged.

As planned, Mokbel also attended Oaks Day that year and again his police tail followed him. There was a close shave when a female undercover officer dressed up for the races caught Mokbel's eye. As the drug bigwig made a determined beeline straight for her the cop thought her cover was blown. But Mokbel was oblivious and offered the undercover officer a free cocaine sample. The pusher man's generosity was calculated – each free snorter was a potential long-term paying customer. And there were more supplies in the post coming from Mexico.

The federal police allowed the parcels, still containing some cocaine that had not been removed, to travel to Melbourne airport. There a UPS driver picked them up and dropped them at the company's warehouse, where they entered the customs control bay under police surveillance.

Cassar told Mokbel the goods had arrived and on a Sunday night, after the cleaners had left for the day, he crept into work. Buddha disconnected the warehouse's security cameras then entered the customs area and emptied the parcels of their important contents. Secretly installed police cameras were still rolling and his actions inside were caught on tape. When he stepped out into the dead of night federal police crews swooped, catching Mokbel's inside man red-handed. With Buddha behind bars the police pounced on Sonny Schmidt, the strongman's brother Pale, who had a minor role, and then – to keep up appearances – the Grifter. Everyone, that is, except for the mission's mastermind.

Police had Mokbel cold for the cocaine import, but authorities had learnt imports like kilograms of pure coke were just icing sugar on Fat Tony's cake. The Mokbels had established a dauntingly huge drug empire. And there were other things Mokbel had said into the Grifter's microphone that police wanted to watch play out. For the moment Tony would remain free.

Inside man Ron Cassar copped six years' jail and the Stooge was condemned to always be looking over his shoulder. But for the strongman, for whom a short prison sentence proved the beginning of the end, the punishment was life.

It seemed anyone who went near the cursed cocaine scheme ended up behind bars, including a melancholy Mexican locked up in the US. A telephone intercept on the Stooge's line recorded his chats with Gino Brunetti. The sting made the AFP the first organisation in the world to have such a senior ranking member of the Mexican syndicate talking openly about narcotic importations on the telephone. The Australian tapes of phone calls between the Stooge and Gino were forwarded by the feds to the US Drug Enforcement Agency. It was Gino's third strike and soon after the Americans locked him up in a US prison cell for life.

Before he started pumping iron with Mokbel, the Stooge's criminal forays had been minor. Aside from driving offences, there were two court appearances when he was eighteen. There were four charges over a fracas at a hotel and a property destruction charge which attracted a fine and a bond. There was another fine for an unregistered rabbit-shooting rifle and a cannabis possession charge. 'He was otherwise of good character with a very strong commitment to work,' a judge found.

But if being sprung on his first major criminal endeavour was hard luck, it was soured further by the revelation that Mokbel was not a foul-weather friend. The Stooge lamented that he realised much too late what he had got himself into. 'I just didn't know how to get off the treadmill,' he said.

* * *

Devonport lad Jarrod Ragg always wanted to be a copper. When the Tasmanian police knocked him back because he was eighteen, he applied to the AFP and became a fed instead. He had gone to the mainland and ended up handling the cocaine prosecution of the nation's biggest drug criminal. Agent Ragg said the Stooge may not have turned Crown witness had Tony treated him a little nicer when it all fell apart. 'He was angry with Mokbel because Mokbel had attempted to intimidate him to stay staunch and not say anything,' Ragg said. 'His pride was injured. He saw the light. He decided that he was better off helping the cops rather than doing time with the Mokbels. He possibly would have stayed staunch if Mokbel had have kept paying for his legal fees and hadn't tried to intimidate him. But instead he was highly offended.'

The Stooge said he had loved Mokbel but in the end Mokbel 'didn't give a shit about me' and just brushed him off. 'I was duped by Tony. He used me in the importation of cocaine to try to shield himself from direct involvement ... by blinding me with his vast wealth, power and trappings,' he said.

But perhaps the most tragic figure in the disastrous episode was Sonny Schmidt. Photographed at court by the press he reverted to his muscleman competition poses, ready for his close-up like a bodybuilding version of *Sunset Boulevard*'s Norma Desmond. Sonny copped a three-year maximum term and became a born-again Christian who would get around his prison hellhole in a 'Jesus is the Lord' T-shirt. Shortly after finding God he found a tumour under his arm. He was diagnosed with cancer in December 2003. Sonny was released from prison early to be nursed by his brother at home, but he died just a month after being diagnosed, aged 50. Sonny was survived by his siblings, whose unique mix of names reflect their German and Islander parentage – Sara, Bismark, Fritz, Fossie and Paletasala.

Medics said cancer killed him. The intake of steroids and other bodybuilding drugs to achieve the perfect glistening beefcake look had not helped. But his family said it was the fall from grace that killed Sonny. 'That done him in,' a close relative said. 'The heartache that came from that ... they say stress can destroy you and that's what happened to Sonny.'

11

Bent

There was a crooked man who walked a crooked mile.
He found a crooked sixpence upon a crooked stile.
He bought a crooked cat, which caught a crooked mouse.
And they all lived together in a crooked little house.

– English nursery rhyme

Police recruits in Victoria pledge an oath to keep the peace, prevent offences and discharge their legal duties 'without favour or affection, malice or ill will'. But in the late nineties and new millennium an alarming number of the state's drug investigators forgot all that. Bent. On the take. Crooked. Dodgy. Rotten. Plain corrupt. Whatever euphemism, it fitted. They were completely out of control and could not lie straight in bed.

Some officers who had been entrusted to sell drugs to criminals for policing purposes forgot it was just pretend. Somewhere along the line greed, arrogance and envy turned their play-acting at being drug dealers into a rotten reality. Other police ran with the role of drug criminal without even being asked to fake the part. Specialist drug cops traded in their specialist drugs. The Three Musketeers, a trio of officers from the drug squad's heroin-busting unit, were jailed for conspiring to traffic massive amounts of heroin. The bent cops would give patronage and immunity from arrest to chosen heroin dealers, who would pay the cops handsomely for the green light.

Over a generation the drug trade had cheapened values in the criminal world, leading old crooks to shake their heads at some of the behaviour of the new gangsters. And it proved equally corrosive to those who started on the right side of the law. It had got to the point where a drug lord like Tony Mokbel would boast of his power over the forces of law and order. At different times he was caught on tape telling fellow crims how he bribed cops to relax his bail conditions and of his attempts to bribe a Victoria Police laboratory scientist to ruin drug evidence that would have had him convicted.

One judge decided it was more than idle chitchat and the comments showed Mokbel 'had a relationship with police and a capacity to pay money to influence police to interfere in investigations and prosecutions'. But Mokbel's fingers stretched deeper into the force than even that. He would tell acquaintances he had police on his payroll and could get to witnesses. He would tout that his bent jacks would tell him if any of his cronies decided to tell tales. 'If there's a rat, they'll tell me,' Mokbel said.

Corruption investigators believed Mokbel was involved in long-term corrupt relationships with an unnerving number of serving and former police.

At the sentencing of one police officer, a judge even fingered Mokbel as the personification of crime's corrupting influence on police. 'You, as members of that squad in particular, see criminals such as Tony Mokbel living what could be described as the "high life", splashing out hundreds of thousands of dollars on gambling, restaurants, fast cars and a party lifestyle,' Judge Betty King said. 'Police are on modest salaries by comparison to this and there is no doubt that the comparison ultimately appears unfair to some members of the police force. The temptation is there from the lowest members to the highest members of the police force.'

Of course Mokbel was much more proactive in recruiting the local constabulary than simply driving by in a nice car and flashing a shit-eating grin. And it is a matter of debate whether the rot started from Mokbel's side or that of the drug squad. 'Mokbel was effectively created by the drug squad. He was a fucking no one,' one senior lawman said. 'They were buying pseudo. No one else could get pseudo. He was buying it off the coppers. Obviously he was able to make the gear, sell the gear, get the money. He was dobbing in his opposition to the cops. So he was effectively made – he was a creation of the Victoria Police drug squad.'

Bent cops were indeed vital to the running of the Mokbel empire. The value he placed on useful people with useful skills, powers and contacts extended to cops and ex-cops, just as it did to jockeys, parcel workers and easily led pizza chefs. And Tony boasted he had plenty of Victoria's finest on the payroll. The exposure of corruption itself later won Mokbel a get-out-of-jail-free card on a swag of charges.

Jim O'Brien is a defender of a brotherhood mentality in the force because, he says, loyalty is needed in such a tough environment. But, he says, when brothers go bad and cross over it becomes toxic for everyone. 'I know I've lost a couple of my people to corruption along the way, [they've] decided to join the enemy – again it's the greed factor,' he said. 'There's nothing more gut-wrenching or soul destroying. I've seen fifty people standing there crying when it's happened.' Strangely enough, it was in the pursuit of Mokbel that one of the most rotten lawmen came undone.

Detective Senior Sergeant Wayne Strawhorn was one of the shining lights of the Victorian force. Aloof and quiet, Strawhorn could, when necessary, curse like a wharfie and hold his own in the force's competitively macho atmosphere. He was beanpole tall and thin, with vanilla features and light hair combed long down his neck, and even the occasional dainty gesture. What he did have was smarts of both the book-learnt and cunning-as-a-shithouse-rat variety.

As the state's longest serving drug investigator he was considered a veteran with scalps on his belt. Strawhorn had risen through the ranks at the drug squad for more than a decade. He became the head of the chemical diversion desk. (Just how aptly named that desk was would only become apparent in time.) His appeal was such that even as internal affairs later zeroed in on his true nature, he was still being feted. Reformist anti-corruption Chief Commissioner Christine Nixon, who ultimately disbanded the disfunctionally crooked drug squad, moved him to the major fraud squad in February 2002.

The end was nigh for Strawhorn at that point. But in 1996 he was still a star. That year Strawhorn travelled to the UK to study how the English police force, home to the gunless bobby, hunted amphetamine tycoons. He returned to Melbourne singing the praises of a controversial policing approach involving 'controlled deliveries', and, with others, persuaded his reluctant bosses to allow a trial of the scheme locally.

One of the key ingredients for cooking amphetamine – pseudoephedrine – was common in cold and flu pills at that time. Under the UK plan police would enter an arrangement to buy base ingredients like this cheaply from drug companies. They would get informers in the underworld to sell the drugs to criminal figures, then use those snitches, bugs, phone taps, video surveillance and tracking devices to follow the illicit goods to their ultimate destination. The beauty of the scheme was the way in which following the 'pseudo' would lead police up the criminal hierarchy. When it worked it gave police a map to bust clandestine speed laboratories hidden in suburban houses and rural caravans. When it worked even better it gave police leads and evidence on the Mr Bigs controlling the speed trade. But the scheme was inherently fraught with danger and it was regarded as pure madness by some senior police.

The controlled delivery scheme assumed that police successes would outweigh the damage done by authorities releasing more drugs into the market. It involved police, regardless of arrests, proliferating illicit substances and contributing to the deadly drug trade. It required enormous trust to be placed in the officers, who would be able to purchase valuable chemicals cheaply and strut the other side of the street with immunity from the usual consequences. And it required those officers to have almost superhuman resistance to the temptation of money, drugs and turning into cowboys.

Strawhorn's plan was pitched as a way to take down defiant Mr Bigs like Mokbel, the Moran clan and mendacious drug cooks and couriers in outlaw bikie gangs like the Bandidos. A retired cop friendly with Strawhorn had a contact who was well placed to provide underworld information. After Strawhorn's cop mate resigned in the late nineties his underworld contact told him if chemicals were provided to certain crims, including a then little-known character called Mark Moran, they could lead authorities to another person of interest, Antonios Mokbel. The retired cop, who cannot be named, passed this information on to Strawhorn, pointing out that it was a unique chance to take down the drug squad's primary target – Mokbel.

It was the birth of the covert campaign Operation Vere and at the helm was Wayne Strawhorn. Below Strawhorn in the pecking order was Detective Sergeant Malcolm Rosenes and below him Detective Senior Constables Stephen Paton and Paul Firth. Rosenes and Paton had been involved in busting the Grifter and were his handlers in his subsequent incarnation as the police informant eavesdropping on Mokbel. The handlers, Paton and Rosenes, would not have liked everything the police bugs on Mokbel recorded. Tony was taped boasting he was 'in sweet' with Paton and had paid $200,000 to police to help him with court cases. Strawhorn also brought his ex-cop mate back into the picture as the best person to handle his contact in the underworld.

Chemicals were sold cheaply by drug company outlets to the drug squad and at some point the arrangement proved simply too tempting. Strawhorn and his dodgy crew started making unauthorised chemical withdrawals and selling them to crims, including Mark Moran, for their own profit. Paton's role in the controlled deliveries scheme was as a glorified pick-up boy. He would liaise with the drug companies and drive out to their suburban factories, picking up and paying for pseudoephedrine and cold and flu tablets from Sigma Pharmaceuticals. Paton would usually phone ahead, security would let him in and he would buy highly sought-after chemicals at bargain basement police prices.

Over the course of the operation a drug cook's cornucopia of Sudafed tablets, red phosphorous, caffeine and lactose gel for a bonding agent passed down the chain to the criminal target. The chemicals would go from the drug company to Paton to Strawhorn to his retired cop mate to the retired cop's underworld informant to Mark Moran. The money for the drugs would often have travelled the other way along the chain days earlier, stopping at Strawhorn.

After a while Mark Moran let the underworld informant know he wanted not just flu pills but straight pseudoephedrine. Through the usual go-betweens a loose arrangement was made for the police to sell Mark Moran two kilograms of the chemical for between $12,000 and $14,000. In May 2000 Strawhorn sent Paton to pick up two kilograms of the drug from Sigma. Like many crooks, Senior Constable Paton had two mobiles – one of them in his real name, the other in the name of an imaginary friend called Craig Grundy. He used the Grundy phone to call security at the factory and took a work car out to pick up the drugs. The drugs, with a purity of 99.7 per cent, were measured out into a strong plastic bag bearing a batch number, then put into a brown paper bag. The cost for the two kilograms of pseudo for police was $340.10. Converted to speed it would be worth between $200,000 and $300,000.

Paton drove the drugs to a Shell petrol station near the West Gate Bridge where Strawhorn was waiting in a carpark at the rear. He put the brown paper package in the back seat of the green Toyota Strawhorn was driving. Strawhorn met his ex-cop mate and swapped the parcel for cash and the chemicals were spirited down the chain into Essendon to Mark Moran.

Mark Moran was gunned down outside his Aberfeldie home in June 2000 – a gangland killing Carl Williams would falsely boast used the bullet dug out of his own stomach (put there by Mark's brother Jason). The day after Mark Moran's killing, the bungalow of a Moran friend, used by the dead man as a drug storage locker, was raided by the drug squad, including Paton, Firth and Rosenes. The police seized laboratory glassware, drug paraphernalia and amounts of white powder including a two-kilogram bag found in a cupboard which Paton recognised as the one he had passed down the chain from Sigma in May. The officers seized the haul, arrested Bungalow Bill, and drove back to their crooked little house at the St Kilda Road police complex. Detective Sergeant Rosenes was testing the powder samples for amphetamine when Strawhorn stuck his finger in one, stuck the finger in his mouth and declared to the squad it was pseudoephedrine.

Rosenes snuck the biggest of the drug bags – which had boomeranged back to them after they sold it – and two smaller half-kilogram bags of white powder down to the station's basement carpark. Ostensibly on a dinner run for the day's raiding crew and their detainee, Rosenes took the squad's Nissan four-wheel drive to Toorak Road and ordered a batch of pizzas. While waiting he zipped across to a South Melbourne supermarket and bought two packets of Glucodin powder and grabbed several extra shopping bags. He then picked up the piping hot pizzas, drove back into the cop shop's basement, dropped the food at the office, then returned to the car.

Inside the car Rosenes took half the contents out of each of the three bags pouring them into a bag for himself to take home to try to sell. Using the shopping bags he mixed the Glucodin in with what was left to pad out what he had taken, spilling only a little in the back seat. He took the three bags back upstairs to the drug squad offices and checked that they were still the correct weight. As it turned out Rosenes had assumed all three bags contained pseudo whereas the smaller two were actually ketamine. As a result his takeaway bag was a virtually worthless mongrel mix of ketamine, pseudoephedrine and Glucodin that even the black market shunned.

But if the unscrupulous squad occasionally bungled their dirty deeds, there were plenty of opportunities to get things right. Five times Strawhorn's pick-up boy Paton had bought substantial amounts of pure pseudoephedrine from the official outlets and all had so far escaped attention. But the police profiteering was not limited to off-the-radar chemicals-for-cash swaps. The chemical-toting cops were also flicking the ingredients to the crims, giving them the green light to cook them up then splitting the post-sale profits. Sigma pseudo was being passed through a criminal informant to Bandido bikies and money was flowing back to police.

Not surprisingly the confidence and resolve of some very dangerous criminals were bolstered by the knowledge that not only was big brother not watching, he was actively on board. When half-brothers Jason and Mark Moran brazenly shot Carl Williams in the guts in daylight in a suburban park in late 1999, it flagged a downward turning point in the gangland war. But the Morans acted knowing they had some important police on side.

Williams recalled that during the shooting the Moran brothers told him: 'You don't fuck with us. We are working with the police. We've virtually got a licence to do anything.' Williams knew Strawhorn was a senior police figure and he knew he was supplying the Morans with chemicals. Williams claimed the police knew who shot him but did nothing because they were protecting the Morans.

As he lay in a hospital bed with a hole in his belly, Williams pretended to an attending detective that he did not know he had been shot. It was a strange thing to do but Williams said the ruse triggered an angry but revealing spray from the cop. According to Williams the detective said: 'That is a fuckin' lie. You were shot in Gladstone Park. You were hit with a bat first and then you were shot by the Morans. We have got them bragging on [a] listening device.' The Moran brothers were never charged with shooting Carl.

The closest the corrupt cops got to acting straight was when, having pocketed sufficient profits, they reneged on deals made with their criminal partners, arresting them to plaudits from force command. It is hard not to feel a skerrick of sympathy for the betrayed crims. They would be left with two options. One: take their lumps. Two: try to persuade little old ladies in a jury box that the nicely dressed, tattoo-free senior policeman over there had also been dealing drugs and it was all a police conspiracy. There is a reason police call their uniform, when worn at court, the 'truth suit'.

If Mokbel was a foe and target of the drug squad it was a compromised and ambiguous enmity. Melbourne's ganglands had a way of making strange bedfellows of police and criminals, and in the carnival atmosphere of the 2000 Melbourne Cup, Mokbel and Strawhorn met up. As they shot the breeze the drug squad chief offered the state's biggest drug menace tickets to a Victoria Police function. Strawhorn said it would be a good idea for Mokbel to attend 'so the other coppers don't hate you anymore'.

Perhaps the free-flowing booze on Cup Day had knocked the senior police officer's already erratic sense of the appropriate further askew. But even Mokbel was taken aback by the foolhardiness of the idea. The gobsmacked gangster replied: 'You want me to go to a bloody coppers' do? Are you kidding?'

Mokbel would have been wise to keep his hands on his wallet while chatting with the senior cop. At one point Strawhorn was overheard talking with another officer about robbing Mokbel of his racetrack winnings. A judge gave Strawhorn the benefit of the doubt in characterising that discussion between the two cops as light-hearted banter.

12

Dirty deeds

*Power tends to corrupt,
and absolute power corrupts absolutely.*

– Lord Acton

The man responsible for Sigma Pharmaceutical's security was former police officer Graeme Sayce. As police purchases of flu pills and pure pseudo increased in volume and frequency and the requests became less formal, Sayce decided to audit the transactions. Senior Constable Paton reacted by telling others to keep Sayce out of the loop, as the police operations were covert and Sayce was not a current member of the force. When word of this reaction got back to Sayce, the security worker began to suspect something strange was going on.

As Sigma closed in on the unauthorised buys, Strawhorn tried to quell the drug company's concerns. He also attempted to distance himself from his lackey's actions, saying he too had been troubled by Paton's reaction to Sayce. At Sigma's pressing, Strawhorn faxed the company a list of the squad's authorised transactions but he only listed Sudafed tablet withdrawals.

In December 2000 Rosenes told Paton there were issues with the Sudafed transactions and it was best for everyone if

Paton resigned. Three days before Christmas Paton offered his resignation letter to Strawhorn. Paton later gave a statement to police asserting that, full of yuletide spirit, Strawhorn, a force luminary, told his young, freshly unemployed charge: 'If you ever say anything about me I will hunt you down and kill you.'

Paton's resignation itself raised further suspicions and the police launched Operation Hemi to police the police and probe the Sigma transactions. Strawhorn further distanced himself by preparing his own report into discrepancies found in the purchase of the chemical compound acetic anhydride from another pharmaceutical plant. But the police probe was closing in. Sigma had handed over documents showing five separate purchases of pure pseudoephedrine. There were also another dozen unauthorised purchases of Sudafed tablets bought for $70,000 with a black market value of more than triple that.

More than three months after suspicions about the controlled delivery were raised, Strawhorn was still not directly in the sights. In fact he was asked by his bosses to conduct an audit of varying Sigma and drug squad records on pure pseudo sales. Somehow Strawhorn kept his head under daily pressure, attended senior meetings, worked his regular hours, answered inquiries about the controlled delivery scheme, and made Paton the fall guy, denying any knowledge of Paton's chemical pick-ups.

Smart police, even the bent ones, learn on the job where criminals come undone, what holds up in court as proof, and where maintaining a story can get even the guilty off the hook. Corruption investigators would need a breakthrough to get beyond the drug squad's sacrificial lamb and their scripted story.

* * *

The Nissan four-wheel drive that Detective Sergeant Rosenes mixed the drugs in had been sold by Victoria Police to Peter and Jenny Nugent. When investigators tracked the vehicle down they were relieved to find the original interior had not been altered. Tests on the rear bench seat, floor and floor mat found residue containing pseudoephedrine and ketamine. Police arrested Detective Sergeant Rosenes in mid-2001 while he was trying to complete the purchase of thousands of ecstasy tablets. Paton was arrested two days later. By the end of 2001 Strawhorn was moved out of the drug squad but remained on the force.

Corruption investigators had more luck with Strawhorn's retired cop mate, who they managed to turn, and one of Strawhorn's criminal informants, who gave evidence against him. The crim informant wore a wire for the toe-cutters, recording a cornered Strawhorn's self-serving version of events and increasingly angry diatribes.

Wayne Strawhorn: 'Can you say that at any stage anyone sat down with you and said, "We are gonna do something fuckin' corrupt here. We'll divvy up the proceeds of it?"'

Informant: 'Never.'

Wayne Strawhorn: 'Well, what the fuck are they talking about?'

Informant: 'There's no blue, Wayne. You've fuckin' done the right thing by me all the way. I don't want to give evidence against Paton. I'm being straight with ya.'

Wayne Strawhorn: 'I tell you what would be good for us. It would be good not to have the squad fucked over. ESD [Ethical

Standards Department] have been coming to me and trying to insinuate that I have been doing bad things with you. I find it pretty insulting.'

Strawhorn told his ex-cop mate the West Gate Bridge pseudo drop 'never happened' and to let his contact know the same. Strawhorn and the retired cop met in the exclusive Birdcage area at Oaks Day in 2002, where Strawhorn handed over a copy of the script – a purported list of 'all' the buys that were done but only containing the authorised ones.

The pair met again in the new year in the less glamorous surrounds of the Moorabbin McDonald's. Strawhorn was still unhappy he might be called into an interview, saying he would refuse to comment. 'I'm not going to give them the pleasure of giving them a thousand answers to a thousand questions when they might find something that's just not quite right.'

He viciously lashed out at Paton and Inspector Peter De Santo, who was pursuing him. 'All we have done is try to lock up the best crooks in Melbourne and we have achieved that. I just can't believe the things [Paton's] done,' Strawhorn said. 'He has now decided to go and spill his guts to ESD about everything he can think of, true or untrue, in a view to get himself off completely and I'm the number one target. If I ever saw the cunt walking down the street I would fuckin' just run over him.'

Self-pity gave way to threatening words when he broached the topic of De Santo. 'The bottom line is my life in the police force is over. My hope to get that thirty-year pension is gone,' he said. 'They have fucked me terribly and I will not rest until De Santo is dead.'

Two days later, on St Patrick's Day 2003, Strawhorn was arrested on seven charges, including trafficking a commercial quantity of pseudoephedrine and making threats to kill. The jury struggled with the credibility of less than ideal witnesses and Strawhorn was only convicted of one trafficking charge. He was sentenced to seven years' jail with a minimum of four. There was some evidence that Strawhorn was splashing about ill-gotten cash – but the provable amounts were minor compared to the $99,500 Strawhorn allegedly received from his corrupt activities.

Strawhorn, as well as being a hard-nosed, ultra-shrewd detective, was a widower who had raised his children himself. Instead of consistently locking up major criminals like Mokbel and Moran, who were heads of larger crime networks, he fell in with them and it profited him little. Indeed there was something tragically banal about the way Strawhorn spent his hard-won drug money. He made cash payments of $1300 to Carpet Call, $990 to Crystal Shower Screens, put a $1500 cash deposit in his bank, and bought $3605 worth of shares with cash. But perhaps it was never about the money for the slightly odd Strawhorn so much as the excitement, and the mental and political challenge of getting away with being a double agent. The judge reminded him: 'You committed the very crime which you were entrusted to detect and eliminate.'

Strawhorn was recently released and refused to comment except to pass a message to the author through an intermediary that my contact details, left in his flyscreen door, had been put in his bin.

A jailed drug squad detective, pressured during the course of Strawhorn's trial to explain his conduct, could not keep his cool.

The witness seemed to morph into Jack Nicholson in *A Few Good Men*. But his blurted comments captured the unbelievable state of the drug squad. 'If you want explanations, I'll give you explanations,' he vented. 'I worked in the drug squad. It was a cesspool. It was full of corruption.'

13

Nabbed

Champagne for my real friends and real pain for my sham friends.

– Traditional toast

His amigos were all in the clink, but after some initial nervousness, Mokbel was increasingly confident he had dodged a bullet on the Mexican coke import. Three weeks after his cocaine crew was picked up, Mokbel told the Grifter he reckoned he had once again given the jacks the slip.

When Buddha Cassar was nabbed red-handed he tried to persuade his arresting officers he was simply seizing the cocaine parcels as part of his role with UPS. The ruse was not successful given the furtiveness of his after-hours swoop and the fact that almost the whole perfidious plot was caught on tape. But what was important to Mokbel was that Cassar had not blabbed. Mokbel told the Grifter he had warned his cocaine crew to be wary of the Mexicans. He bemoaned that he would not see a grain of coke from the venture but now had to financially support the family of his jailed inside man. Mokbel was not always so benevolent, but since he was footing the bill he let the street know that loyal foot soldiers who stayed staunch got repaid for their discretion.

'He was a fucking top bloke, poor cunt,' Mokbel said of Cassar. 'Doing the right thing, ya know ... now I've got to give a grand to his family every week. Now I've got [to pay] the fucking solicitors.'

Mokbel's criminal associates had maintained the code of silence before and he assumed his latest crew were being stand-up guys now. But while Buddha was feeling the love, Mokbel was less certain about the Stooge. Mokbel said the Stooge was greedy and needed to be killed. Threats to kill made by Mokbel were not to be trifled with. But the Stooge, in jail for his part in the crew's failed cocaine caper, had more immediate problems.

Upon entering the prison system the Stooge found a card on his pillow from the homosexual convict sharing his cell. It read: 'You are unique. Welcome to my harem.' But no amount of sobering reality could cure the Stooge of his basic naivety and he managed to get duped again behind bars. The flamboyant cell mate conned the newest member of his harem into believing that his influence extended into the nation's centres of power. He convinced the Stooge that he could bribe three High Court judges into reducing his sentence. The Stooge handed over thousands of dollars, which his fellow prisoner simply kept while pretending to call High Court judges to discuss the Stooge's case.

Mokbel's plan for the Stooge was cold-blooded but his underlying instinct about the Stooge turning dog was right. Still fuming at being duchessed then dumped by Tony, the Stooge leapt at the chance to turn witness for the prosecution. Mokbel's antennae were less astute when it came to the Grifter – the man from the same criminal streets as Tony who posed a far greater threat to his epic ambitions.

Since his arrest and turning by police in August 2000, the Grifter had made massive inroads with his target. His established reputation as a lifelong crook, his status as a talented and pioneering speed cook and his strong links with the Morans saw Mokbel breezily take the Grifter deep into his confidence. The two men would discuss sexual conquests and the Grifter shared with Mokbel details of his love life – including a short dalliance with nubile television current-affairs host Naomi Robson.

'So how's Naomi?' Mokbel would ask.

'She is all right, she's made, yeah,' the Grifter would reply.

The brunette TV host met the Grifter through friends, and dated him for several months in 2000 – or, as she said, 'caught up with [him] on a handful of occasions'. Ms Robson said the Grifter had presented himself as a successful corporate executive with brochures to fit his story, and insisted she knew nothing of his heavy involvement in drugs and crime.

But whether it was women or work the Grifter, much like his quarry, did not do things by half. When he got frustrated with the capacity of his police-supplied tape recorder, the Grifter used his own money to get a superior device.

His police handlers were providing him with money, and where necessary, drugs, to make deals with Tony. The Grifter and Mokbel would come to an arrangement then Tony would send his corrupted chef Pizzaboy to make the broad daylight exchange in TJ's carpark just metres from the Brunswick cop shop. Over just two months in 2000 Mokbel used Pizzaboy to deliver to the Grifter around half a kilo of amphetamine worth at least $50,000 on the street, a thousand LSD tickets, five sample ecstasy tablets, another six sample Es from a different batch, and then an ounce (thirty grams) of amphetamine. The Grifter's tape was rolling when he and Mokbel negotiated their deals and he kept it rolling when Mokbel boasted of his other drug ventures. Mokbel had a seven-figure corruption war chest set aside for stealing and destroying any evidence against him, corrupting police and generally subverting any Crown case, prosecutors later alleged.

At the Brunswick Market Mokbel met 45-year-old Fawkner man Joseph Parisi and made him his drug 'gopher'. Tony got Parisi to pick up and store drug deliveries and bring samples to him at the Grove Cafe in Sydney Road. Parisi trafficked kilograms of pseudoephedrine, Valium and hundreds of LSD tablets. Police later warned Parisi that Mokbel regarded him as a 'weak link' in his syndicate and had issued a contract for his murder.

Tony was adept at using corporate structures and financial schemes and blending them with a criminal version of paperless community banks. But he was less sophisticated at avoiding police scrutiny. Amazingly for a Brunswick boy who built a drug empire large enough to attract the interest of the federal authorities, there was little subtlety to the successful operation. But if Tony was arrogant enough to think his brash, blunt appoach would work forever, he had a reasonable foundation for that view – it always had. Loyal lawyers had kept him mostly out of jail despite a long string of prior convictions dating back to when he was seventeen.

His high-powered legal eagles had busted him out of prison despite being caught talking drugs with a fellow drug kingpin and it was not the last swifty they would pull for him.

Within weeks of the cocaine import going awry Mokbel imported $2 billion worth of pseudoephedrine hidden in a shipping container carrying ceramics, basins and toilet bowls. A short message – 'the girls have arrived' – heralded the entrance of the staggeringly large illegal import. The motherlode contained barrels of the chemical weighing more than half a tonne and capable of being turned into forty million pills. The container travelled from Yugoslavia to Melbourne's waterfront then, following the Mokbel blueprint, it was taken to a factory in Coburg and furtively unloaded by three shadowy figures.

Mokbel was taped admitting he drove into the bush and hid the 500 kilograms of amphetamine precursor which police never found. Again he thought he was home free but again he was wrong. His day of reckoning was fast approaching. The drug boss had engaged in cosy trackside chats with Strawhorn, the state's peak drug cop, and been invited to the police ball by him. It must have been nice for Mokbel to know the man who could do the most damage to his drug empire was without principles and entirely compromised.

Mokbel could convince himself the hashish bust was the work of the federal police and the cocaine debacle was sparked by a Mexican cock-up such as the use of wooden containers alerting customs. But with connections to dodgy cops in the debauched drug squad he expected to be forewarned before any bust or arrest involving Victorian officers.

Mokbel had grown up with police who charged you and dragged you in the second they had enough. Even as police nabbed two of his successive crews he had failed to imagine an operation devoted almost solely to him, patiently stacking up evidence for multiple charges over multiple imports and deals. Tony was confident he would be left alone or at least forewarned. But even bent police have to make occasional collars and Mokbel's confidence in Strawhorn was as misplaced as his candour with the Grifter.

Mokbel was taped by the Grifter boasting about the arrival of the half tonne of pseudoephedrine and that another similar load was on its way. Police later recovered an empty shipping container with pseudo traces. The Grifter recorded Mokbel telling how he had sold one tub of the drug for half a million dollars and had twenty-one tubs left. The Grifter expressed interest in buying and Mokbel gave him a small sample which police forensic scientists found was chemically identical to traces of the drug found in the dumped container. The jig was up.

Before the sun rose on Friday 24 August 2001 more than one hundred officers swooped, raiding eighteen premises across Melbourne and arresting van-loads of slumbering crims. Serious crime-world figures, including Mokbel, Lewis Moran, Bert Wrout, Mokbel crony Lucky, 'weak link' Joseph Parisi and Mokbel's corrupted chef, Pizzaboy, were all charged. When police stormed Pizzaboy's house they found forty-six grams of methamphetamine, a set of scales and $3500 cash, seemingly indicating he was more than just a delivery boy and had graduated to a Mokbel street speed-dealer.

Mokbel was arrested at dawn by police, who took his beloved red Ferrari and a jet-ski from out the front of his large Pascoe Vale home. Authorities seized and froze an estimated $20 million of his assets including the beachside palace, the Merc and his Templestowe units. For all the straight state and federal police who had taken a daily interest in Mokbel there was no more pretending they had not been watching him.

It was the end of Victoria's largest ever drug sting and of monitoring Mokbel's efforts to bring in cocaine, hashish and pseudoephedrine. Months of patience by the operation targeting Mokbel and the Grifter's year of living dangerously were rolled into a super brief that police hoped would lead to super sentences. It had taken a cast of hundreds, the involvement of federal police and customs. It had also taken months of endurance and a superstar grass with breakout talent and more front than Myer. But now it was over. Mokbel, the infuriatingly flashy and cocky crim, was finally behind bars. His red Ferrari would be replaced by a red tracksuit. And that Friday night straight and bent cops alike charged their glasses.

14

Snitches get stitches

Anyone can rat, but it takes a certain amount of ingenuity to re-rat.
– Winston Churchill

He had put a major criminal in jail but the Grifter, although a conscientious police informant, had not exactly turned his back on his criminal past. Just three months before Mokbel's arrest the Grifter, on behalf of Lewis Moran, was shopping in the underworld for a hitman to kill Carl Williams. When small-time drug dealer Terrence Hodson was still alive and a one-time detective, Senior Constable David Miechel, was a policeman not a prisoner, Hodson told Miechel that the Grifter had offered him $50,000 to take out the Morans' arch enemy, Williams. (Terrence Hodson and his wife, Christine, were later to be executed in their home, just prior to giving evidence about alleged dirty dealings in the drug squad involving Miechel, and their murder remains unsolved to this day.)

Even when working with his police handlers, Detectives Paton and Rosenes, the Grifter's dealings were not squeaky clean. If Mokbel quoted the Grifter $10,000 on a drug deal, the police handlers would tell their bosses they needed $140,000 and then the treacherous trio would split the difference. When it came to how much illegality was too conspicuous, the Grifter had more nous than the bent coppers. Fearing the detectives' greed outweighed their sense, the Grifter took out his own insurance policy by recording their dodgy dealings on the extra space of his self-bought recorder.

One day the Grifter wandered into the police's Ethical Standards Department to turn his technology against his malignant police masters. He brought with him his own extended remix of his law and order tapes. He played his explosive director's cut. And he almost single-handedly detonated the drug squad. Paton and Rosenes were arrested, tried and jailed for drug trafficking as more details came to light of misuse of speed chemicals by other bad boys in Strawhorn's squad.

The new female chief commissioner, Christine Nixon, brought in from interstate to sweep the force clean, ended the controversial chemical diversion program and ordered a probe into the drug squad which by the end of the year saw it disbanded. Sergeant Ray Dole, who had written Mokbel a reference, was probed for a time by anti-corruption officers but ultimately resigned and was never charged.

Nixon's campaign to expose corruption would have a positive flow-on effect for those like Mokbel who were caught by drug squad officers. It is even possible the Grifter – as a double agent running with the fox and the hounds – foresaw it could play out that way. Whatever the case, the prisons were getting a steady stream of new inmates – ex-detectives and Mr Bigs alike – with a serious grudge against the Grifter. Mokbel, like all accuseds, was entitled through his lawyers to learn the specific evidence against him. The Grifter's name would not need to have been included for the scales to be lifted from Mokbel's eyes as to who was behind his recent run of bad luck.

Mokbel had been arrested in August 2001 and by the following month his legal team persuaded a magistrate to bail him on a million-dollar surety. It would have been a nervous time for the Grifter, who won bail on his drug charges in recognition of his hard, risky work. But the dangerous decision to let Mokbel loose was corrected a month later, in October, when the Supreme Court overturned the magistrate's decision. The somewhat bewildered judge described Mokbel in arachnid terms. He said if the police claims were true, Mokbel 'propounded a web of illegality and corruption' with himself at the centre. The judge said that given Mokbel's potential to pervert the course of justice, 'It is manifest that the Magistrate fell into serious error in concluding that exceptional circumstances existed which justified the granting of bail.' Mokbel was sent back to the slammer. But the man once christened 'the Octopus' by the press still had tentacles everywhere.

The Grifter had made a powerful and ruthless enemy and would have had plenty of cause to be nervous. But in the meantime he decided to live it up. While on bail his car was firebombed and even his attempts to party away any fears were spoiled by a failed bid to abduct him from a nightclub. The Grifter's bail conditions meant he was forbidden from leaving the country and regularly had to check in with nominated police. But to simplify some of the onerous requirements, the grass with the gift of the gab made a unique arrangement with police (who could monitor the location of his mobile phone) to make his regular check-ins by SMS.

Police were still getting the text messages, their origin reassuringly traced to near the Victorian–New South Wales border, when the Grifter left the country. Never one to give a sucker an even break, the Grifter had left his phone with a friend near the Murray River. He packed his fake passport and in late 2001 jumped a jumbo for a refreshing overseas holiday. Months later, the day before he was due back in court, he casually flew back home. Grabbed by annoyed cops as he landed at the airport, his bail was revoked and he was thrown into the prison system where the Mokbel menace machine was in full swing.

At the Melbourne Assessment Prison a guard approached the Grifter on behalf of Mokbel and told him all would be forgiven if he just walked away from testifying. A million-dollar bounty then materialised on the Grifter's head. Writing from prison the Grifter said: 'My life is in danger because I exposed police corruption. I've been promised, pledged, reneged on, lied to – you name it. My family is copping threats [from] persons threatening me and them harm. I have sacrificed my life, as it will never be the same or safe for me.'

One claimed kill plot targeting the Grifter involved notorious prison pest Greg Brazel, who was locked up for decades after being convicted of killing three women. Brazel told police he was hired to poison the Grifter while both men were in Barwon prison together. Brazel said he shunned the contract and instead blew the whistle on the plot. He swore in an affidavit to police: 'I had received certain messages from other criminal identities requesting that I take action to prevent [the Grifter] from being in a position to give evidence against certain persons charged with, or about to be charged with, criminal offences.'

Brazel would not name the plotter but the spectre of Mokbel hung heavy in the background. 'I, in fact, warned prison staff that it would be prudent that [the Grifter's] milk etc be stored in the staff fridge, rather than the fridge within the Acacia Unit for prisoner use. I did not tell staff why this would be prudent, but knowing me over a long period of time they accepted this advice without question.'

Brazel said after he told the Grifter he was a murder target the Grifter reciprocated the trust and confided another reason he feared for his safety. '[He said] that he was involved in a sexual relationship with this woman and that she was the woman of another criminal, that is, the wife or girlfriend of another criminal,' Brazel said. 'This is commonly referred to as "back-dooring" and is a cardinal sin within the criminal community.'

When the author visited the state's two highest security units at Barwon, a padlock had been added to the communal milk fridge. The warden offered the benign explanation that it was to stop the prisoners nicking each other's milk.

By mid-2003 when he got a discounted sentence on his drug charges, the jailed Grifter was somehow still staying alive, beating the odds and dodging inmates trying to claim Mokbel's million-dollar bounty. But an underworld source said the incident that really spooked the Grifter while he and Mokbel were 'in boob' was not overtly violent at all. 'The pair of them were in there together, separated, one to a cell, high security, the whole bit,' the man said. 'Then one day a guard opens [the Grifter's] door, he looks up and there's Mokbel standing there at the entrance to his cell.' Mokbel said 'Hi' and the Grifter's real name and then the guard Mokbel had clearly bribed closed the Grifter's door and returned Mokbel to his cell. It was not an overtly violent visit but Mokbel's message was clear: there is no place I cannot get to you.

The Grifter was released on parole in September 2003, the bounty on his head still weighing on his mind, but nevertheless in one piece despite what he claimed were multiple attempts on his life in jail. Mokbel's influence and connections did not stop at the prison gates. The crime boss's network of eyes, ears and enforcers was everywhere and once out of prison the Grifter decided he needed to be out of sight and out of mind. He needed to at least get out of the city and ideally flee the country. Leaving Melbourne's September winter blues would not be hard. Still, the Grifter would miss the upcoming AFL Grand Final and the thrills of the Spring Racing Carnival. There would be hard times ahead for the Grifter if he left Australia. But in his mind these compromises were balanced out by the complete lack of Mokbels in Holland.

After his last escapade got him sent back to the big house for a volatile stay with his would-be killers, the Grifter was a little more reticent to flee the country without permission. He successfully applied to the parole board to vary his conditions allowing him to leave Australia because he feared for his safety. He was given a green light but authorities expected the Grifter to return to testify against Mokbel when his case eventually slouched to court. But in

May 2004, as Melbourne shrank to a patchwork of farmlands out his plane window and his jet trails marked the sky, the incorrigible Grifter had other plans. Or, as the underworld source summarised it: 'After that surprise visit from Mokbel in boob he just said fuck this I'm gone.'

The Ethical Standards Department probe into the conduct of the drug squad was delaying and even destroying police cases and having an open-sesame effect on the jail cells of underworld figures. Mokbel's old street dealer Carl Williams, locked up awaiting trial on drugs charges, had walked out into the fresh air because of the probe.

Mokbel, betting the corruption clean-up could help his cases too, refused to plead despite the strong evidence against him. Depending on one's view of the justice system it was either a big gamble or the type of delay-and-defend tactics that are a sure bet for rich defendants. Either way it paid off. By the time Mokbel's committal rolled around, drug squad Detectives Paton and Rosenes were in jail. And the police informant who had fronted court on the Friday of the dawn patrol over Mokbel's pseudo import – Sergeant Paul Firth – was no longer above suspicion. The same month that Paton and Rosenes went inside, Firth was suspended from the force pending an Ethical Standards investigation. Firth later resigned, which meant the ESD probe could go no further and he was not charged with any criminal offence.

Defence lawyers were at the ready to make a meal out of the emerging corruption in the drug squad. They would have a particularly good time with those involved in the operation that targeted Mokbel. Adding to authorities' woes their star witness had gone feral. The Grifter and his hidden wire had been the scourge of the underworld, then of bent drug detectives. As Mokbel's trials approached, the absent grass was making yet another powerful enemy – the prosecutor's office. From his overseas hideout the Grifter said he was not coming back to testify in the trial. There was anger that the career crim had fled and was not fronting up to do his duty. But the anger would have become blind rage had anyone known what the prodigal perp was really up to overseas.

The Grifter had a rough time leaving Melbourne to fall off the radar. He told a friend how he lost five months of his life stuck in a Spanish jail before flying by seaplane to an island without security checks. Reborn yet again with a new identity, the charismatic conman eventually fell on his feet in Holland where he set about creating a new drug empire while on the lam. As Mokbel was counting the days waiting for his court dates, the man he wanted dead was setting up an international team of drug mules spanning Europe to South-East Asia. The Grifter's mules would each swallow up to a kilogram of cocaine wrapped in condoms and smuggle the drugs into Canada and Australia in their stomachs. Australia's most wanted fugitive had learnt the secrets of counter-surveillance from bent drug squad detectives. And for three years he would pull off the ultimate feat of criminal multitasking, presiding over a global drug ring while on the run.

Back in Victoria the Grifter's absence meant prosecutors had to re-evaluate their prospects against Mokbel. The Commonwealth

Department of Public Prosecutions asked its Victorian counterpart to commence action against the Grifter to have him re-sentenced for failing to honour his undertaking to give evidence. The Grifter's barrister, Nick Papas, defended his client's decision not to testify against Mokbel in the wake of the execution of the Hodsons, who paid the ultimate price for snitching on cops and crims alike, and other gangland slayings. 'We're not whistling Dixie here,' Mr Papas said. 'Everyone else is dead.'

Prosecutors were left with the bitter task of cutting Mokbel's charge sheet down to the offences they could still establish beyond reasonable doubt that would not give rise to a courtroom carnival about police corruption. The vast majority of the trafficking and possession charges against Mokbel – relating to drugs like ephedrine, LSD, cocaine and ecstasy – were dropped. The only ones left – and paltry compared to his $2 billion import and the true scale of Mokbel's real operations – were the carpark drug deals and a federal charge over the cocaine import. Mokbel's corrupted chef, Pizzaboy, had ten charges dropped and others in the crew also won out of the big shrink.

On the cocaine import the prosecution still had the Grifter's tapes and the Stooge's willing testimony and Mokbel was committed to trial. But against his own lawyers' advice Tony – who boasted of keeping a seven-figure kitty for stealing evidence and ruining trials – would not plead to it. That meant remaining in jail, the novelty of which had worn off for Mokbel over successive visits. But the jailbird did not plan to stay locked up for long – and nor would he. He needed the two things that always got him out of trouble: a little of his legendary luck and his loyal platoon of high-powered lawyers. An initial application for bail was refused at the first legal hurdle and did not get to court.

Mokbel's lawyers argued in a three-day Supreme Court hearing that their client should be bailed because police corruption probes were delaying his case, meaning an untried, presumed innocent man was spending longer and longer in jail. Mokbel's barrister, an expensive QC presumably not acting on a pro-bono basis, argued that his client was $8 million in debt to the bank, a situation that was getting worse because being locked up prevented him from managing his assets. His lawyers also sought to rely on the absence of the Grifter as a changed circumstance justifying bail. The argument ignored the fact that the Grifter had fled because Mokbel put a $1 million price on his head.

The bail application was dismissed but less than four months later Mokbel's lawyers tried again, arguing that Tony's trial looked certain to be delayed even further. The same judge found that despite the unfortunate delays the risk of Mokbel jumping bail, reoffending or interfering with witnesses was too great and again refused bail. Undeterred, Team Mokbel tried again a month later, arguing that delays meant the prisoner could be jailed for up to three years from his arrest before getting to trial. It was third time lucky and in September 2002 Mokbel got bailed on strict conditions.

Near the height of his bigwig status Mokbel had once more been saved by a very lucky twist of fate – bailed to the bewilderment of the public because of police corruption bloodletting. He even seemed to get a promotion from the judge from witness tamperer to messianic figure. 'This is not an occasion for the court to act as Pontius Pilate by washing its hands of the matter,' the judge said before freeing Mokbel and washing his hands of the matter. As the drug tycoon once more walked from jail, shocked police and prosecutors were more convinced than ever that Mokbel was not the Messiah, just a very naughty boy.

15
Tony on the town

> For a single man gets bottled
> on them twisty-wisty stairs,
> An' a woman comes and
> clobs 'im from be'ind.
>
> – Rudyard Kipling, 'Loot'

After a year behind bars Mokbel was bailed in September 2002. Walking free from custody he said he just wanted a good night's sleep. But there was to be little rest for the heavy gambler and notorious pants man.

Upon release Mokbel made a sombre pilgrimage to Fawkner cemetery to visit his father's grave. He then lived his next few years like they were the last he had, painting as much of the town as red as possible before his bailee's nightly curfew of 10 pm. He moved to a central city pad, was seen dropping bundles trackside, indulging at expensive restaurants, and getting chauffer-driven to the Grand Prix. Within two months of being released he got his bail altered so that for ten days he could take his children to the Gold Coast and the strip of giant theme parks south of Brisbane on the Pacific Motorway. He then spent his nights living it up in his luxurious accommodation at Jupiters Casino.

In June 2004 Tony visited a friend locked up at the Melbourne Custody Centre, turned on the charm and slipped the prison guards $350 for officers to order forty super special and Hawaiian pizzas and dozens of Cokes from a gourmet city pizzeria. The cash splash treat for all the inmates and guards was highly welcome but also highly illegal. As an accused on bail Tony should by law have been excluded from visiting in the first place. But not for the last time, when Tony turned on his highbeams, logic seemed to go out the window.

All charm, braggadocio and bogus bonhomie, Tony had lived the first act of his criminal life as if everyone was watching. He had been the hail-fellow-well-met drug boss of Sydney Road, conspicuous in power suits and his zippy red sports car, dropping big drug-money tips to grateful waiters. If you had thrown a rock in the Brunswick air it would have hit a Mokbel mate, possibly one in a blue uniform. But in reality, during that period Tony was a legend in his own overloaded lunchbox and little known outside police, crime, clubbing or northern suburbs circles. That all changed with coverage of his dawn raid arrest, his brothers' growing notoriety and the deepening gangland war.

The Mokbel moniker and even the tag 'Fat Tony' became household names. Out on bail and in the second act of his criminal life Mokbel kept living as though everyone was watching. The difference was that this time they actually were. With court pending, the prospect of more jail in the offing, bullets flying and cameras flashing, it might have been wise for Tony to take a break and retreat into the shadows. But Mokbel did what his particular sect of aggressive flashy gamblers, known as 'blasters', always do – he doubled down and raised the stakes.

Detectives figured Mokbel had multiple crews working for him on a national basis and that he upped the ante as he became a criminal celebrity. 'From August 2001, that was the period when he was most prolific, believe it or not,' Detective Sergeant Jim Coghlan from the Purana anti-gangland taskforce said. 'During that period he would have made over maybe a hundred million dollars. Probably about the GDP of a small island,' he said.

But a man is not an island in all aspects. And by then Mokbel was estranged from Carmel. If at any point he had maintained a moment of monogamy, he now quickly shunned it to return with relish to the life of single Tony on the town. When he was not importing or snorting cocaine – sometimes called 'the white lady' – Mokbel's head was turned by white ladies of a non-inhalable variety.

He stood, balding, tubby and 167 centimetres short, on the precipice of turning forty, but when it came to seducing beautiful women Mokbel was a rotund Romeo without peer. Police watching him around the clock could not help but notice his all-hours meetings with his glamourpuss solicitor Zarah Garde-Wilson. A federal agent and a Purana detective swore in court that Tony had a constant on-off sexual relationship with the raven-haired beauty. Mokbel might have been a charmer but with Garde-Wilson he had big shoes to fill – her old flame had been a real killer boyfriend.

The love of Zarah's life had been Lewis Caine, a gangland thug not long for this world, whose sperm she kept on ice after the zip went up on his body bag. Caine, who was Zarah's client before becoming her lover, was less a tactical underworld Mr Big than a senselessly violent career crim. One night in 1988 he was ejected from a King Street nightclub after having a row with a stranger over a woman. When the stranger left the club Caine followed him in a taxi to Spencer Street then kicked him in his head until his skull gave way. The man died and Caine then walked back to the nightclub in bloody shoes and boasted of his kill. He copped a dozen years for what became known as the 'pizza head murder' because of the state of his victim, and then he met Zarah.

A farm girl turned private-school princess turned legally licensed crime groupie, Zarah tended to go that extra step for her clients. Well endowed, with a leaning towards the skimpy, her prison visits became legendary among female-deprived inmates. A coquettish woman of few words, Zarah has not been averse to posing in beach showers or suggestively with her pet python, Chivas, in racy photo shoots for lads' mags. But on issues of more substance she has otherwise been notoriously shy of the spotlight. When chequebook media outlets or even judges have asked her tough questions, her answers have been stunted, legalistic or missing in action. She was convicted of contempt of court for refusing to testify against the two gangland killers who gunned down her boyfriend Caine. She said her defiant silence was not part of a gangland code but 'so I don't get my head blown off'.

Her family originally ran a 6000-head merino farm near Armidale in northern New South Wales. When wool prices went south her family went north to Queensland and Zarah boarded at

Toowoomba's Fairholme Ladies College. She got her law degree at the University of Western Australia then landed on Melbourne's mean streets as an articled clerk under colourful bouncer turned lawyer George Defteros. Her legal mentor momentarily handed in his practising certificate after he was charged with a gangland plot to kill Carl and George Williams. The charges were later dropped.

Zarah met Caine when she represented him on a driving charge and the pair fell into bed. They became qualified reiki healers together – a method of spiritual healing drawing on life-force energy. But all Caine's life-force energy left him when he was gunned down then dumped in Brunswick Street. Zarah included the dead killer's name in her new law firm – Garde-Wilson and Caine – and told a lads' mag she still spoke to his spirit (which was presumably kicking in the heads of other spirits in the sweet hereafter). A psychological report described Zarah's posthumous attachment to the dead thug as pathological and abnormal behaviour.

Police feared Zarah was too close to the underworld and could be passing briefs of evidence and witness statements to third parties with criminal connections. Her unique presence in the staid Melbourne legal community as a snake-owning solicitor with a double-barrelled surname saw her dubbed 'the hyphen-with-a-python'. But Zarah's designer wear and sexy reputation distracted from her steely survivor streak. She came back from professional death to beat perjury and gun charges and to overturn a legal watchdog's ruling that she was not a fit and proper person to be a lawyer.

Her stock agent father is believed to have passed away and she seems to have little to do with her mother. Zarah has amiably refused various interview requests stating, 'I don't like journalists,' and refusing even to comment on the health of Chivas – 'None of your business.'

Police said the gangland solicitor who would house-sit for Carl and Roberta Williams lived in an apartment bankrolled by Mokbel. Questioned in court about Mokbel, Zarah said, 'I'm waiting for my counsel to object to relevance.' The leggy lawyer and pint-sized paramour made an unlikely couple, but Zarah's flirtatious mix of vulnerability, self-confidence and plunging necklines meant that within minutes of meeting her Tony would have been smitten. In the same way Mokbel just had to have the latest Ferrari, Zarah would have gained an instant number on his must-have list.

Mokbel was in the same callous human trade as the head-stomping Caine, but unlike her last boyfriend Mokbel had money, brothers and associates to take care of the rougher edges of his business. Tony once combined two of his loves by taking Zarah to a Queensland casino, where she was seen collecting his thousands of dollars of winnings. His charm, charisma and sheer front, combined with some conspicuous displays of wealth, saw Mokbel punch well above his not insubstantial weight when it came to women.

Zarah was a prize conquest and handy contact, but since the turn of the millennium the main woman in Mokbel's life was Danielle McGuire.

Like Zarah, her raven-haired rival for the balding man's affections, Danielle was also a thin, buxom underworld vamp with a dead gangster on the ex-boyfriends list.

Her poor taste in men may have been genetic – her mum, Joan Madin, dated a gunman who police later linked to the Hodson killings – and at fourteen Danielle was dating a twenty-year-old. She had a daughter, Brittany, from a subsequent abusive relationship that lasted only six months.

When police raided her Collingwood home in 1998 McGuire was living with her new beau – a male model – and her then two-year-old daughter. As the raiding officers discovered, McGuire was also sharing house with pill-making equipment, 7300 speed tablets worth about $400,000, cocaine and $9200 in cash. The pretty and feisty young mum was an ecstasy- and amphetamine-using party girl who did not know when the party was over. She left her daughter with her mother most weekends so she could rave until Monday, cutting a drug-fuelled swathe through the city's nightclubs.

McGuire also had an affair with married mobster Mark Moran. When Moran was gunned down outside his family home in 2000, McGuire recovered sufficiently from her grief to begin an affair the same year with Mokbel. But while Mokbel was clearly a charmer, his wandering eye meant his main molls never rested easy. There were heated scenes between the balding man's blonde and dark-haired companions when Danielle learnt of Zarah.

Moon-faced millionaire Mokbel could excite a lot of passion among his envious coterie of admirers. A Melbourne gumshoe said his private detective agency was hired by two different women to watch Mokbel. Each client was unaware of the other's existence but both had a nasty hunch their man was straying and wanted

Mokbel tracked. McGuire took her concerns into her own hands and bugged Mokbel's car. What she learnt led her to angrily confront Zarah. Someone then, in return, smashed in the windows of McGuire's luxury Toyota Lexus.

Roberta Williams was friends with Danielle (just as her husband Carl was mates with Mokbel) and was relatively close to her and Carl's criminal solicitor and occasional house-sitter, Zarah. Roberta said Zarah denied an ongoing affair with Mokbel so she warned Danielle off going the scrag against her. 'I had a falling out with Danielle because I said to her, "If you fucking go near Zarah we will punch on because I am not going to let you hurt Zarah,"' she said. But Roberta said her loyalties changed when she realised Zarah was lying to her and living high on the Williams hog while secretly sleeping with her close friend's man. She has successfully maintained the rage against Garde-Wilson ever since.

Roberta and Danielle were no longer 'great mates' at the time of writing but Roberta said she still regretted Zarah getting between them. 'I'm spewing I didn't listen to Danielle in regard to Zarah. I should've believed her and a few other people instead of listening to Zarah's lies,' Roberta said. 'Zarah did the wrong thing and I should have listened to other people and I lost good friends out of the lying whore in the situation.'

Years earlier Danielle McGuire had pled guilty to her drugs charges. As those charges had slowly crept through the courts she had met Mokbel and been won over by his admit-nothing-and-unleash-the-lawyers approach. She appealed to the Supreme Court to change all her guilty pleas to not guilty. But it didn't work. Not even borrowing Mokbel's legal dream team of Nicola Gobbo and Con Heliotis, QC, could save her from the big house. McGuire was given a blue tracksuit and sent to do a minimum of nineteen months, allowing Mokbel to revert to his preferred status as single Tony on the town.

One night Mokbel drank too much and got thrown in the drunk tank without charge by Melbourne West police. Mokbel associates would not say what the usually temperate drinker was celebrating. Whatever it was, when Mokbel stepped out of the cells hungover at dawn, there was a bright side. It was his only walk to freedom that would not cost him a fortune in legal fees.

When Danielle McGuire was released from her substantially longer stay at Her Majesty's pleasure, she and Mokbel set up home at a Southbank penthouse reportedly owned by bookie Frank Hudson. The expensive luxury accommodation came with multiple personal carparks. A fellow resident could never undertand why his portly, balding neighbour always parked his luxury cars wherever he wanted – often in the resident's own spaces. The resident raised it with the body corporate and eventually Mokbel himself only to be told, 'Don't you know who I am, mate?' It was only later that the resident saw Tony's face on the news and realised why he could never get the building authority to act on his carpark complaints.

McGuire established her own business, Hollywood Hair Extension & Beauty Salon, in the yuppie belt of Toorak Road, South Yarra, in July 2005. More than $250,000 was reportedly channelled through the business to Betfair in London. The great thing about betting accounts is you can be penniless – like if you're stuck in a prison or a fugitive from justice – and with a telephone and a password can move money around. Milad's wife, Renate, later became a co-director in the South Yarra salon with Danielle.

Crown Casino is a modern megalith rising from the banks of the brown Yarra River. Giant flame-throwers at the entrance spew fireballs into the air and, according to local legend, roast the occasional disoriented pigeon or bat. To mega-gambler Mokbel, who had grown up on illegal backroom games, the casino was a devil's playground. He was a regular at the high-roller Mahogany Room and was treated to free and discounted room rates due to his Very Important Punter status. Crime colleague Lucky was also a Crown VIP and Tony's brothers, Milad, Kabalan and Horty, regularly used the casino as a rendezvous point. At the height of the gangland war Mokbel would hunker down in the palatial suites of the Crown Towers hotel.

Mokbel had been banned from about five hundred bars and clubs in Prahran and neighbouring suburbs after police adopted a rare procedure allowing people of 'notoriously bad character' to be excluded. He had already been banned from owning racehorses. And then in June 2004 the Chief Commissioner, Christine Nixon, used special police powers to ban dozens of gangland figures from the casino. All four Mokbel boys got letters from the chief telling them their days of spread misères, rivers and flops were numbered. Tony's increasingly notorious protégé Carl Williams and his pa, George, were banned. So too was Carlton Crew figure Mario Condello, who once robbed a fellow high-roller at knife-point in the Mahogany Room toilets. Some gangland figures took the news better than others.

One day the author had a sit-down with Mick Gatto – also on the casino banned list – followed by an interview with the state's top cop, Nixon. On learning of my next appointment Gatto said: 'Tell her thanks for banning me from Crown – she's saved me a fortune. I was gonna send her a diamond ring but I don't want her to get the wrong idea.' Nixon got the joke, laughed, and said: 'I remember signing those letters.'

Mokbel loved the casino but as far as he was concerned the sweetest gamble around was the legal system. It was the only game totally stacked in the player's favour, one where the house has to play with an open hand while the punter keeps his hidden. So he pointed his one indulgence at the other and asked his lawyers to sort out his casino problem. Though Mokbel initially attempted to mount a legal challenge to the ban he ultimately dropped his appeal, wistfully comparing himself to Joe Pesci's character in Scorsese's mob movie *Casino*. 'If a casino is good enough for Nicky Santoro it should be good enough for me,' Mokbel said.

Horty Mokbel also attempted to legally challenge his casino ban as a deprivation of liberty, even summonsing the Chief Commissioner who had issued the bans to appear in the Supreme Court. But Horty had a more pragmatic fall-back plan. He was listed as a Conrad Club member – the high-rollers clique of Queensland's biggest casino, Conrad Jupiters, on the Gold Coast. While Horty headed north in the pursuit of income detached from work, Tony went back to the track.

Mokbel boasted he made $380,000 at the 2004 Melbourne Cup as crowd favourite Makybe Diva chalked up her first of three historic consecutive Cup wins. He won the princely sum, more than seven times the average wage, from home, laying phone bets with a rails bookie. But the flamboyant gambler was no good at being a homebody. Two days later, amid growing public notoriety and while on very contentious bail, Mokbel surfaced at the 2004 Oaks – one of the biggest events on Australia's racing calendar – to splash the cash.

Undercover police had watched him at the Oaks four years earlier, aghast at the openness with which the crime lord distributed cocaine to the celebrity in-crowd. Now while on a controversial million-dollar bail, with $20 million in assets seized and facing very serious drugs charges, Mokbel brazenly returned to the scene of his earlier infamy.

Looking like a short, balding Johnny Cash, Mokbel made his grand entrance dressed from head to toe in black designer wear. He horsed around with mate Sam Greco, ex-world kickboxing champion and cafe owner. He mingled with high-profile sporting, business and social figures in the members' betting ring. And he even gained access to the exclusive Birdcage section of the track which hosts prestige marquees, international celebrities and supermodels. 'I've been betting from home,' Mokbel, wearing a dark pinstriped suit, black shirt and black tie, said on the day. 'But this is a nice day and everybody gets dressed up.'

Mokbel said he put an $80,000 bet on a short-priced winner and before the seventh race picked three firsts in a row. One of his suspiciously serendipitous steeds was the ominously named Oaks winner Hollow Bullet. Tony was either very tinny on the day, had an inside word or more likely was loudly inflating his winnings for the benefit of the tax man and forensic accountants.

He was photographed smiling alongside bookie and associate Frank Hudson, who had copped the fine and ban for the unlicensed wagering in New South Wales and was technically Tony's Southbank landlord. The defiant display led to headlines like 'BAIL IS A CARNIVAL' and prompted an inevitable backlash, with politicians drafting laws to help keep crime bosses away from the track. But then just days after his ostentatious appearance at Oaks Day, Mokbel was excused from the grind of attending his cocaine committal hearing, after his lawyers argued he could not attend court because he feared for his life. They were very good lawyers. Hundreds of thousands of people attend the Spring Racing Carnival each year, entry can be bought with a $60 ticket and, unlike the Supreme Court, there are no metal scanners at the entrance.

The police had seized the Mokbel assets they knew of, amounting to a $20 million big freeze. There were undoubtedly millions more in names and from sources they could not connect to Mokbel. But the cash-flow problems did hurt business and, in Mokbel's mind, made it more necessary to do more business – even while on bail awaiting his cocaine trial. Mokbel had a new $80,000 pill press made so his syndicate could up production and had an underworld killer show him how to work the press. 'Tony then started punching pills out with a fox symbol on them,' the killer said. 'I would estimate that Tony Mokbel would have made over $100 million through his dealings in the drug world.'

Mokbel wanted to bring in a shipment of the chemical MDMA to turn into millions of dollars of ecstasy tablets for the Australian market. He urged two men to import an initial delivery of 100 kilograms of the powder, agreeing to pay $8000 per kilo, and was caught on tape bragging how he had police and federal agents on his side. But the men he was dealing with were an informer and a federal agent. 'Mr Mokbel claimed he was producing MDMA tablets and he could make $15 to $20 million in a fairly short period of time,' AFP agent Glen Meredith later told a court.

At some point Mokbel must have smelt a rat and he rang the undercover agent telling him to 'stop the project' and that he never 'had any intention' of going ahead. He was arrested near his Southbank apartment carrying six mobile phones and $38,000 in cash in a Prada bag. He was caught with the impressive wad just six days after telling his cocaine trial judge he would need taxpayer funded Legal Aid because he was too broke to pay his lawyers.

Mokbel became the first person in Australia to be charged with inciting others to import MDMA. He claimed he was not really trying to import ecstasy ingredients, just seeking drug world information he could then give police as a 'bargaining chip'.

Con Heliotis, QC, told the court he could only appear for Mr Mokbel thanks to the generosity of friends paying his bills. He claimed the cash Mr Mokbel was arrested with had been given to him by one of his brothers to pay outstanding legal fees. The feds opposed bail saying Mokbel was a flight risk and unreconstructed crim.

'What an extraordinary thing to do when you are facing serious Commonwealth matters whilst you are on bail,' the prosecution said. 'This man plays according to his own rules and no others.' Magistrate Phillip Goldberg disagreed and Mokbel was again granted bail less than a month after his arrest.

Mokbel was perhaps the most notorious Victorian criminal since Ned Kelly to remain free while his infamy rapidly increased. Unlike Ned, he could defiantly thumb his nose at authorities without going into hiding. But in place of a sound prosecution case or a tougher court system, a tapestry of rarely used bans were applied like bandaids to a gangrenous leg. There were casino bans, local bar bans and horserace bans. The police described their casino ban as a 'form of public shaming'. The bans sprang up to try to cope with the peculiar problem of Tony Mokbel – guilty as hell, presumed innocent.

Mokbel got his cocaine trial delayed because he was waiting for public funding – necessary, he said, because police had frozen all his assets. The judge allowed the postponement but claimed his lawyers, including Zarah Garde-Wilson, had sat on their hands. He also noted it was odd that Tony claimed to be cash strapped given he had varied bail several times in the past year to holiday in Queensland. 'That does suggest there is some money,' Judge Gillard said.

* * *

Mokbel's lingering cocaine charge continued through the wheels of justice. A police witness appeared by video-link from a secure location. But the court television had folders taped to the sides like blinkers. Mokbel's latent menace and ability to get to people was apparent in a cordon of crime-scene tape strung up across the court, keeping the public and media back and all but the lawyers from seeing the face of the witness on the television screen. The menace was made more palpable when gangland patriarch George Williams – father of Mokbel's mate gone large Carl – later wandered into the court followed by two known Mokbel associates.

There was further drama at court the day arrangements to protect the Stooge were discussed. His testimony would be another blow to the defence case and an angry Mokbel confronted Agent Ragg outside the courtroom. 'He was in a temper because he denied being the financier. He got hold of me outside the court and said, "I'm not the financier." He made a number of admissions which were unrecorded and got into a right temper,' Agent Ragg said.

Mokbel's lawyers tried to calm their client down saying, 'That's enough, Tony.' But when he refused to relent they vacated the ugly scene.

'He had a lot to say. He made admissions to his involvement,' Ragg said.

'I'll do two years,' Mokbel offered.

Ragg responded that it was not up to him how long Mokbel did. He told Mokbel that yelling outside the Supreme Court was not the way to get his side of the story across. He said if he wanted to dispute the witnesses he should do a record of interview. But Mokbel wasn't interested. 'He had an unrealistic perception of my ability to influence the judicial process. He thought just by talking to me he could come away with a two-year jail sentence,' Ragg said. 'I tried to say to him it doesn't work like that, it's up to a court, not me.'

There was a dark underside to Mokbel's time on bail. It had been busy, pleasurable and high paced – perhaps because he sensed the evidence against him was stacking up and the walls were closing in. But while Tony on the town was ostentatiously embracing his passions, in the background bullets were flying. Murder and death were stalking the drug trade and the bodies of people he liked and people he detested were piling up. The gangland would provide a carnival mirror showing how every one of Mokbel's jovial indulgences had a distorted and dark flipside.

Mokbel's cool in a crisis and efforts with the opposite sex were legendary. He once combined both to flirt with a policewoman who was searching his house, even asking her to come and work for him. But his charm extended only to those who could help him and did not stand in his way. Coked-up airheads willing to laugh at his jokes would meet a charming cherub of a man. Others – like the female prison guard Mokbel threatened to kill – found him less chivalrous.

Mokbel got in an argument with the woman during visiting hours at the Melbourne Assessment Prison. He eyeballed the woman trying to earn a basic wage and, as he was walked to the officer's station for a strip search, he spat his venom.

'I'll make one phone call and I'll have her knocked tonight,' he said.

He repeated the threat loud and clear twice more and then exclaimed: 'She is dead!'

16

Fat Tony and the gangland war

Bang, bang, you're dead.
Fifty bullets in your head.

– Playground chant

When the litres of blood spilt in the gangland war had been mopped up and the dozens of dead gangsters lay mouldering in their flashy graves, Mokbel, a rare survivor, looked back with faux regret. 'We were all friends and it was the saddest thing happening. It was just sad,' he said. His outlook during the underworld war itself, however, was more opportunistic than melancholy.

The tiny truth in his crocodile-tear-stained recollection was that Mokbel was at some point friends with most of the hunters and their human quarry. Mokbel has generally been regarded as peripheral in the perception of the gangland war as a shoot 'em up between Carl Williams's north-western suburbs crew and Mick Gatto's Carlton Crew. But in recent years an alternative history has emerged in which Mokbel was a major player in the bloodbath.

Mokbel had managed to get to the top of the local crime scene and muscle in on others' drug profits with very little overt violence, as a result of his skill as a freewheeling diplomat and a salesman unaligned with any faction. He had a fellowship with Lebanese crims and had established relationships with outlaw bikie gangs that played a crucial role in chemical distribution.

Mokbel had been close to the Morans, who, through Lewis's friendship with Mick Gatto, became a kind of Anglo-Celt crime subsidiary of the Italians. Tony's Mediterranean looks, gourmet tastes and decidedly mafiosi nickname 'Fat Tony' saw him fit in easily with the Melbourne Calabrians and their approved franchisees. Mokbel had cousins who were close to Carlton Crew consigliore Mario Condello. In his gold chain and dark suit Tony also looked more like the coffee-sipping Carlton gentlemen of crime than the suburban bogans snapping at their heels. If there had been bad blood over pinching the Morans' cook it was not so serious that anyone was going to spill anyone else's claret over it. In hindsight that cook, the Grifter, had ended up being more trouble than he was worth, and in any case it is likely Mokbel patched up hurt feelings with cash or a joint venture.

While there was plenty of money coming in, Mokbel was of the view that a rising tide lifted all boats. The way Tony saw it, all comers were welcome, particularly those dopey enough to take the fall in times of inclement fortune. It was this attitude that endeared him to Carl Williams, Tony's long-time acquaintance, sometime prison pal, protégé in perfidy and street dealer gone very large. As well as their history Mokbel fitted well with Williams's aspirational suburban crew because of his down-to-earth wag personality and view of the drug business as a non-hierarchical merit-based cash bonanza.

The Italians had the ties that bind. Duty, honour and omerta. Kissed cheeks, burnt saints cards, tamped down secrets, and firmly closed mouths at family reunions. For everyone else there were the non-cultural universal ties that bind – filthy lucre and the prospect of violent retribution. Mokbel, largely linked to, liked by, and respectful of all, was uniquely placed in the web of Melbourne crime families and factions. The future could only be bright. And then it all went to hell.

When the badlands bells toll for the gangland dead the list of victims usually starts with Alphonse Gangitano, who died in his jocks after getting three in the head at his Templestowe home. Next there was a series of murders of Italian 'family men' with links to the fruit and vegetable markets – Vince Mannella, Joe Quadara, Gerardo Mannella and Frank Benvenuto.

The links between the deaths of those men and what was to follow are not strong except for the consistent involvement of a couple of guns for hire: Walsh Street killer Victor Peirce and Sunshine young gun Andrew 'Benji' Veniamin, and probably their employer. Those two handmaidens of carnage were linked to Italian executions and would reprise bloody roles as the new underworld combusted. But the gangland war as most know it started on a clear day in a suburban park when up and coming Broadmeadows drug dealer Carl Williams got shot in his belly.

Carl's old man, George, was a career crim and drugs were the constant family business despite workplace accidents like Carl's brother, Shane, dying of a heroin overdose. On Carl's twenty-ninth birthday crime dynasty half-brothers Mark and Jason Moran met him to settle a dispute involving drugs, money and bitterness over the ownership of a pill press. Bubbling under the surface was a twisted history of two proud, cocky, trigger-happy crime families with more baggage than just guns, drugs and money. Roberta Mercieca had been married to a mate of Jason and Mark's before she went on to become Mrs Carl Williams. While on that scene she had been unimpressed with the Moran wives. She found them stuck-up and likely informed them of this. Carl had previously had a Romeo and Juliet (without the double fatal ending) style dalliance with Sue Kane, sister of Jason's wife, Trish.

The meeting in Gladstone Park in Melbourne's north ended with Jason firing a single .22 slug from a Derringer into Williams's gut. Mark appealed to Jason: 'Shoot him in the head.' But in a rare instance of mercy – or perhaps as a pragmatic decision because a debt was owed – Jason wavered.

Had Williams at that point elected to play Gandhi, move north and live out his days eating fried chicken in the Gold Coast sunshine, the bulk of what we call the gangland killings would not have happened. Instead, in precision strikes, the Williams crew gunned down a mad mate of Mark Moran, Richard Mladenich, and less than a month later Mark Moran himself. Williams would also use the kill-or-be-killed logic to justify having Jason, then father Lewis, Moran killed by different teams of assassins. 'I am guilty of defending my loved ones from being killed,' he said.

While contracts on Carl's life no doubt existed, few shots were fired at Williams as his 'self-defence' killing spree spiralled out of control. A major cause of the cold and calculated crime-land slaughter was the paranoid Williams adopting the bloodthirsty Benji Veniamin as his own personal executioner. The unhinged partnership of Carl and Benji turned out to be as deadly as that of Smith and Wesson – and their union was all Mokbel's fault.

In November 2002 Mokbel was just two months out of jail and still celebrating when he attended a sit-down with the Carlton Crew at a Lygon Street restaurant. A Mokbel mouthpiece later said he was 'hijacked or abducted' and dragged to the rendezvous. But police believe Tony simply responded to a gentlemanly invite from Mario Condello, who could have ensured Mokbel's attendance by mentioning La Porcella served good pizza.

When Mokbel arrived at the Carlton meeting the teflon don Domenic 'Mick' Gatto was there. So was then Gatto associate and hitman Veniamin. Coffin Cheater bikie Troy Mercanti and drug dealer Fabian Quaid, both friends of fellow sandgroper and bad boy footballer Ben Cousins, were also there. Nik 'the Russian' Radev and John Kizon – a colourful Perth identity, Gangitano pallbearer and Gatto mate – may also have been present.

It is not clear what Mokbel did – or more likely said – that attracted violent retribution. Whatever it was it was about as popular as a Mohammed joke in Mecca. Or perhaps it was a trap all along and Mokbel had been invited as the party's piñata – destined to be put in his place either for a gangland faux pas or simply his runaway success. Either way the result was not pretty.

Mercanti and Quaid attacked Mokbel and gave him a serious

working over. Others may have been involved as well. According to gangland folklore Mercanti and Quaid objected that Mokbel had been telling others they were 'dogs'. But when Tony failed to back down from his comments things got bloody. It was a nasty public beating that would have instilled resentment in a victim with less pride and ego than Mokbel. He went down hard outside the restaurant and was kicked in the head by men in solid boots. 'There was blood everywhere,' Gatto said.

Tony's cheekbones were broken, bruising from his two black eyes met in the middle like a raccoon, and his head started to swell up like a melon. The flash king of Sydney Road was helpless to fight back as the near fatal beating was dispensed. Senior Carlton Crew figures Gatto and Condello watched on without intervening.

When the assembled crims had finished their lesson in humility Gatto pointed the bloody heap of contusions and proud flesh out to Veniamin. 'Andrew, do us a favour – take him and get him patched up,' Gatto said. Veniamin put Mokbel in a car and drove him to a private doctor who would not report the incident to police. But Mokbel got a doctor's note for missing his bail-mandated police check-in and, according to his lawyer, was laid up for a week recovering.

As a business decision it had always made sense to Mokbel to keep as many Mr Bigs as friendly as possible. But now, nursing a head the size of a pumpkin, his blood boiling, he changed his mind.

Senior police and long-time Mokbel watchers believe the bashing had a profound effect on Tony's outlook on the gangland war. Detective Sergeant Jim Coghlan: 'That would have been a factor. Getting beaten up and Big Mick not lending him a hand.'

The head of the Purana taskforce and successor to Jim O'Brien, Detective Inspector Bernie Edwards, concurred: 'He wouldn't have thought too nicely about that happening.'

Something changed as Veniamin drove Mokbel to the medics. Most likely it was Tony's silver tongue still working through the blood. Until that time Benji had been Gatto's enforcer, but Mokbel might have mentioned his up and coming friend Carl. He might have said how the goons that had just bashed him were a spent force. He might have told how many millions he and Carl were making and how they always paid top price and didn't have to be chased to settle on a contract.

Benji had killed for the Italians before and was believed to have been the triggerman in the supermarket carpark hit on Joe Quadara in Toorak in the late 1990s. Mick Gatto, an ex-boxer, must have seen a little of himself in Benji, also a graduate of the ring, and had taken him under his wing. Benji had gunned down his old Sunshine schoolmates turned drug dealers Dino Dibra and Paul Kalipolitis – the latter a hit, police suspected, for the Carlton Crew. But before Benji met Tony on that fateful day and drove him to the medic's, there was no clear-cut case of Veniamin killing for Williams. Gatto also noticed how close Benji and Tony, who he called 'the Mediterranean', became after Mokbel's beating.

'Before long they'd formed a tight working relationship,' Gatto said. 'Andrew also became close to Carl Williams through the Mediterranean, and as a result more people died at Andrew's hands. They both offered Andrew easy drug money, which I couldn't. There was big money there, and Andrew tapped into it.' Gatto claimed Horty Mokbel was embarrassed by Tony's behaviour at La Porcella and it led to the brothers falling out for a couple of years.

Word of Mokbel's anger and desire for vengeance travelled far. An unrelated murder trial in the West Australian Supreme Court heard that Mokbel was rumoured to have put a price on the heads of senior Perth Coffin Cheater bikies Troy Mercanti, Eddie Withnell and Darren Whittaker. The whispers prompted one criminal enemy of the Coffin Cheaters to draft a letter to Mokbel asking: 'How much for Troy? How much for Eddie?'

After the bashing a rattled Mokbel sought sanctuary in the bosom of Crown Casino, a haven from which he had not yet been banned. He stayed in a luxury hotel suite on the twelfth floor of Crown Towers for nearly a month. Room 1223 is spacious, contains a comfortable puffy white lounge suite, a glass table, marble work desk, and a giant flatscreen TV. The curtains draw back to reveal a semicircular wall of glass outside of which is a sweeping vista of the city across the Yarra River, unrolling north over the city's skyscrapers. And from room 1223 Mokbel plotted his revenge. His enemies, real and perceived, would soon start dropping like flies.

Police and crims warned Gatto that Mokbel had taken out a contract to have him killed. The don himself was concerned enough to step up his security. Gatto turned down a Purana offer of protection. But he chopped and changed his routine, and made sure he, or someone with him, was always packing heat. Gatto said of Mokbel: 'He used to be a friend of mine but he's no friend of mine anymore. Simple as that. I don't worry about him or anyone. He's got his own headaches and I'll just let him worry about his own headaches.'

There was a suggestion that Nik Radev was initially offered $400,000 to kill Gatto. Radev was apparently willing to have Gatto executed at La Porcella by a man with a machine gun riding pillion on a passing motorbike – assassination South American-style. But Mokbel never paid Radev's requested $50,000 upfront fee. And soon circumstances changed and Radev too was removed from the picture.

Nik 'the Russian' Radev was perhaps the most ruthless and wicked of a gangland brimming with megalomaniacs and psychopaths. He had come from Bulgaria to Australia as a refugee but in time proved he was more familiar with the dispensing end of brutality. He once broke into a 71-year-old man's home with another doomed goon, Housam 'Sam' Zayat, and bashed the resident before tying his five-year-old granddaughter to a bed and threatening the little girl with a gun. Underworld folklore claims Radev, who had 'taxi' tattooed on his penis (because 'it would go anywhere'), would also rape victims of both genders as a means of intimidation.

Radev bought drugs and chemicals from Mokbel and Williams but when he got ambitious about sourcing one of Mokbel's speed cooks, Tony and Carl got nervous. The pair knew Radev was likely to kidnap their cook and use him as lucrative slave labour. And, according to informed sources, they decided to strike before the ambitions of the vulgar Bulgarian consumed them all. Tony had a pick of motives. One: avoid losing a good cook. Two: Radev had also stood on the sidelines and said nothing – or even joined in – as he was beaten to within an inch of death at La Porcella. And three: 'the Russian' had once firebombed his mate Willie Thompson's car.

At a council of crims believed to include Mokbel, Radev was told he could meet the cook he was interested in if he went immediately to the northern suburbs. The Russian was near his parked Mercedes in Coburg when Mokbel's new mate Benji emerged and fired up to seven bullets into Radev's head and chest before being whisked away in a car driven by a killer called 'the Runner'. Tony and Carl kept their cook, and Radev, flashy to the last, went off in a gold-plated coffin.

Just three months later Mokbel's mate since school, clubbing guru and drug dealer Willie Thompson, was gunned down in his new car. Radev had been behind the firebombing of Willie's old car and had Radev been alive at the time he would have been prime suspect over Willie's murder. Perhaps, some surmised, the hit on Willie was a payback from Radev sympathisers, and the killing of the Russian's surviving associates soon followed.

In perhaps the most sordid gangland death, Benji murdered Radev associate Mark Mallia. A crim said Milad Mokbel also claimed he was present at Mallia's killing. Drug dealer Mallia had fallen for the romance of crime but there are few things less glamorous than the desolate way he left the mortal coil. Mallia was tortured with a soldering iron and strangled to death. His burnt remains were found in a wheelie bin in a drain in West Sunshine. Another Radev associate, Housam 'Sam' Zayat, was shot dead by Nicholas Ibrahim in an outer suburban paddock. 'Mokbel was devastated about Willie and he wanted someone to pay,' a gangland source said.

According to a police witness a meeting was called at a location convenient to Tony and with a cuisine appropriate to Williams – the Red Rooster in Brunswick. Allegedly present with Carl and George Williams and Tony, and later to tell the tale, were the gun for hire called 'the Runner' and his driver. Mokbel believed the man behind Willie's death was drug dealer and hot dog vendor Michael Marshall, who some believed was Thompson's business partner. Mokbel knew the Runner from his last stint in Port Phillip prison. The Runner had worked in the jail kitchen and would smuggle Tony food to add to his cell stash of alcohol and mobile phones.

The Runner and his driver had form for killing parents in front of their children. Carl had used them to blast Jason Moran and Pasquale Barbaro to pieces in a van full of little kids as they left a football clinic. It was a crime that shocked the nation as the gangland bloodletting spilled into the public arena.

Police were told Mokbel, galvanised against the Carlton Crew, helped tip off Williams as to Jason Moran's movements. According to the Runner their unholy alliance was further forged with murderous plans hatched over fried chicken. But if Mokbel really wanted to get his hands on Willie's killer he may have only needed to reach over the table to the portly fellow in beachwear at the other end of the twisters and drumsticks. The police prime suspect for Willie Thompson's execution in Chadstone was actually Carl Williams (although the motive remains hazy). But Mokbel thought the killer was Marshall and neither Carl nor the Runner were about to disabuse him of the notion.

The Runner claimed Mokbel offered them $300,000 to roll the hot dog vendor. They decided the execution team would get two-thirds, and Carl, as boss, the remainder. The Runner said: 'When I shook hands with Tony he passed a piece of paper to me which had the details of Marshall's address ... It also said he drove a white Hilux.' Mokbel would provide guns and money for Marshall to be executed within weeks. 'Carl was keen to do the job quickly so Tony did not become suspicious about Carl's involvement in Willie Thompson's murder,' the Runner said.

Mokbel's life had been littered with low acts. He traded off others' misery. He found fidelity a challenge. And he routinely advocated murder as the solution for weak links and snitches. There would be time for a few more low acts in his future. But, if the Runner was telling the truth that Mokbel bankrolled the Marshall job (and there are plenty in the gangland who believe the Runner just told the police what they wanted to hear), what happened next would be his lowest.

At dusk on Saturday 25 October 2003, kickboxer, drug dealer, hot dog vendor and family man Michael Marshall was returning from a bakery with hot dog rolls for his night's business. On the narrow roadway of Joy Street in leafy South Yarra, Marshall hopped from his van and went to open the rear door to let his son, just five, out of his booster seat. The boy watched on helplessly as a stranger ran up and fired at least four shots into his father's head from close range.

The effect on a five-year-old child of seeing his protective kin's head blown to smithereens is unfathomable. It was the sort of horrific sight that regularly leaves hard-as-nails cops, emergency workers and soldiers reeling with a lifelong crippling stress disorder. Michael Marshall's five-year-old son had seen something terrifying from a world of nightmares. He just wanted to get to the sanctuary of his mother. But before crossing the road he still stopped and looked right, left, right. The distressed boy alerted his mum at home nearby to what had happened. The two people in the world closest to Michael Marshall then watched him lying in the gutter dying with severe injuries to what used to be a head.

The Runner admitted he pulled the trigger but he said the ugly scene was Tony's bastard – it was just how the multimillionaire chose to spend his money, he claimed. Mokbel consistently denied involvement and though charged had the charge dropped due to insufficient evidence. Williams later pled to the murder but denied Mokbel's involvement. However, at Carl's hearing the no-nonsense Betty King, Australia's version of Judge Judy, was having none of it. Judge King had ended up with nearly all the gangland cases. She was a woman who stared down homicidal maniacs during work hours, had a penchant for leopard skin boots after hours, and barely suffered anyone gladly, particularly not fools.

'What is now clear is that the murder was not done at your initial instigation but that of Tony Mokbel,' she said. 'It was a callous, brutal execution of another human being ... one of the worst types of murder that may be seen.'

And if the Runner's version of events is at all right, all Mokbel achieved was the murder of his dead mate's friend in front of his child and the gift of $100,000 to the real killer of his mate Willie Thompson.

By late 2003 chaos in the badlands had cost at least eighteen people their lives, but it was the murder of Graham 'the Munster' Kinniburgh that hit too close to home for Mick Gatto. Kinniburgh, an ex-painter and docker, had survived Melbourne's last major underworld slaughter – the war on the wharves. But twelve days before Christmas 2003 it was the Munster's turn to die.

It is not clear who came calling for the Munster. Some close to the Williams crew claim credit for the killing as part of their aggressive anti-Carlton Crew campaign, while other gangland insiders say the driveway execution was over something completely different – 'something personal', or even a preemptive strike by a targeted assassin. Whatever the case it was one dead friend too many for Mick Gatto, who called a council of war at Crown Casino with Carl Williams and the shooter who had done both groups' bidding, Veniamin. The two leaders' ample frames were caught on camera demonstrating that while ultimately crime might not pay, short-term it can certainly put you in a good paddock.

At the meeting Gatto told Williams: it was not his war but it needed to stop there and then. Gatto said all parties could walk away and there would be no more to pay. But he warned his younger adversary that if Williams kept going – look out.

Williams had justified his killing on business and preemptive strike principles. Now he had put the two Morans who antagonised him, and many others besides, in the cemetery. Williams wanted to know if Gatto could be trusted to honour his pledge. Williams asked Benji his opinion and Benji gave the only answer he knew: 'Kill him.' Things would play out slightly differently.

The last time Benji went to La Porcella there had been more red sauce on the ground outside than on the pizzas within, after Mokbel was bashed almost to death. On that occasion Benji had been the one to chauffeur Tony away. This time, when Gatto summoned Benji to the pizza house, there would be no 'nearly' about the killing and Benji would leave chauffeured away by the coroner.

Gatto had been told a number of times that Veniamin was gunning for him but could not believe it. Gatto admitted firing the bullets that killed Benji out the back of the restaurant but said he did so only after wresting the gun from his would-be assassin. Gatto took Veniamin out the back to talk and the barney between the ex-boxers was settled with multiple blasts and a dead Benji.

One of those lunching with Gatto when it all went down recalled: 'After they had been gone for a few minutes I heard what I thought was gunshots from the back of the restaurant. I looked in that direction and Gatto came in. He did not come to the table but went straight to the restaurant owner and said, "He tried to kill me, ring the police."'

Benji's death, one of the few scalps worn by the Carlton Crew in the supposedly tit-for-tat battle, dealt the ultimate penalty to a gangland turncoat. It also dealt a devastating blow to Williams, very close to home. Self-defence or not, Benji's death was the old guard warning off the rabid contenders to the throne. While banged up awaiting the murder trial, Gatto was told by another prisoner: 'I was part of a surveillance team that was hired by Carl Williams and the Mediterranean to have you killed. Me and [two others] were paid to sit off your house, follow you, watch your movements and try and kill you.'

Gatto was defended at his trial by super-wig Robert Richter. But there were striking aspects of the case that even Richter could not completely discount. Gatto had a body bag in his boot. It was Gatto's home turf. Veniamin's other hits were not public, broad-daylight affairs. Not one pizza muncher saw a thing. And Gatto's story changed nine months after Benji was shot: a Gatto friend said that just after the shooting Gatto handed him his own gun. The prosecution thought this was a ruse to portray the remaining gun as Veniamin's. But the character evidence against Veniamin was toe-curlingly unsympathetic. He was, after all, a serial killer with HOTSHOT number plates who had murdered old childhood friends. By contrast when Mick took the stand – an option many accused killers refuse because it allows cross-examination – he was his usual charming everyman self. Gatto was acquitted on self-defence grounds.

Once he was free, though, Mokbel's contract still weighed heavily on Gatto's head. He said he knew he was still a target and Mokbel had a lot of money, power, police and crooks on his side. 'Many people I knew – acquaintances – had sided with him. People are like sheep: they follow the money,' Gatto said.

Jim O'Brien was appointed officer in charge of the Purana taskforce in November 2005. He was worried what sort of monster would emerge top of the pile from the gangland war's brutal evolutionary dynamic. 'People have said the police must be pretty happy that these people are shooting each other – none of them are any good,' O'Brien said. 'I'll pose this question if you think that way: at the end of the shootout, who's the last man standing? Is it the strongest or the weakest? It will always be the strongest.'

Mokbel had been a silent, largely invisible partner in the underworld's spilt blood, but at Veniamin's funeral he publicly and ostentatiously declared his loyalties. A motorcade of four stretch limousines and a Rebels bikies escort brought the funeral party to St Andrew's Greek Orthodox church in Sunshine. Benji's holes had been patched and his body placed in a $20,000 coffin parked under the noses of three solemn black-clad priests. A congregation of hundreds wept in the church pews and monitored who had turned out. Mokbel walked up the centre aisle, leant into the open casket and kissed the bandaged face of the young corpse. In poker it is called 'all in'. You push all your chips in the middle, show your hand and live or die by your decision.

Mokbel placed a newspaper obituary to his recent, and recently deceased, mate: 'To a friend I haven't known for very long.

You were a true friend. My deepest sympathy to all his family – Antonios Mokbel.'

Tony spoke with Carl at the funeral. The following night Lewis Moran was gunned down by two bandits in balaclavas at the bar of the Brunswick Club. Carl and Tony were to go halves in the contract price, police claimed, and they recruited their kill squad at a Sydney Road venue linked to Mokbel. Foul fortune had caused a big realignment of gangland loyalties since Tony and Lewis were simpatico speed barons and horse fanciers a decade earlier.

For obvious reasons it is hard to describe what it feels like to be the victim of a gangland hit. Lewis Moran can't tell us but Bert Wrout – who was shot with him and survived – can. Wrout was Lewis's accomplice, driver, drinking companion, and one-time mate. A long-time Moran associate, Wrout says he died after the shooting but was brought back by medics. It left him with an unusual motto: 'Don't kill me again.'

Wrout recalled: 'We knew we were marked men. We had enough phone calls from Carl Williams every second night – "We're coming now to get you, you pair of whatevers."

'We got to the stage we were both out on bail at the time and it was pretty hard to carry protection, so to speak. If we'd been pinched again of course we wouldn't have gotten out on bail. With all the trials at the time and corruption in the old drug squad, trials were getting held up for years … the point is we would've been rotting in jail if we'd done the wrong thing, so to speak.

'We were just going and I turned around to the bar to pick up the change and Lewis was gulping his last beer and … actually cheap beer got us killed – Lewis was always looking for a cheap alternative to anything. Anyway, I'd turned around and the next thing I know we hear the boom boom boom of boots.'

Lewis Moran saw the balaclava-wearing gunmen and said, 'I think we're off here.'

Wrout continued: 'The bloke they've convicted … supposedly the one who did the actual shooting, he burst through the middle of us, sort of stuck a shottie in Lewis's groin, pushed him away and turned to me and half smiled.'

Wrout headed for the exit door. 'I ran behind Lewis and the gunman … well, it was probably a stupid thing to do but you're not thinking about it at the time. The next thing I know I'm running into the second gunman. I was wearing a suit and I thought, oh shit, I'm off here. By this time Lewis was dead. Not that I heard any shots or anything but he was dead by this time. I'm pretending I got a shooter in my back and I'm trying to get it out, hoping the bloke would turn around and go out the door but he didn't. I'm about two foot from him and he's still holding the gun right at my head.

'I tried to kick him actually, I tried to spin around and kick him. The next thing I know, bang. I was conscious for a while. I was conscious when the ambulance people got there and then they must have knocked me out in the ambulance. The next thing I know I wake up there three weeks later or something. I was on life support for three or four days, intensive care for four weeks – three or four weeks – and they were pretty drastic injuries so I had to wear like a big cage that holds your arm together because it took two centimetres of bone out. Actually the bullet that hit me went through my arm, broke [it] in two, and then two bullet holes in my chest and one of those bullets went boom boom boom through five or six organs and including my spleen which they eventually had to take out and I've [got the bullet] still lodged in my spine.'

The ricocheting slug also caused damage to his liver, kidney, diaphragm and lung.

Shrapnel is typically the preserve of returned servicemen, however, Wrout was left carrying around a bullet six decades after the end of the last world war. He said that strange claim to fame hardly made him Robinson Crusoe.

'There's a lot of blokes in my position. Plenty of blokes, you grow up in this scene knocking around with different blokes, lots of them been shot by the coppers, shot by associates etcetera, and once a bullet gets, well they tell me, once a bullet gets near to your spine and lodges in, it's too dangerous to remove it.'

The driver in the Lewis Moran hit – brother of one of the gunmen – later made a statement to police about the execution. 'I spoke to Carl Williams on the phone,' the driver said. 'His exact words were, "Good one, mate, you have 150,000 reasons to smile."'

The driver said he met Mokbel to get paid. 'Tony was congratulating us on a good job,' he said. 'He handed me an envelope. It was a big yellow envelope. He mentioned that he was dirty on them [the Morans] because he was set up and bashed by their crew.'

The execution of Lewis Moran occurred in a Sydney Road pub in the heart of Tonytown. The death in Brunswick echoed the

Quarry Hotel shooting just a kilometre away when Tony was a teenager. It is safe to say Mokbel had become a lot more involved in neighbourhood affairs in the interim.

Like the police, Lewis's partner, Judy Moran, believed Mokbel was one of the men behind Lewis's death. 'All I know is he was friends with Carl Williams. That's as much as I know about that. What caused him to turn on my family I have no idea other than Carl Williams,' Judy said. 'I think he's a lowlife,' she added. 'Tony must have [been involved], he was involved in all the murders. He must have been involved in that.'

Purana went to court to get permission to interview Milad Mokbel, who was doing a stint in Barwon prison. As part of the application the court heard that Milad knew of the plans to murder the Moran patriarch and was present when the two hitmen were paid. Milad appeared by prison video-link at the application hearing. The magistrate ruled there could be a maximum four-hour interview. Milad, who had never cooperated with police, said: 'It will take five minutes.' It was unlikely he was planning a speedy confession. The magistrate replied: 'That's a matter for you.' Milad's estimate ended up being right.

The Australian Crime Commission also summonsed Milad to give evidence at a secret hearing about the gangland killings of Lewis Moran and Victor Peirce. But the belligerent Milad's involvement did not last long and he refused to take the oath. He was warned that refusing to answer the hearing's questions was a serious crime. 'If you say so, yeah,' he replied. He was charged and when a magistrate added eight months to the eight-year minimum stretch he was serving, Milad either benevolently or sarcastically thanked her for her time.

On a separate occasion Milad threatened another crim to do as he said or he could expect an appointment with the reaper. A cook for Tony and Milad told a court he lived in fear of the brothers. 'I am afraid if I don't do what I am told I could end up just another statistic,' he said. 'I blame myself for getting involved with these people, I fear them greatly ... I know their capabilities,' he said.

Milad reportedly told the fretful crim: 'I was there when Mark Mallia was executed. So don't push my buttons or you'll end up the same way.'

Judge Bernie Teague described the Sydney Road killing of Lewis Moran in stark terms. 'I will moderate the language that I use to describe the murder of Lewis Moran. I nonetheless say that it was a callous, planned, premeditated execution for money,' he said. 'To some people, life is not sacred, as it should be. To some people, life is cheap.'

Carl Williams's feeling that he was a hunted man was justified – the Morans certainly wanted him dead. But every time Williams killed – purportedly to make peace – he then decided the last killing necessitated more deaths. Having buried his mate Benji and knocked off his enemy Lewis Moran, Williams decided surviving members of the Carlton Crew might now come after him. And indeed part of the Carlton leadership team, Mario Condello, was making spectacular plans for an Uzi-toting motorcyclist to carry out a triple homicide on the Williams crew in the heart of the city.

Police believe Williams hired Zarah Garde-Wilson's boyfriend, Lewis Caine, to whack Mario Condello. They believe Caine himself became the target when a shooter he recruited to help with the job betrayed him. The recruit leaked the 'Get Condello' plan to the Italians and got a more lucrative contract on his would-be partner, Caine, from the Italians. The last victim, as families buried their dead and the Purana taskforce jailed the culpable, was Mario Condello. Police intercepted one attempt on Condello's life but in February 2006 he was killed in Brighton ten minutes before his curfew, the last of the gang to die. By then the dogs were barking for Williams and, locked up in reprobates' row, in Barwon he was a spent force. But Mokbel, still at large, never forgot his beating and was intent on keeping the bloody faith. He paid the private school fees of Carl and Roberta's daughter Dhakota (before police took over the bill) and, police suspect, continued the executioner's role. In a statement to police a crim fingered Mokbel as the bagman in the murder of Condello, who had earlier invited him to the perfidious pizza parlour La Porcella, and Purana consequently considered him a person of interest in that crime.

There were other factors allegedly linking Mokbel to knowledge of the Condello kill plot. According to a detective's evidence in a Melbourne Magistrates Court, Tony's brother Milad reportedly told a friend to make himself scarce as Condello was about to get killed, just forty-five minutes before his prediction became grisly reality. There was another link – a suspected shooter in the Condello murder was Tony's almost-relative the Duke, one-time live-in lover of Danielle McGuire's mother, and suspected gunman in the Quarry Hotel shooting back when Mokbel was a teen, and who was also suspected of killing the Hodsons.

Mokbel said when Jason Moran was still alive he sat down with him and told him the war was stupid and getting out of hand. 'The standard thing was we were all mates – it started over a silly thing and suddenly there were just bodies falling all around me,' Mokbel said. But the multi-generational slaughter of the Moran speed dynasty, in which Mokbel was at the very least quietly complicit, left Tony with an unnatural amphetamine monopoly.

While 'the war' was generally bad for everyone's business, Mokbel, less on the radar than others, did quite well out of all the right people dying or getting banged up. Tony's beating might have pushed him into the war but the booming bottom line kept him from straying back to pacifism. His good fortunes at the end of the war were in stark contrast to other gangland leaders.

Carl was the visible figurehead against the old guard. Tony was unseen. Carl grew the ulcer waiting for all his hits to ricochet back. Tony was ulcer free. Carl in the end copped the immediate jail time. Tony was a free man. Carl, with father, George, made an estimated $15 million during those years of turmoil. Tony made – on a crim's conservative estimate of the period – $100 million.

17

Into thin air

'All right,' said the Cat; and this time it vanished quite slowly,
beginning with the end of the tail, and ending with the grin,
which remained some time after the rest of it had gone.
'Well! I've often seen a cat without a grin,' thought Alice; 'but a grin
without a cat! It's the most curious thing I ever saw in my life!'

– Lewis Carroll, *Alice in Wonderland*

Mokbel stood accused by the Runner of bankrolling the execution of a man before his child's disbelieving eyes. But to children whose parents Mokbel liked, Tony could be doting and kind. 'He's caring and he's kind and he loves children ... My kids love him. He's just so kind to any kids,' Roberta Williams said.

Mokbel had dozens of godchildren and, shacked up with Danielle McGuire at his Southbank penthouse, he was a father figure adored by McGuire's daughter, Brittany. It was there the quasi-nuclear family held a party to ring in the new year of 2006 so Tony wouldn't breach his 10 pm curfew. Few knew at that point, possibly not even Tony, that it would turn out to be a farewell party.

In early March Mokbel met his leggy lawyer Zarah Garde-Wilson for lunch. Police believed that at their repast she passed him more than the salt. An Australian Federal agent told the

Supreme Court that police suspected Zarah tipped Mokbel off to impending murder charges. Defence lawyers had been provided with a killer's statement implicating Tony and Carl in a gangland hit. Joining the dots it was clear a murder charge was imminent for Tony.

'A statement had been provided to this effect and is suspected to have been made available to Mokbel by his former solicitor and former girlfriend Zarah Garde-Wilson,' AFP Agent Ragg said.

Zarah confirmed the lunch but denied tipping Tony. 'I wasn't acting for Williams or Mokbel at the time. I wasn't in possession of these statements,' she said.

On St Patrick's Day 2006 prosecutors, in a prescient move, begged once more for bail to be withdrawn because the cocaine case against Tony was so strong. There was no mention of Mokbel being increasingly in the frame for one or more of the gangland killings, despite Victoria Police the same day telling the feds they planned to arrest Mokbel for murder. Federal investigators were willing to introduce the Victoria Police information, but prosecutors were unwilling to lead evidence before the judge that was technically hearsay of hearsay.

Justice Bill Gillard denied the application. He said the conditions on Mokbel's bail prevented him being a flight risk. Being a Friday the court then retired for the weekend. That Sunday at 5 pm Tony walked with Danielle to the South Melbourne police station to check in according to his bail conditions and the pair retired to their top-floor inner-city penthouse apartment.

The following day, Monday, at 10.30 am everyone arrived back at court. Mokbel's lead defence barrister, Con Heliotis, QC, appeared. He made a simple but resounding five-word statement to the judge that would rock the nation: 'We don't have Mr Mokbel.'

Fat Tony had left the building. And a political firestorm would erupt in his wake.

Was he dead, drunk or deliberately departed? Mokbel's lawyers cautioned against jumping to the conclusion that their client had done a runner. Tony had met with foul play from enemies before, they said. And in the bullet-riddled city a month after the killing of Condello, it was a prime possibility that Mokbel had simply become the latest smoking corpse. But the more anyone thought about it the more there was only one inevitable conclusion about the fate of the criminal chancer who had played the system like a violin and seemed to have a thousand second acts. While diligently appearing for court, checking in with police twice a day and keeping to curfew, Mokbel had always kept one eye on the horizon.

A police delegate was dispatched to tell an irritated Deputy Commissioner Simon Overland the bad news of Mokbel's departure.

Later, as Chief of Police, Simon Overland told the author: '[They] came and told me that he'd gone. There was nothing we could do about that so we just had to work out what we could do. My initial reaction was obviously really annoyed but then we pretty quickly thought through what that could then allow us to do.'

Overland still fronted the public to talk tough to the prodigal perp: 'You can spend five years on the run. That's fine. We will find you eventually, and we will bring you back to face justice.'

AFP Agent Jarrod Ragg told the Supreme Court: 'Mokbel is the head of a Lebanese organised-crime syndicate based in Melbourne. Mokbel has sufficient contacts and financial resources to support a fugitive lifestyle overseas.'

Ragg also told the court that Mokbel and Zarah had been involved in an amorous affair. There was speculation that it was a ruse to provoke Danielle's envious rage so she would attempt to contact Tony and give police the lead they so desperately needed. 'I was answering questions asked during cross-examination. The fact that the questions were asked was not by design. But it would have been advantageous to us if Danielle had have decided to take umbrage and speak to Tony about it,' Ragg said.

If alive, where in the world was Fat Tony, a Kuwaiti-born Arabic speaker from a Lebanese family, hiding? In Lebanon, Mexico or Dubai? Theories abounded, including that he left the country and slipped into the Middle East disguised as a Maronite priest. As the horrible truth sank in for the authorities, rattled top cops and lawyers entered a public spat over who was at fault. Police blamed bail-happy judges as being fundamentally naive about the criminal character. Deputy Commissioner Simon Overland, a law graduate, questioned the need for committal hearings and said some lawyers were silent partners in crime. He highlighted that nine of the gangland victims were on bail when killed and four of the suspected hitmen were on judge-granted bail when they committed their murders. Judges and lawyers returned fire, pointing out that it was inquiries into police corruption that had delayed Mokbel's prosecution to such an extent he could no longer justly be kept behind bars untried.

Police Minister Tim Holding said he wanted Mokbel brought to justice. 'We want to see him serve his time in jail. We want him to pay his debt to society. And that's why we want him found as quickly as possible,' he said. But many were wondering: why had Mokbel spent more than three years on bail then flown the coop at the eleventh hour in his cocaine trial? The logic of his vanishing act seemed to lie in the fact that the judge might not have known police were looking at Mokbel's gangland activities but, after his lunch date with Zarah, Tony apparently did.

Mokbel later said he fled after a tip-off 'on the street' that he was about to be charged with murder. He also candidly elaborated on his disappointment at sometimes not being a better crim. 'I wasn't worried about the drug case. I knew I was going to be doing serious time, like double figures, so the jail was not a worry,' Mokbel said. 'I wouldn't even have been convicted on the drug charges if I hadn't been stupid and talked about the strategy of our defence on the phone to some mates. It's my fault. I'm stupid, and I know that a few times I said on the phone, "Things went well today, we're going to win and this is why ..." The police were listening to my calls, it's my own fault, I should have known that, in fact I did but I was just careless.'

The jurors in Mokbel's cocaine trial were told a warrant had been issued for the arrest of the man who was supposed to be in the dock but that the trial would proceed. All evidence had been led and there were only closing legal statements to go. But Mokbel's legal team of Heliotis, Nicola Gobbo and Michael McNamara said they were going to withdraw as they could not possibly continue without their client.

It had already been a rough month for Justice Bill Gillard. The judge had declared Mokbel no flight risk only three days before he became the nation's most wanted fugitive. Gillard just wanted to sail his criminal trial sans criminal through to the finish patched up with string and wire. And now the defence team was threatening mutiny. In polite but firm legal language the judge suggested the defence's premature evacuation was a bad idea. It could be regarded as a cynical set-up for a retrial in the event that Mokbel was found guilty and ever actually found. The defence team listened to the judge's strong words, contemplated them, and then walked anyway.

The jury took ninety minutes to find the absent Mokbel guilty over his Mexican cocaine import. He was convicted of knowingly being concerned in the importation of almost three kilograms of cocaine. The empty dock was sentenced to twelve years with a minimum of nine. Two federal agents soberly shook hands over the pyrrhic victory.

The authorities' embarrassment worsened after Danielle McGuire publicly left the beauty salon she was running with Renate Mokbel and headed overseas. After Tony vanished his connections had squirrelled her $60,000. Less than four months after Mokbel disappeared, Danielle, with daughter, Brittany, and carrying her and Tony's baby in utero, flew out of Melbourne. As she did so she flamboyantly told of her passion for the missing Mokbel and backed his criminal escapades. 'You can't help who you fall in love with ... I'd rather Tony out there somewhere than sitting in a cell,' she said.

The federal police followed in hot pursuit. An AFP spokeswoman said: 'From our perspective, we're not aware of any Commonwealth offences so she's free to travel, as would be any citizen. You can't stop people from travelling.' In truth authorities, already scouring the globe for Mokbel, were ecstatic. Danielle would ultimately lead them straight to Tony, they thought. All they had to do was not lose one pregnant, ex-Collingwood druggie travelling with eleven-year-old daughter, Brittany, in tow. How hard could that be?

Just weeks after Mokbel vanished Justice Gillard – the judge whose name would forever be entangled with that of the criminal he let get away – sentenced Mokbel's corrupted lackey Pizzaboy for speed and ecstasy trafficking. 'I have seen enough of Mokbel to know that he is a very engaging person; friendly, determined and cunning,' the judge said.

You could sense Mokbel's self-impressed grin still lingering. But it was a grin without a cat. The cat was long gone.

18
The Company

> 'Twas an evening in October, I'll confess I wasn't sober,
> I was carting home a load with manly pride
> When my feet began to stutter and I fell into the gutter
> And a pig came up and lay down by my side.
> Then I lay there in the gutter and my heart was all a-flutter
> 'Til a lady passing by did chance to say
> 'You can tell a man that boozes by the company he chooses.'
> Then the pig got up and slowly walked away.
>
> – The Famous Pig Song

The company Mokbel chose was a strange group of greedy private-school-educated misfits. Before vanishing into thin air, Tony did as he had done with his cocaine and hashish ventures and reached into his extensive network to assemble a crew. The syndicate he created to make and deal amphetamine was much more sophisticated than a simple rip and lift team. It was a lucrative business that kept detailed financial accounts and even adopted a legitimate-sounding corporate moniker: The Company.

Joseph Mansour and Bart Rizzo had been mates since they had together gone to elite Melbourne Catholic college Whitefriars.

Since graduating in the class of '96 Mansour, who had a borderline low IQ, and Rizzo, who had been diagnosed with attention deficit hyperactivity disorder and had been ostracised because of his morbid obesity, had led bland, aimless lives. Mansour's parents had migrated from Lebanon and worked hard to give their sons the best opportunities in life.

Not long after hanging up their school blazers both Mansour and Rizzo were rudderless twenty-somethings who had dropped out of higher education and fallen back into family businesses. Rizzo joined his parents' bed linen and gift shop in Templestowe. Mansour worked at his mum's restaurant then at cafes co-owned with his uncle.

In September 2005 Mansour came across Mokbel in the dodgy nightclubs of Melbourne's crime-riddled Chapel Street and was given the highbeam treatment. By the end of the year Mansour and Rizzo were hanging out with Fat Tony, the Mokbel brothers, friends, and girlfriend Danielle McGuire. Rizzo even bought a motorbike for one of Tony's kids. 'They met just from clubbing. They'd do you a favour. One favour led to another favour. Before you know it, he's got ya. Doesn't take much,' a detective said.

For their dress rehearsal Mansour and Rizzo were sold two pounds (about a kilo) of amphetamine by a Mokbel connection and were able to source enough of their own customers to onsell it all. Mokbel installed them at the apex of The Company and filled the pyramid below with contacts and cronies with specific criminal skills. When the boss had to go on sudden and indefinite leave the duo's responsibilities multiplied and they became the absent tycoon's left and right hands. Even when he was off the scene, Mokbel would call the pair and direct them to a particular spot for a specific task – like picking up 200 litres of acetone.

Sometimes the boys would be directed to buy hundreds and thousands of dollars worth of chemicals from Tony's brother Horty. Mansour and Rizzo were to oversee the speed making and selling process from start to finish and pay the component cogs for their efforts.

Joe 'Coffee Shop Max' Ferola was substantially older than the rest of The Company's young turks. He was also, according to authorities, the best illegal chemical converter in the state. Coffee Shop's role in The Company was to change phenylacetic acid, used in some perfumes, into a different chemical called P2P. Brothers George Elias and Chafic Issa then 'gassed' the P2P oil converting it to methamphetamine. The siblings with matching goatees earnt a pretty penny for their perfidy. Issa alone was paid more than $1.2 million for his efforts over less than a year. University student Andrew Ryan was paid as a consultant to improve the quality of the final product and to try to source better chemicals.

Three smaller time members almost completed The Company's terrible ten. A young man named Robert Benedetti brought in cocaine which Rizzo onsold. Another, Jamie Saro, offered a dial-a-storage service and helped package the drugs for street sale. And another ex-Whitefriars boy, Christopher Ferraro, acted as a courier and dealer of the drugs and provided storage for them. Ferraro had a rough childhood and had suffered teasing because cerebral palsy had given him a distinctive gait and one finger permanently stuck out in a claw. The tenth member would only become necessary later. An extensive log of The Company's finances was maintained by Rizzo and nicknamed 'the Raymond Weil'. It was either an aspirational reference to the luxury Swiss watch the profiteers fancied or perhaps a nod to Swiss bank accounts where some of the ill-gotten funds may have been destined.

The misfits seemed to find their groove in the high-end drug making and selling of what judges call a 'large commercial quantity' of speed – an offence which can attract a life sentence. They used hotel rooms to cut and package the drugs and hire cars to courier them. Company members switched between multiple mobile phones and SIM cards and found camera black holes for deal meetings. When transporting drugs or equipment they used anti-surveillance driving tricks like late turns, U-turns and false indicator flashes. And when talking on mobiles they used codenames for drugs, places and people. Tony was 'our friend', 'our mate' or 'our friend overseas'. His brother Horty was always 'the Greek'.

Mokbel had a deep knowledge of amphetamine-related chemistry and it extended to different cooking methods. But he did not like to spend too much time around the toxic vapours and potentially explosive speed kitchens himself. Despite his lower risk remote overseeing role, the arrangement Mokbel laid down was this. Once a pile of powder had been produced Mokbel's two chiefs would pay him the bulk market value of that yield less the costs of producing it. Mansour and Rizzo then got the proceeds of the onsell of the whole broken down into a multitude of smaller, more profitable deals. Not bad, when even the pre-broken-down whole could be increased by up to fifty per cent of its size by Mansour and Rizzo cutting it with other ingredients.

Chasing dough: Mokbel opened a suburban fast-food restaurant as his second legitimate business and named a pizza in his own honour.

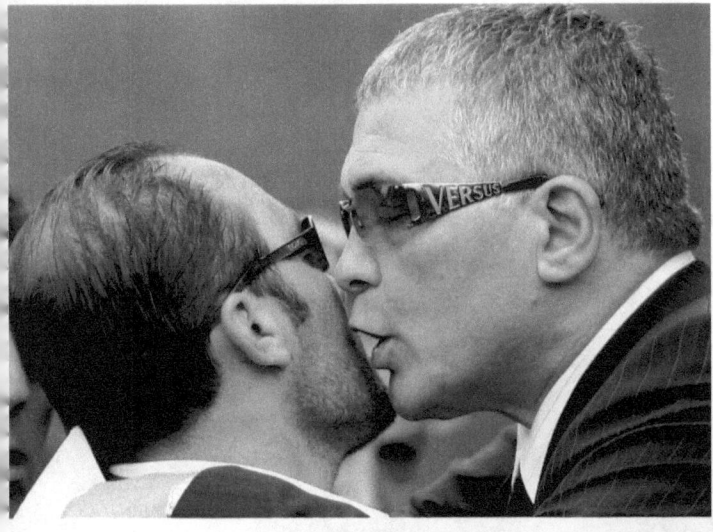

Old school: Mick 'the Teflon Don' Gatto at yet another funeral. He and Mokbel fell out after blood was spilt on the streets of Carlton.

Life's a beach ... and then you die. The new school – Carl Williams and Andrew 'Benji' Veniamin – splash around at Surfers Paradise in 2004.

At work: Glamorous criminal solicitor – and alleged Mokbel love interest – Zarah Garde-Wilson at court.

And play: Posing up at the beachside showers on the South Melbourne foreshore in 2003.

Trackside Tony: Mokbel at Flemington for Oaks Day 2004, having a laugh with bookie Frank Hudson.

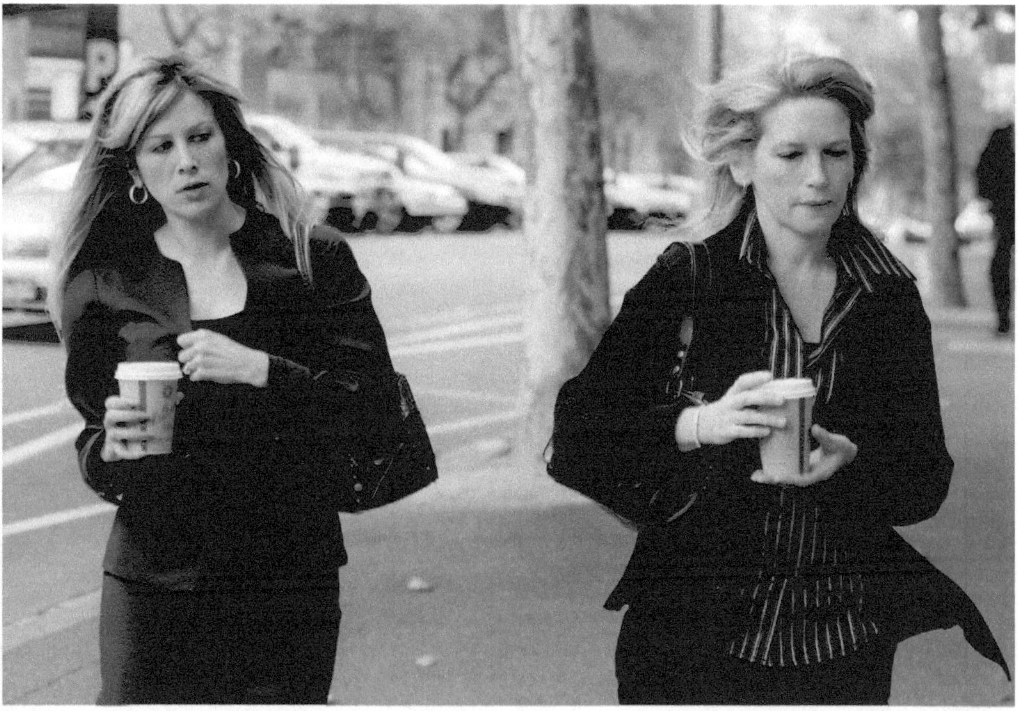

The Herald and Weekly Times Photographic Collection

Stand by your man: Tony's girl Danielle McGuire and Mrs Milad Mokbel – Renate – attend court.

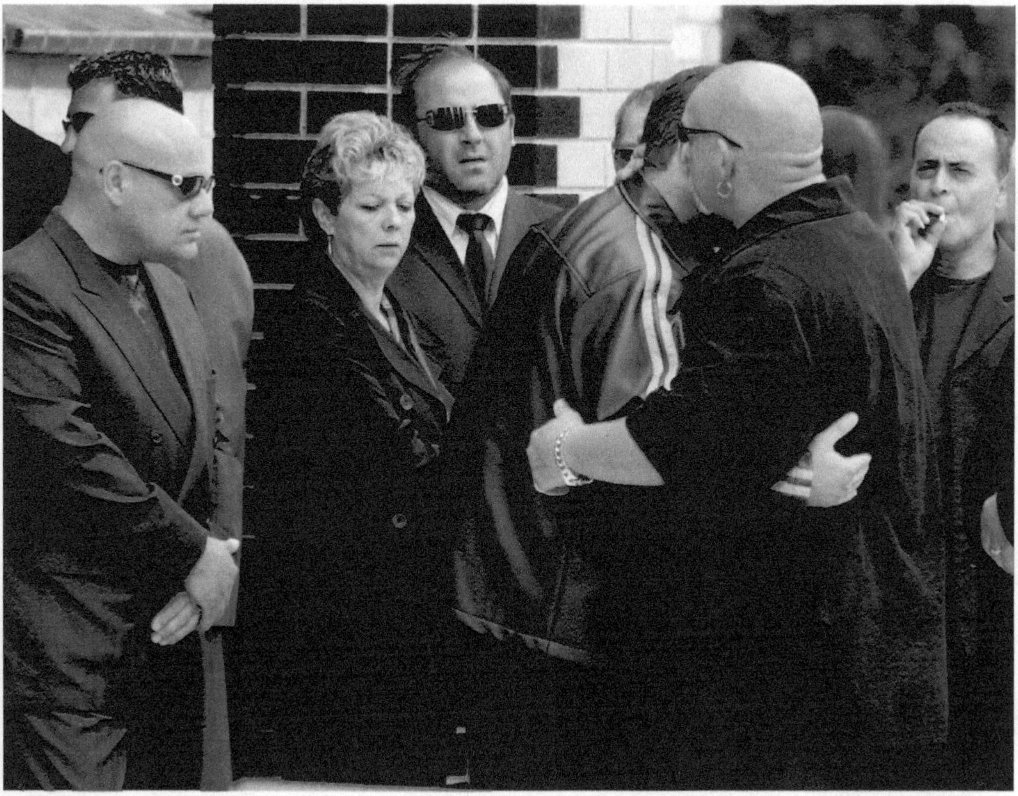

The Herald and Weekly Times Photographic Collection

Taking sides: Mokbel casts his lot in with the Williams crew, standing next to Carl's now-deceased mum at Benji's funeral.

The Herald and Weekly Times Photographic Collection

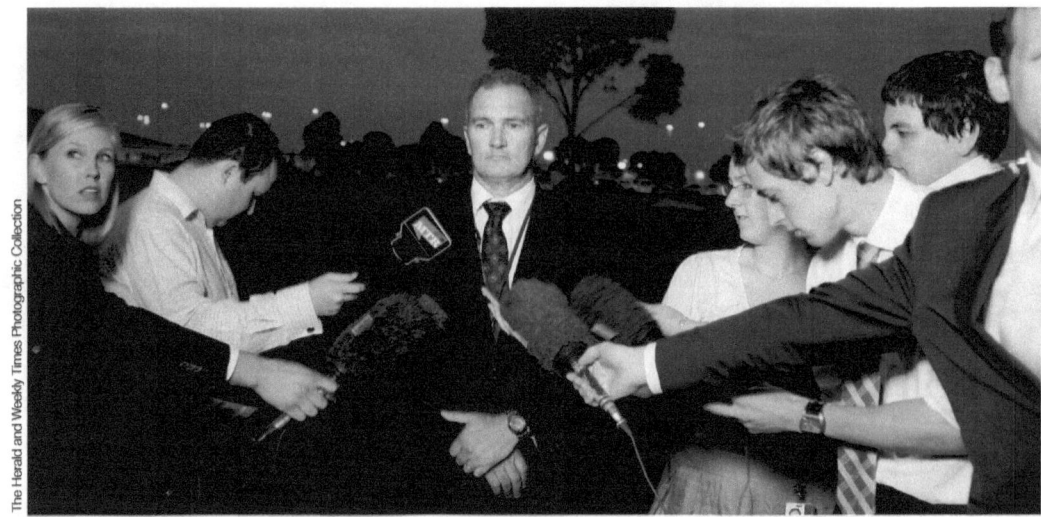

Press-ganged: Purana chief Bernie Edwards, who oversaw Operation Magnum's probe into Tony Mokbel, fronts the media pack.

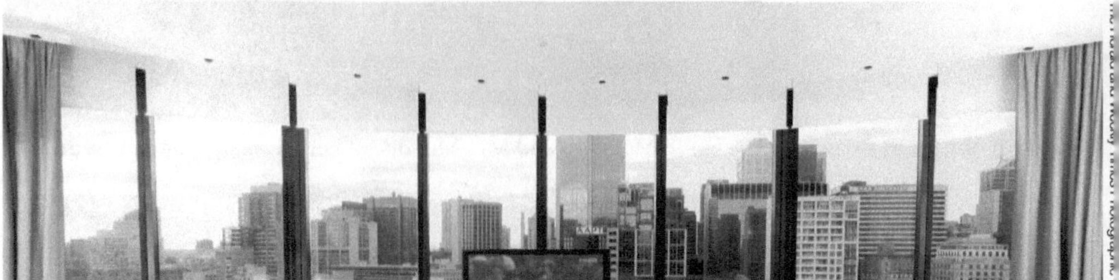

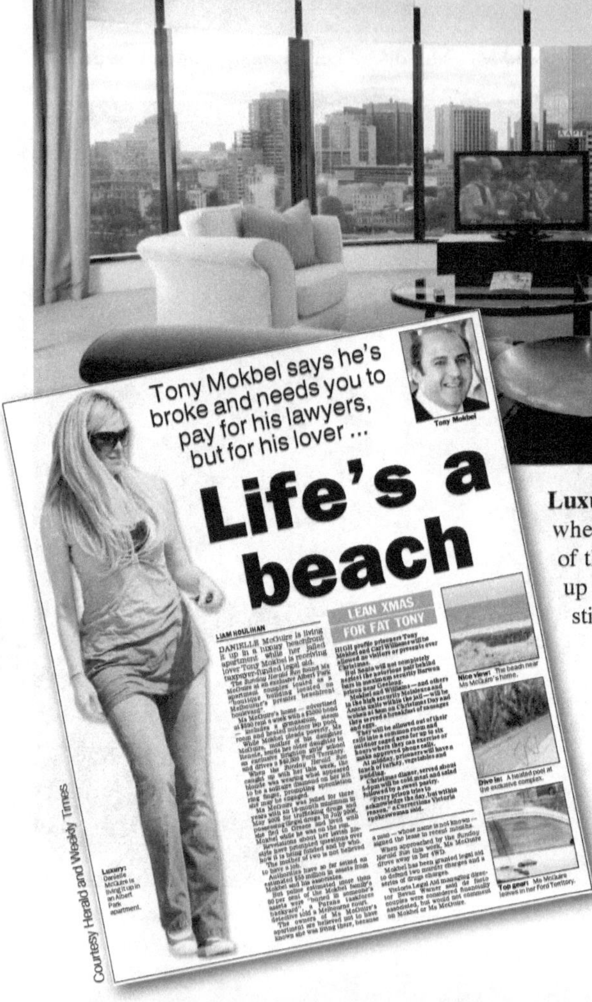

Tony Mokbel says he's broke and needs you to pay for his lawyers, but for his lover ...

Life's a beach

Tony Mokbel

LIAM HOULIHAN

LEAN XMAS FOR FAT TONY

Nice view! The beach near Ms McGuire's home.

Dive in: A heated pool at the exclusive complex.

Top gear: Ms McGuire leaves in her Ford Territory.

Luxury: Danielle McGuire is living it up in an Albert Park apartment.

Courtesy Herald and Weekly Times

Luxury: (above) Room 1223 of Crown Towers, where Mokbel hunkered down during the height of the gangland war; and (left) with Tony locked up and crying poor, unemployed Danielle was still living in coastal bliss.

Bent: Wayne Strawhorn, a shining light in the force until he was jailed for being a drug criminal.

Straight: AFP Agent Jarrod Ragg pursued Mokbel for years.

Cops and robbers: Officer in charge of the Purana taskforce Jim O'Brien fought to take a bite out of the Mokbel family syndicate.

Vaudeville: A relaxed Mokbel vamps it up outside the Melbourne courts.

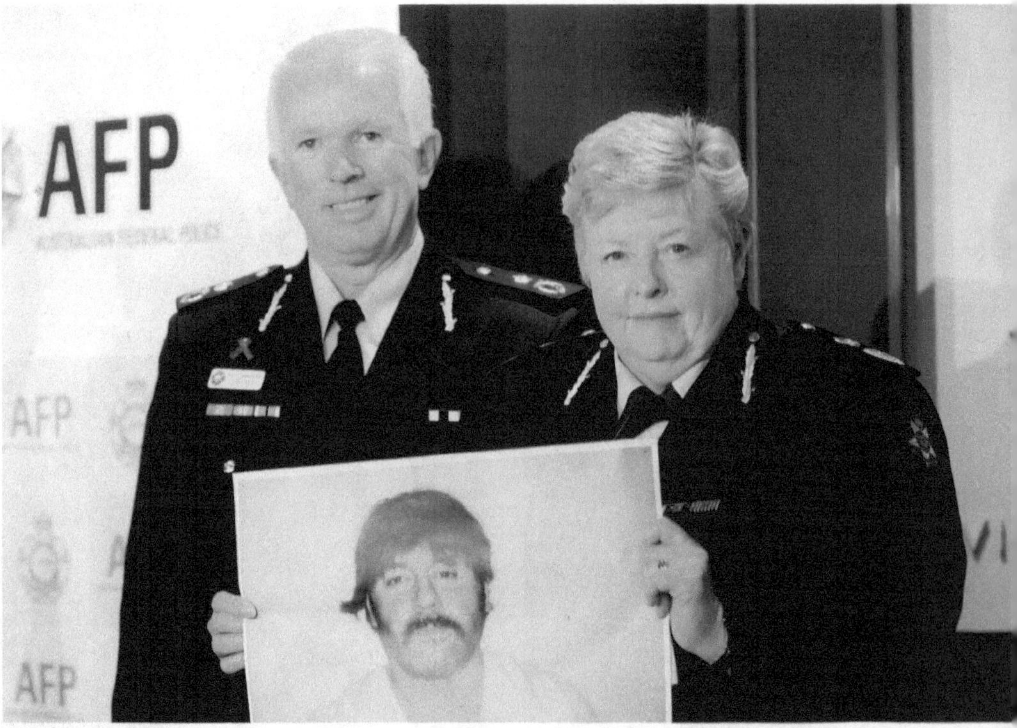

Richard Cisar-Wright © Newspix

Gotcha: Chief Commissioner Christine Nixon with an image from Greece of Mokbel in disguise.

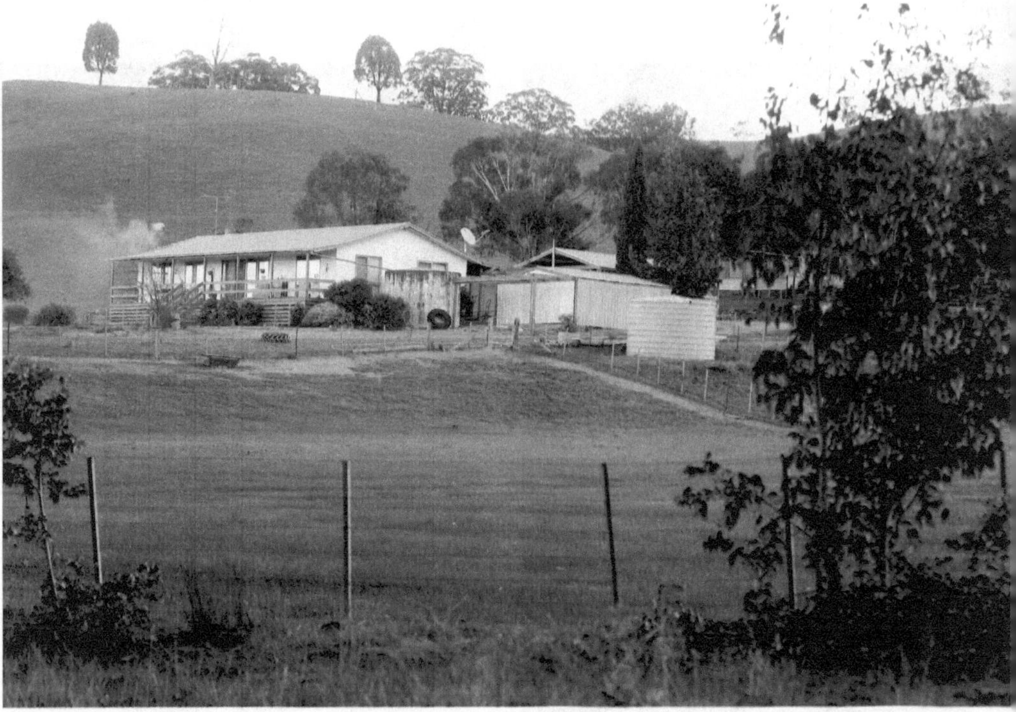

Solitary man: In Bonnie Doon, Tony got more enforced 'me time' than he may have liked.

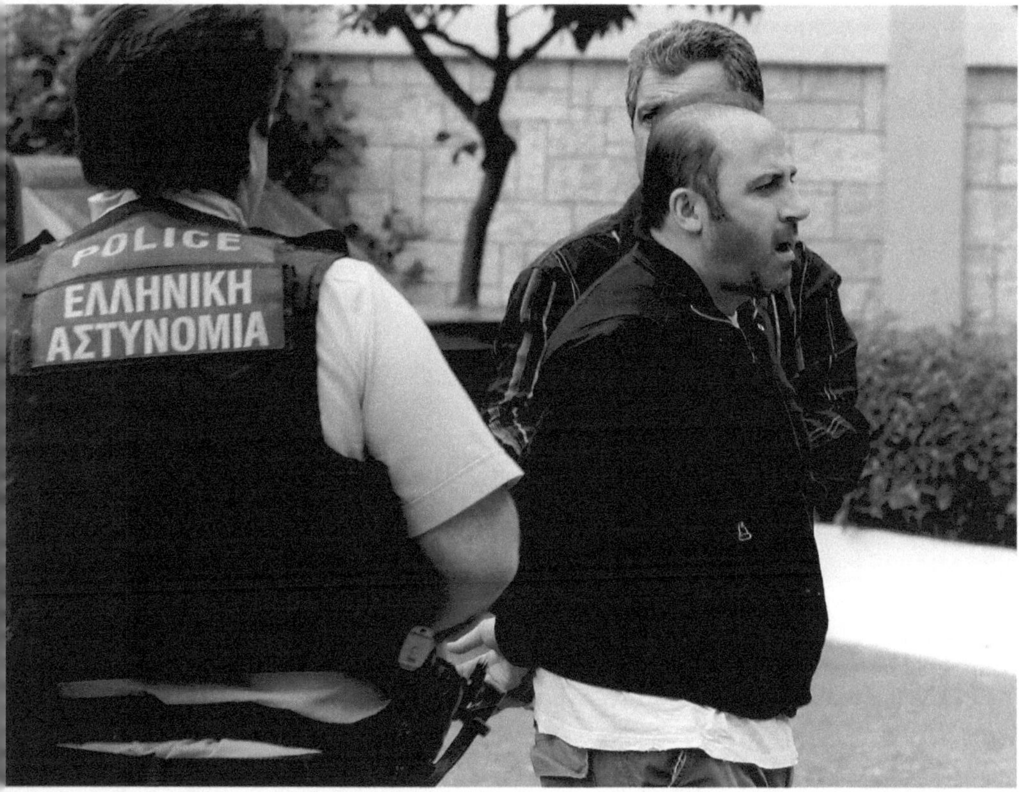

Greek unorthodox: Another country, another perp walk to court for the man who would become a crook in any language.

The Herald and Weekly Times Photographic Collection

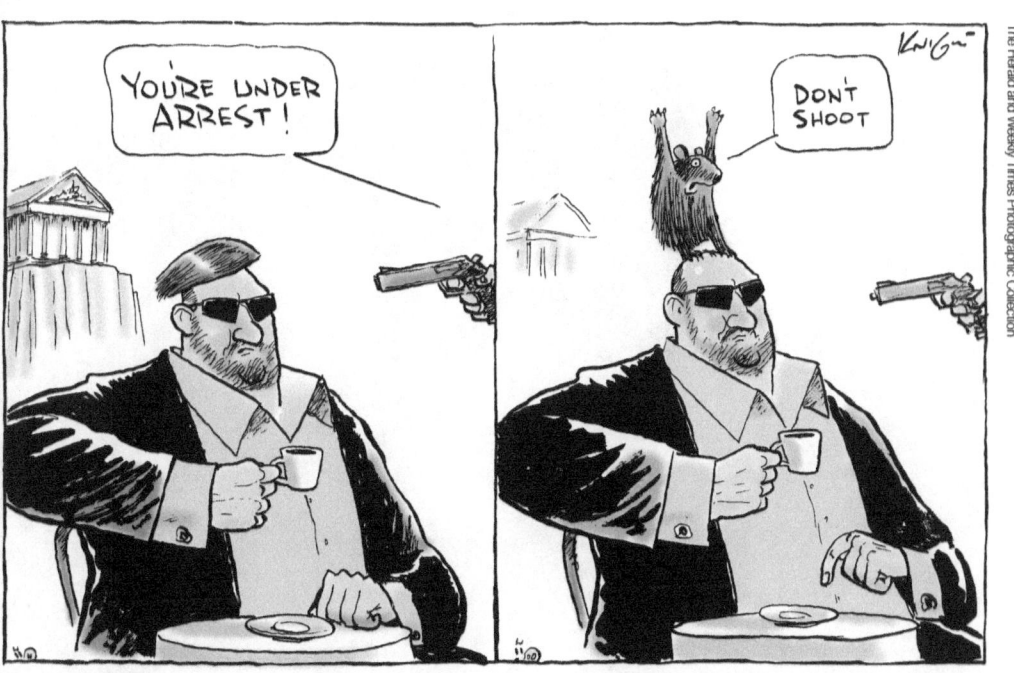

Wigging out: Mokbel's hairpiece became as notorious as its host, as in this celebrated Mark Knight cartoon.

Apple of her eye: Ma Mokbel backed her boys to the bitter end (above); and (below) Bigwig no more – Tony looks less than impressed by the twist in his tale.

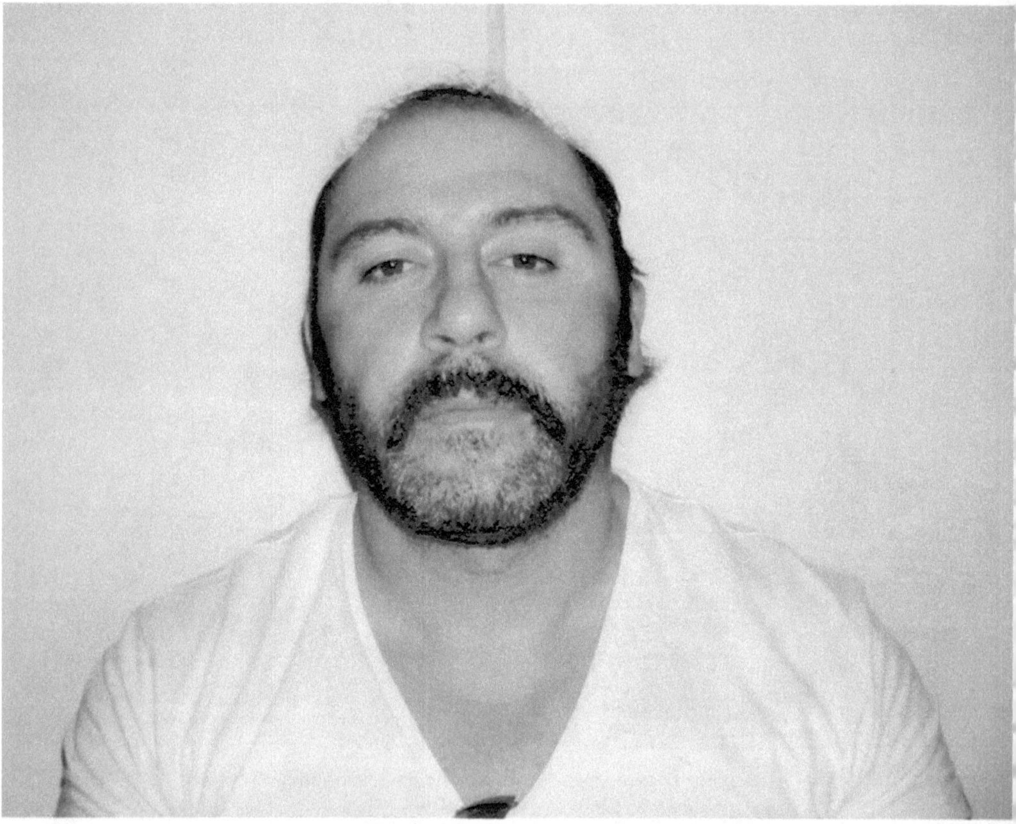

Drugs were their business and business was booming. A blizzard of white powder was sweeping the nation and The Company was behind it. In less than eighteen months (between January 2006 and June 2007) The Company churned out at the very least forty-two kilograms of amphetamines worth tens of millions of dollars on the street. When the good times were rolling, even their smaller hobby industries of ecstasy and coke were going gangbusters. The money was huge. The risks seemed low. Everyone knew what they were doing and everything was in its right place. The possibilities looked endless. And then in February 2007 Coffee Shop Max, converter par excellence, upped and died and the major operation hit a sudden snag.

Mansour was concerned and phoned Mokbel to inform him of the crisis. Tony had a brainwave. Coffee Shop Max had a son – David Tricarico – who could take over the family business. Tricarico had been given the best education money could buy – another Whitefriars lad, he went on to become a graduate of Xavier College. Brains and the blueblood boost had got him into chemical engineering which would come in handy once seconded to Mokbel's kitchen. Tony successfully persuaded Tricarico to take over his father's role in The Company.

But amphetamine production is no simple science. There is a reason why good cooks can charge $50,000 per conversion and face kidnapping as an occupational hazard. Since Coffee Shop Max's demise, Mokbel's mob of spotty wannabes often got it wrong. Ryan was regularly brought in to improve poor quality yields and was seeking sophisticated amphetamine glassware that could also improve their product.

The Company was created to mirror a legal business but when the product was bad its attitudes about corporate responsibility and consumer rights were found wanting. When one of their amphetamine batches made users violently ill, some having to receive emergency medical attention, there was no product recall. Instead the price of the poisonous product was lowered and the pushers told to push it harder to clear stocks. Continued sales were the main priority. We'll get it more right, less poisonous, on the next batch, was the attitude.

The misfits comprising The Company would become known to police through the next job Mokbel gave them. But Tony was really remotely running a series of drug 'companies'. According to Detective Sergeant Jim Coghlan: 'These members of The Company would go to other associates of Tony for glassware and chemicals. You've got to remember he had six or seven phones. It only stands to reason there are other groups he operated with,' he said. 'It only stands to reason that there's other people around Australia, not just in Melbourne, that he would have dealt with. The Company wouldn't even know who they were and they wouldn't know who The Company were. He was a great one for distancing everybody from everybody else. That's why he's so successful. He just wanted to keep the peace. If anyone caused any problems then they're out of the loop.'

The Company had been good to its creator. The junior criminals had made Mokbel millions while he rarely had to lift a finger. On the odd times he did, it was simply to punch a number into his mobile phone and have a conversation on his favourite topic – the finer points of amphetamine production.

The ragtag band of misfits had indeed been useful to Mokbel. But The Company's most important role yet – the one that would either enslave or liberate their master – was about to begin.

19

Escape

There is a tide in the affairs of men
When taken at the flood leads on to fortune
Omitted, all the voyage of their life is bound in shallows and in miseries.

– William Shakespeare, *Julius Caesar*

In the days before he fell off the face of the earth Mokbel was secretly laying the foundations for one of the most inspired fugitive escapes of all time. Through a devastating combination of desperation, design and dumb luck, Mokbel's disappearing act was an absolute triumph. It fiendishly manipulated people's assumptions that he would make a flash first-class getaway. It played on expectations that smooth-talking Tony with a cash-filled suitcase would have bribed his way to the other side of the planet overnight. And like all good magic tricks the real action went on out of sight while all eyes were fixed on the compelling spectacle playing out on centre stage.

When Danielle McGuire flew out of Melbourne just months after her boyfriend disappeared, those in her camp loudly proclaimed she was not going to reunite with Mokbel hiding out in a distant exotic locale. 'I'm sure they're following her anyway. And they'll find out she's just on a holiday,' Danielle's mum said.

It turned out that was the truth. Or at least a half-truth.

The federal agents following Danielle as she jetsetted around the globe, and others who had their heads turned from their work, were being drawn like sirens' victims half a world away from their target. France, Italy and Turkey were some of the glamorous locations in which Mokbel was said to be hunkering down. But the whole time Mokbel had never left the garden state. The banal reality was that he was stuck in a small white Victorian homestead at the foot of a grassy hill, off a red dirt road in Bonnie Doon, nursing a case of fugitive ennui.

Despite the generous Scottish adjective, Bonnie Doon is a bland town at the desolate northern tip of Lake Eildon, about two hours north-east of Melbourne. It is a place where families like the Kerrigans in the film *The Castle* go to race jet-skis and speedboats on the big lake, smell the two-stroke and take in the serenity. Tony made his emergency tree change there after his last police check-in on that Sunday night in March. The rural property was owned by Company cook and trusted Mokbel man George Elias, and Mokbel shared the house with Elias, his wife, Sharon, and their daughter. Tony paid his way as a tenant at Bonnie Doon.

Elias's wife didn't necessarily, at least initially, know the true identity of her husband's mate on the permanent sleepover. But as the months ticked by Elias must have warned his daughter, about twelve, not to mention 'Uncle Tony' to anyone. The fugitive passed the days watching the walls, phoning through speed-making tips to The Company and liaising with his ecape-plan mastermind. Remarkably enough, given the heat on him, he did get at least one special visitor to break the monotony.

The federal police had launched a massive operation to investigate Mokbel's escape and hunt him down. They interviewed his girlfriend, Danielle McGuire, but in the weeks after Tony vanished it seems no one was tailing her. Under the noses of the authorities Danielle made the trek to Bonnie Doon and visited Tony. There among the lowing of the Bonnie Doon cattle the lawless lovers were reunited. And while police scoured the globe, Australia's most wanted man and his girlfriend conceived a fugitive baby in country Victoria.

No one had been watching Tony when he legged it. But then he had been deemed fit for bail and conditional freedom by the courts. If police had caught him immediately after he vanished on Monday morning, it is likely his only offence would have been failure to appear. It is less comprehensible that after Tony vanished and became the nation's most wanted fugitive, no one was watching his girlfriend.

Victoria Police still unofficially blame the feds who had carriage of finding Mokbel for the monumental slip. But a fair bit of dumb luck saved Mokbel's bacon too. When Danielle made her move Melbourne was in the thick of hosting the Commonwealth Games. The event accommodated more athletes and meets than the 1956 Olympics in the same city, shutting down roads and bringing waves of visitors into the inner city. Public transport was extended and a massive law-enforcement contingent was supplied to prevent disorder, disaster or political embarrassment.

Given the global political climate at the time, the primary focus for the AFP when allocating staff was preventing a terror attack, a source said. Another long-time Mokbel watcher added: 'You've got to have a mind to what was going on in Victoria at the time Tony left. It was the Commonwealth Games.' And so while the sporting event was in full swing, the nation's most wanted fugitive was able to have his girlfriend casually drive up to meet him for a rural date undetected.

Danielle was not Mokbel's only visitor. Tony rarely left the indoors at Bonnie Doon but every so often he would walk through the farm to a nearby forest. There prearranged visitors would pop out of the bushes to discuss drug trafficking or nautical matters with him.

Mokbel conceived a child and watched a lot of television in the seven months he spent at Bonnie Doon. It is not clear what else, if anything, Tony did for fun in the great indoors deprived of gambling, epicurean delights, and with next to no female company. Police later found cannabis in the farmhouse, so it's possible Mokbel fended off cabin fever by getting stoned and watching the sand fall through the hourglass on *Days of Our Lives*. Farmhouse living may have been a far more spartan existence than Tony was used to, but it was a mundane although necessary first step. Bonnie Doon was phase one of Mokbel's plot: get the hell out of Dodge and fall off the radar at all costs. For the subsequent more complex phases of his extraordinary escape Tony would have to rely on his own personal Mr Fixit.

As a high-school dropout turned millionaire Mokbel was a big fan of rough diamonds. You could lord it over them, they showed more respect, and – the narcissist's favourite reason – they reminded him of himself. Mokbel built a multimillion-dollar speed syndicate out of a disparate group of private-school misfits. And the man he chose for the epic task of squirrelling him out of the country was an equally unlikely character. The figure who would mastermind the million-dollar escape of public enemy number one was a workshy 63-year-old pensioner from Reservoir called Byron.

Byron Pantazis and Tony Mokbel had met through their mutual love of gambling. The duo had a long history of playing together at backroom card games around Coburg and Brunswick. Byron was a serious gambler and would have found an easy use for the chunky cash prize Mokbel would deliver to him if he helped the fugitive to freedom. 'He's a very, very heavy gambler. You've got to remember he's got to keep servicing that gambling habit,' a police source said of Mokbel's Mr Fixit. Under-employed and overweight Pantazis suffered from a number of ailments, including diabetes and arthritis. He had not worked for many years and he walked with a limp. If the devil makes work for idle hands, Mokbel's big fat Greek pensioner was ripe for a diabolical masterstroke.

Mokbel and The Company had nicknamed Horty 'the Greek', but Pantazis was the real deal – a dual national with strong ties to the old country. With Pantazis's help Mokbel would make a dash for Greece to start a new life. The fugitive had all sorts of links to Greece. He was taught how to cook amphetamines by Greeks and there was even a theory that there was a group of people he knew living there. But ultimately Tony's target destination was chosen for him as the country where his Mr Fixit had the most connections. 'Byron was organising it, Byron had the contacts in Greece, so that's the place he's going to head,' Detective Sergeant Coghlan said. 'If Byron had contacts in Libya the same thing would have happened [there].'

While Mokbel was stuck indoors in Bonnie Doon, the grey-bearded, bespectacled Pantazis and his wife, Foula, made a number of trips to Greece to pave the way for Tony to slip out of Australia and pursue his Grecian getaway. As part of the preparations Pantazis reached out to a long-time friend in Greece called Theo Angelakis. As well as associates in Greece, Pantazis was also willing and able to drag in family members as extras in the escape conspiracy.

Byron Pantazis had married Foula in 1982 after she left a failed arranged marriage. Foula had come to Byron with her toddler daughter in tow, so Byron got a new four-year-old stepdaughter, Yvonne, in the deal. More romance blossomed at their wedding, with Byron's best man, George Verykios, and Foula's sister, Angela, hitting it off. The wedding of George and Angela – the groom's mate and the bride's sister – followed the next year. But unlike Byron and Foula's union, George and Angela's marriage was a troubled one. George, like his best mate, Byron, was not what you would call a workhorse. Two years into his marriage he hurt his back working at Corinthian Doors, and got a settlement and a pension.

His injured back sustained the rigours of begetting three post-accident Verykios babies over the next eight years. But George Verykios's industrial philosophy was to retire undefeated and he refused to ever risk a return to work, door-related or otherwise. That left Angela Verykios juggling a young brood and working in milk bars and factories while George preferred to stay home smoking pot. After nineteen years of this kind of marital bliss Angela Verykios left the lovable George and took their five children with her. And that was it but for one notable postscript: their separation process took a whopping five years because George refused to acknowledge the five children as his own until each had been DNA tested.

Fast-forward twenty-four years from the 1982 wedding of Byron and Foula to the year of Mokbel's disappearance, and what it all meant for Byron is that he had a solid cast of reliable women for his escape plot. Byron's sister-in-law, Angela, may have had profound buyer's remorse about Byron's best man, who had robbed her of the best years of her life, but she was magnanimous enough not to hold the disaster against her sister, Foula, or Foula's hubby, Byron. And for his part Byron counted Angela in as potentially useful in the Mokbel plot.

By 2006 Byron and his adoptive daughter, Yvonne, after so much shared history regarded each other as kin bound by something as good as blood. It had been a long time since Yvonne was sent by Byron to school (ironically to St Joseph the Worker), and she had grown before his eyes from a toddler to a woman in her thirties with a baby of her own. So Byron counted Yvonne and her baby into the Mokbel plot too. Her seven-month-old baby boy was much more to Mokbel's Mr Fixit than a bouncing grandson – he was also a great decoy prop for a fleeing fugitive.

When the going got tough for Mokbel, his unlikely escape mastermind, Pantazis, got off the couch and flew to Greece. He added a dash of vaudeville to the escape plot in Athens, recruiting a troupe of Greek sailors willing to fly Down Under for an unorthodox little earner.

East coast ports and air terminals were crawling with police. The nation's airports were too hot for Mokbel to escape by plane. Technology, computer systems, biometrics and the authorities themselves had got smarter since 1981, when Bob Trimbole flew out as authorities prepared to charge him, eventually dying on the lam in Spain.

Bleaching his hair blonde, wearing glasses, growing a beard or changing a digit on his birth date would not be enough for Mokbel. Pantazis had a plan to address these dangers that was simple in design, more complex in execution, but potentially devastating to authorities if it worked. Mokbel would leave Australia by sea, sailing to freedom as a guest of the Greek sailors Byron had recruited overseas. While blanket Mokbel media coverage raged on the east coast he would depart from the opposite side of the country. Western Australia considers itself independent from the rest of Australia. Its capital, Perth, the world's most remote city, is closer to Singapore than Canberra. Fremantle, just south of Perth, would be the launching place for Mokbel's getaway vehicle. But first Pantazis needed to get Tony a nice big boat.

Pantazis sweet-talked his wife, Foula, and sister-in-law, Angela, into catching a train from Melbourne to Sydney to help him with some business. By law Australian-registered vessels require at least partial ownership by an Australian national. Byron told his sister-in-law some friends were having trouble with a boat so it would be put in her name. As instructed Angela Verykios handed over cheques, signed the documents and was made, with some strange Greek sailors, the proud co-owner of a $330,000 yacht. She was then put on a plane back to Melbourne.

The 17.3-metre-long yacht, known as a cutter sloop and named *Edwena*, had twice sailed around the world. The buyers told the New South Wales businessman selling the yacht that they wanted to fit it out to be used as a cruise vessel in Greece. One of the Greek sailors then flew from Sydney back home. The remaining trio sailed the boat to Newcastle, where Pantazis pimped Tony's ride, adding secret hiding holes for Mokbel and a desalination unit for an ocean journey. The massive yacht was then lifted onto the back of a truck and transported nearly 4000 kilometres across the continent from Newcastle to the west coast at a cost of $350,000.

The tricking up of the *Edwena* continued en route, police said, with giant fuel tanks and a self-righting mast added. Slowly over six days it made its way through three states with wide load signs, flashing lights and pilot cars. In Western Australia tens of thousands more were spent on a life craft, generators, new sails and a specially fitted toilet, as Team Mokbel raced to be ready for the seasonal winds that would whisk them halfway across the world to Greece. The Greek sailors flew from Newcastle to Fremantle to hook up with their ride. And in early October the *Edwena* was lowered into the Indian Ocean at Fremantle harbour to await her controversial cargo.

* * *

Police from around Australia were still desperately chasing any lead that came their way. Officers raided the homes of Mokbel family members, cronies and any known Tony haunts. AFP Agent Ragg said: 'Every security camera in Melbourne and surrounding areas – South Melbourne, where Tony lived, we had all the tapes of that. We had customs, all-ports alerts out. Obviously we had all the airports on alert.

'We were at one point a day behind him. The information we were receiving from AFP informants had us a day behind him. He never went direct to Bonnie Doon, we think. We suspect that he was in Melbourne for a short amount of time and we were effectively a day behind him. He moved around a couple of times. We had some informant information that was putting us where he was twenty-four hours behind him. Once he moved on to Bonnie Doon we didn't know where he was.'

The spooks were also adding to the foot traffic in the Mokbels' home village of Achache, Lebanon, doorknocking weary relatives.

'It wouldn't be so bad if everybody just came here to his grandfather's house with their questions,' Tony's first cousin Wajih, then thirty-three, said. 'But the Interpol document has gone to all the security services and been stuck on their walls – anti-drugs unit, general security, all of them – and they all come around separately asking questions. They start by talking about something else, like bird flu, but we know where it's going. They end up asking about Tony.'

By October 2006 the Commonwealth Games had been over for months and was just a collection of fond memories. It had gone off without a hitch, there were no terror attacks and the costume of the lovable mascot, Karak, the endangered black cockatoo, had been packed away. But Victoria's number one crim and the nation's most wanted man was still missing. Mokbel had been indoors with the curtains drawn for seven months. His Bonnie Doon blues were broken only by the thrill of seeing news reports that he still had not been caught. He was tiring of the same four walls and the constant waiting. But the monotony would be shattered when phase two of Mokbel's escape began.

While Mokbel was on the lam his self-sustaining drug syndicate The Company, set up to need little priming from its long-distance puppetmaster, kept pumping out speed. Returning him his profits, the syndicate gave Mokbel a liquidity lifeline and the funds for his escape plan. The Company also paid off family and would-be snitches on behalf of Tony.

Trusted Company lieutenant Mansour was summoned to Bonnie Doon by a Mokbel call. Mansour had known two days before the rest of the country that Tony would not show at court that fateful Monday in March. As instructed he visited Mokbel's Bonnie Doon bolthole, handed him $100,000 in cash and arranged for special phones to enable future contact. Days earlier The Company had placed another $140,000 of profits in an account for Tony for the next leg of his journey.

Mokbel then snuck from the Bonnie Doon farmhouse to another secluded regional property – this time in rural Elphinstone in central Victoria. It was a risky move, as the nation's most notorious criminal had not told his would-be hosts – squarehead family friends of the previous generation of Mokbels – that he was coming. If they didn't call the cops on him they might still just lock him out, leaving him stranded in country Victoria while the massive manhunt closed in.

Youseff and Evette Zeidan, sixty and fifty-two respectively, were hardworking Maronite church members originally from Lebanon. The retired empty-nester couple were understandably reluctant to open their house to the surprise criminal guest. They had suffered enough bad luck with health issues and the failure of their emu farm. The demise of the farming venture had left them living in the small rural weatherboard house Mokbel was trying to crash. They told the fugitive he was not welcome to stay. Mrs Zeidan recalled: 'I told Joe [Youseff] he mustn't allow Tony Mokbel to stay at our place but he's soft hearted and I feel Tony Mokbel sort of pressured him into this. I was just frightened and I told Joe he mustn't let him stay but I think Joe was scared of what might happen if he didn't let him stay there.'

Mokbel was confident he could tug on the ties that bind and appealed to their sense of family and loyalty to his uncle Kabalan. Youseff Zeidan had been a close friend of Tony's uncle Wajih Kabalan for forty years. He had known Tony's dad, Sajih, before his death and had known Tony when he was just a small Brunswick boy. As a young man Tony had gone rabbit shooting on their property until he tired of small game. Tony pleaded: it would only be one night then he would be on his way and out of their hair. Evette Zeidan still said no but Tony's hard words about family and friendship and the invocation of his kindly uncle eventually worked on Youseff, who later said: 'When I had the stroke [Tony's uncle] Wajih would come to us, to my wife saying, "We'll help you." When I was ill Wajih would cook for us.

'When Tony Mokbel asked if he could stay a couple of days my wife and I tried to convince him to give himself up,' he said. 'We felt we couldn't report him because of the family loyalty thing. In any case, I thought he would get caught and I didn't want to get involved. I suppose in a way I felt a sense of obligation because I had such a close friendship with Wajih Kabalan.'

One night turned into two as the Zeidans fretted about their dodgy lodger who did not seem too keen to rush off.

Meanwhile in Melbourne's northern suburbs the 'Reservoir dogs' – Byron Pantazis, his sister-in-law, Angela, his adopted daughter, Yvonne, and Yvonne's baby – were putting another piece of the plot into play. The disparate group met in the morning at Pantazis's Reservoir home, bundled into a hired Nissan Patrol four-wheel-drive and travelled to Elphinstone to pick up their mystery passenger.

Pantazis's crew were told little about the job and seemed deliberately incurious about the unusual adventure. Pantazis had told Angela she would get paid $1000 for taking the trip. As a portly claustrophobic she would earn her fee. His wife also paid her sister to buy two mobile phones in her own name.

Pantazis told his daughter she would also get expenses and spending money for coming on the interstate trip. The unemployed work-shy dad told his stepdaughter it was for work and not to ask too many questions. The women's lack of curiosity was down to

Byron being the patriarch of the Greek family, a police source said. 'More or less what Byron says goes.'

When the Reservoir dogs arrived in Elphinstone the women were introduced to their passenger. He was a man of few words called Yanni, who looked an awful lot like missing criminal Tony Mokbel in a bad wig. The Zeidans were happy to see the back of their imposing tenant. When he left with his pick-up crew the couple gratefully returned to their quiet country life. Before Tony's arrival Youseff had cut down to twenty cigarettes a day but in the uninvited visitor's wake, stressed and dragged into a criminal conspiracy, he quietly went back to eighty.

The Reservoir dogs travelled west towards Adelaide, silently watching cluttered skylines slumping into flat plains, the fauna getting sparser with every mile. Before crossing the Victoria–South Australia border speed siblings George Elias and Chafic Issa pulled in behind the 4WD in a rented motor home to form a convict convoy. The first night they all stayed at a Murray Bridge motel. Issa gave Mokbel another $100,000 from The Company's ongoing profits.

On day two Yanni gave the women hundreds of dollars for food and magazines for the trip. The convoy arced westward around the Great Australian Bight, keeping the big blue on their left and dry paddocks on the right. They cut across hundreds of kilometres of indistinct country where the arid Great Victoria Desert bleeds down into the Nullarbor Plain. In the 4WD Pantazis drove and Yvonne rode shotgun. In the back were Angela, the nation's most wanted criminal and a baby boy. The members of the odd travelling party each quietly kept their own counsel as they made the haunting 3400-kilometre trip across the barren continent. There were lots of deep silences among the travellers, but Mokbel did question Yvonne about her husband, Wes. The conversation ended with Mokbel telling her that if they were pulled over she was to say he was her husband, Wes, and that he was a deaf mute.

The vast space of the Nullarbor Plain is broken only by roadkill, the odd piece of desert art or strange and disconcerting sights like a dozen cats hung by their necks from a tree. There was nothing much to look at on the trip and little to do but think. The female passengers started to wonder about Yanni, the mysterious toupeed traveller. At a toilet stop Yvonne told her Aunt Angela she thought Yanni might be Tony Mokbel, the drug dealer off the news. Or if not that, she said, he's still definitely wearing a wig. Angela was not convinced but a picture in a newspaper later obtained en route, and incidentally paid for by Mokbel, confirmed their late-breaking suspicions. When Yvonne asked her father if their passenger was Mokbel he said not to ask questions about it.

The Nullarbor remained unchanged as the convoy finally passed into Western Australia. As the sun set on their third day Tony's travellers stayed that night at mining town Norseman – one of the first major signs of life after emerging on the western side of the plain.

Tony never left the car the whole trip except for furtive nightly dashes into motel rooms. He had to forgo outback bistro parmigianas as the group would stay only in rooms with kitchens and cook their own dinners behind closed doors. No one stayed in the campervan. It was there simply to add legitimacy to their appearance as holiday travellers and as emergency lodgings if waylaid on the side of the road.

After four straight days of highways – the Pyrenees, Calder, Sturt, Eyre, Great Eastern, Roe and Canning – the convoy finally made it to the other side of the country. They arrived in Fremantle where the *Edwena* was waiting.

Pantazis and Mokbel had loaded up Angela's debit card with more than $48,000. It was used to cover accommodation costs for the convoy crew, and for the Greek sailors' lodgings in the wildflower state. As last-stage preparations for the sea voyage were made, a generator, tools, batteries, a life raft, jackets, flares and long-lasting food were all swiped onto Angela's card. Brothers Elias and Issa bought night-vision electronics for the yacht. Then Angela's magic debit card was used to pay for Yvonne and her baby's flight back to Melbourne. 'Yanni' gave Yvonne $5000 for her company on the most confusing and boring road trip she had ever taken and another $5000 for her bub. Later, once reunited back in Melbourne, Yvonne and her aunt sat down and discussed the trip. Angela said: 'I asked her if she was ever going to tell the baby when he grew up that we went to Western Australia with Tony Mokbel. We decided between ourselves that we would not tell anyone.'

Four days after arriving in Fremantle Mokbel got three new reasons not to be in Victoria. He was convicted in his absence of trafficking a commercial quantity of ecstasy and smaller amounts of amphetamines and cocaine.

* * *

November 11 has long been a portentous date in Australian history. It's the date Germany surrendered in World War I, a governor-general dismissed a prime minister, and our most famous bushranger was hanged on a judge's orders. Tony added his criminal adventures to the ledger, choosing the eleventh of the eleventh 2006 to bid adieu to his adopted country – never, he hoped, to see her coast or constabulary again. On that date customs officers inspected the mega-yacht before it sailed out of its berth at the customs jetty of the Fremantle Sailing Club. The officers were told by the three Greek sailors on board that their destination was the Seychelles. They later watched the yacht sail from the Fremantle Sailing Club marina.

The west coast in November can get oppressively hot, redeemed only by the soothing breeze that comes in from the sea at the end of the long day to cool the coastal sandgropers. What the locals call the Fremantle Doctor would have been blowing in off the Indian Ocean as the *Edwena* sailed up then away from the Australian west coast.

It is possible Mokbel was hidden on the boat as a stowaway when it left Fremantle, but authorities suspect he actually joined the crew later after they sailed north up the coast. One of The Company men drove from Fremantle six hours up the coast to Geraldton. Police suspect it was there that Mokbel was ferried out to meet the *Edwena*, possibly in a small fishing boat or motorised dinghy. Mokbel's father, Sajih, had journeyed across the world with his family to start a new life in a foreign country. Tony hoped to do the same.

Danielle had already left Australia and was somewhere out there in the world carrying his latest child. 'She left the country in July as a decoy for the authorities,' Detective Sergeant Jim Coghlan said. 'That was a decoy run for the feds and they chased her all over Europe and the plan was to do that – put everybody off the scent so he could get his yacht and escape from Australia.'

With the wind in his sails Mokbel cut out of the country that wanted to see him rot in jail. Across the seas Tony hoped he would find a new life and an excellent and lengthy adventure.

20

Bruvvers

> Help your brother's boat across,
> and your own will reach the shore
>
> – Hindu proverb

Back on terra firma the landlubber Mokbel brothers were about to pay for the sins of nautical Tony, plus a few they probably would have managed on their own. The police mission to demolish the supporting pillars of the Mokbel drug empire – the brothers – began in earnest in September 2005. Mokbel's flight six months later simply intensified the authorities' desire for a full house – the four Mokbel men behind bars.

When the feds came knocking in the immediate aftermath of Tony vanishing, the brothers played dumb. Horty felt that 'Tony was OK in that no harm had come to him,' while Kabalan hoped the disappearance meant Tony had fled as an alternative to being killed. Milad told police Tony would not have been the victim of foul play: 'Tony did not consider he had enemies. He was honest in his dealings and would deal with people face to face.' Either way Milad was not expecting his big bro back anytime soon. Four days after Tony disappeared Milad returned Tony's leased $500,000 Mercedes-Benz coupe to the Southbank dealership around the corner from Tony and Danielle's love pad. An acquaintance of Milad Mokbel said the bald brother told him after Tony took off there was a safety deposit box hidden somewhere in the city holding enough ka-ching to pay off all debts left behind.

The bond between the Mokbel brothers had been fired in the crucible of the loss of their father. Others may have called portly Antonios 'Fat Tony', but to Kabalan, Horty and Milad, he wasn't heavy, he was their bruvver. Although one of the younger siblings, Tony had risen to the top of the family tree and led the brothers to a larcenous life of leisure. 'He was more confident about what he was doing. The others were more apprehensive about getting involved,' said Detective Sergeant Jim Coghlan. 'But they got into it and away they went. They made fortunes and people made fortunes from them.'

Kabalan, Horty and Milad purportedly operated an oil company but authorities are sceptical as to whether any of it was legitimate business untainted by crime, laundering or extortion. Whenever the brothers were dragged before court, legitimate occupations would magically appear for them. Tony was a property tycoon, his lawyers would say. Kabalan came before the judge as a truck driver and former restaurateur. Milad was trying to bring home the bacon as a butcher at the Brunswick Market, and Horty listed his occupation on an affidavit as simply 'businessman'. His silk explained he had an interest in a service station.

Others were less accepting of the whitewashed work histories. 'These people don't work. They don't get up like we do at five o'clock and catch the train to work,' said Detective Sergeant

Jim Coghlan. 'They wake up at eleven, do their business in the afternoon, gamble, then play cards all night. That's all they do. They don't have a job.'

Each of Tony's brothers had their own focus in the empire, reflecting their own personality, skills and proclivities. Younger bro Milad was Tony's partner in amphetamine production and a handy bit of muscle for contract enforcement. Horty ran drugs too but was also Tony's man at the track. Kabalan, the eldest and most mild-mannered Mokbel, copped the odd jobs. Occasionally sibling rivalry would derail the smooth running of the family's nefarious trade. 'They had a lot of fights. They had a lot of brotherly bickering over certain chemicals or money. Maybe one was jealous he wasn't getting enough,' Coghlan said. 'So they did follow their own paths at certain points.'

Milad, a bald beefcake with a two-second fuse, had looked up to Tony as a surrogate father since the pair lost their own while still teens. But Milad had surpassed his fraternal mentor when it came to aggression. Police who have had the pleasure of arresting the Mokbel boys over the years said Tony is the nice-as-pie country squire who goes quietly but Milad tends to fire up and throw around his fists and use his bulbous head like a demolition ball. Milad was the most involved in the family's drug enterprises after Tony. His lawyer once said he had become a professional gambler after Tony introduced him to the ponies. But police said Milad was at the top of the tree and at the forefront of drug trafficking and manufacture in Victoria. Milad would scoop up as much as seventy per cent of a lab syndicate's profit.

Milad and wife Renate's Brunswick mansion was a hive of drug activity. A swimming pool had been built where Howden's old speed lab had erupted in flames. And behind the yellow house's closed doors and gates Milad would organise for his pure meth deliveries to be diluted, repackaged and onsold. Cash and loot from their drug running poured in so quickly the family home ran out of stooks to hide the incoming riches. In just three weeks Milad banked $25,000, writing 'gambling wins' on the deposit statements. Renate would put their wealth down to the sale in 2005 of a butcher's shop, and her husband's skill with a punt. 'He was very lucky with his gambling. But how can luck last? That's how I looked at it,' she said.

When Renate's uncle, Garry Gibbs, a mailroom worker, visited his niece and her husband for dinner the pair would thrust bags of cash and jewellery at him, which he buried in his Parkdale backyard. 'There's enough jewellery here to open a jewellery store,' Uncle Garry would say to his niece.

Once Uncle Garry was handed a string shopping bag stuffed with cash pulled from a laundry cupboard. Milad's laundry had been specifically set up for drug processing. Nefarious characters, like a man who had helped organise Jason Moran's death, would pop into Milad's laundry to collect speed, sometimes leaving the payment with Renate. Uncle Garry claimed Milad had pleaded about the cash and jewels: 'Please take it home. I'm sick of my brothers borrowing money off me.' The uncle claimed he believed his niece had been given most of the jewels at family gatherings in line with Lebanese tradition.

Milad, Tony and Horty had moved out to their own places but Kabalan was still living at home with Ma Mokbel when he was in his forties with a family of his own. He had been left the man of the family when Sajih died but this translated to getting the responsibilities while Tony assumed the role of boss. Sometimes in big families these things are decided in a factional vote to which the intended victim is not invited. Kabalan was either the most soft-hearted of the brothers to want the role of dutiful son to his ailing Arabic-speaking widowed mother or, if he didn't want it but got it anyway, he was the one most easily strong-armed.

A psychologist described Kabalan as reserved, accommodating and submissive. Police concurred he had neither Tony's manipulative charisma nor Milad's vicious streak. 'Kabalan – what Tony told him to do – he just went and did it, whether that be transport of drugs and stuff like that, he just did it,' Detective Sergeant Jim Coghlan said. 'Kabalan was definitely more hands on. Tony was the kingpin and everything just sprouted out under him.'

Kabalan had clocked up some priors for dishonesty and street offences, but both Kabalan supporters and those who wanted him jailed agreed he was a follower and submissive to little bro Tony. But if Kabalan was the big friendly giant of the bruvvers he was a Shrek with a shottie. The longarm was kept under the bed where he slept.

In 2003 Kabalan became the subject of an action-packed arrest when police bumped into him, literally, at a high speed. The dramatic confrontation occurred as police busted open a

$6.5 million syndicate cooking amphetamines for Tony from a house in Rye in country Victoria. A team of one hundred police officers had been monitoring the drug ring's actions for ten months. They would wait for the cooks to produce a large amphetamines yield then monitor it as it was delivered up the line. Nabbing any old skrote with the drugs would not do. Police wanted a Mokbel red-handed with a large amount of amphetamine. But the Mokbel heartland of Melbourne's northern suburbs proved to be like a Bermuda triangle for police. Every time the amphetamines left the regional lab and entered Tonytown, anti-surveillance tricks and lucky breaks would conspire to save the Mokbels' bacon.

Police threw a net over the area. Officers were strategically positioned on the expected route, monitoring places and players, and ready to pounce. The first time the delivery happened but not as expected and police missed it. A week later they got a second chance. Officers followed the drugs all the way to their ultimate destination but police believe they 'got made' – were recognised – as the package was taken into a Mokbel house, so they withdrew. Had they raided, they feared the drugs would be flushed and they would seize nothing but drug residue on empty plastic bags. Better to have the Mokbels dispose of the drugs and then doubt whether the police were really observing them.

On the third delivery police watched as a Mokbel cook placed an Officeworks box containing two kilograms of amphetamines worth $300,000 on the front passenger seat of a car being driven by Kabalan. Kabalan gunned his Commodore for a dash toward the Brunswick Street property where he lived with Ma. This time police were taking no chances. Idling nearby was a large four-wheel-drive packed with heavily armed Special Operations Group officers. The four-wheel-drive accelerated around the corner and met Kabalan's vehicle head on. As the Soggies swarmed the crumpled Commodore and arrested its shocked driver, Kabalan told them: 'I'm just the delivery man.' Nobody was under the misapprehension that he was the criminal mastermind. 'With Kabalan he was probably operating for the other two. It would be Milad or Tony's gear and he was the goose doing the pick-up,' ex-Purana chief Jim O'Brien said. 'He was the oldest brother and the lowest on the IQ scale.'

Kabalan was charged with trafficking, and at Ma's police found a fake ID and a stolen shottie under Kabalan's bed. His silk told the court that yes, the delivery looked suspicious, but Kabalan didn't necessarily know what was in the box. Kabalan was bailed and given permission to travel interstate for a sunny sojourn at the luxurious Palazzo Versace on the Gold Coast. His days in the sunshine waiting for trial became months then years due to delays and industrial action at the police forensic lab.

The Mokbels may never have known the chance they missed to walk away from the busted Rye lab unscathed. A notorious associate of Williams later claimed to police that Carl, who was involved in supplying chemicals to the Rye endeavour, was tipped off about police closing in by an allegedly corrupt cop. The crim made a statement saying the cop said if Carl pulled out he wouldn't get busted, but he had to let the Mokbels go down or it would be too obvious there was a police leak and questions would be asked.

'Carl said that we had to let the Mokbels go down on it. I wasn't very happy about this but Carl made me swear to him that I wouldn't tell the Mokbels,' the crim said. 'Not even two weeks after this the lab was raided and Milad Mokbel was arrested.

'Some time after the Rye cook was busted by the drug squad I heard from Carl that Milad Mokbel was whining and sooking in the interview room. [The cop] had told Carl that Milad was complaining about being pinched. I wanted to shit-stir Milad about being a sook but Carl wouldn't let me because then Milad would know that we had a copper on the inside.'

Like Tony, Milad had been raided in the mega-swoop of August 2001. Raiding police had found more than $66,000 hidden in his mansion. But the charges were dropped after Paul Firth, a former drug squad detective and crucial witness, was suspended in the context of a corruption probe. The lucky break made a happy Milad the first beneficiary of the investigation into corrupt police destroying an entire prosecution case.

Arrested again the same year over Tony's $11 million pseudoephedrine import, Milad's luck held out. Despite his fingerprints being on a shipping document detailing the movements of a drugs container, the evidence was not strong enough to proceed. His lawyer crowed that Milad was now a free man. However, Milad had expensive tastes and he used his lucky breaks to return to the drug trade – lucky breaks that were rapidly running out.

Some have said Jim O'Brien's time at the helm of Purana coincided with the most successful dismantling of organised crime in the history of Australian crime-fighting. When it was decided the Mokbel brothers needed to be put away properly, a skilled team and proper financing were allocated for the fight. Said O'Brien: 'I called a team of people together and in that I actually had accountants, solicitors, taxation office people, telephone intercept monitoring people and criminal proceeds investigators all co-housed together in one location. For the first time we started seeing a communication crossflow and a bit of discipline in the organisation to the point where that much more information and intelligence was coming forward. There was an air of electricity when you walked into the room. There was no place for egos.

'I was once a homicide detective so I can say this. There are a couple of things about homicide detectives. They wear the best suits, they don't like getting them dirty and they don't like doing any other sort of investigations except homicide. Well, we stopped that. We had homicide investigators, drug investigators, criminal proceeds investigators. It was seamless. No separation. One team.

'It was my job to make sure the i's were dotted and the t's were crossed and there was no room to be left open for people to exploit and see those prosecutions lost. When you think that we monitored 328,000 telephone calls from September 2005 to July 2007 it'll give you an idea of the level of work.

'It was also the loneliest place on earth. In the two years I was at Purana I had hardly a night when the phone didn't ring about every hour, hour and a half. I'd exist on three or four hours of sleep a night and catch up at the weekends.'

O'Brien had studied American policing and adopted the US Drug Enforcement Agency's three-step approach of investigate, identify the players, then dismantle. American crime-fighters had struggled for generations against mob figures running drugs, including Anthony 'Fat Tony' Salerno. Purana had their own Fat Tony plus his three brothers to deal with. O'Brien: 'Basically from September 2005 our vision was to investigate and dismantle – to a point from where it would never recover – one of the most significant organised crime groups not only this state but this country had ever seen.

'In the past we might have gone out and had a look at a criminal and said, "This guy's fairly active, let's target him." On this occasion we mapped out the whole organisation. We spent a great deal of our time doing nothing, just getting to know who was who, who was playing what part, and how we were going to dismantle in a strategic manner. So if something happened over here we could get a result over there which would deliver evidence and we would prosecute someone down the track.

'It went into the hundreds and hundreds of people involved. It wasn't four or five people. It was a matter of identifying them all and using coercive examination systems to get the evidence to allow us to pull the assets off them. So it was a bit more than Mr Plod just walking along and bumping over things – which is quite often the way the regular police do.'

After Milad's second escape from the long arm of the law he organised a meth lab running out of Strathmore. The lab was hidden in a shop near a primary school and potentially exposed the little learners to toxic fumes. The lab was pumping out $1 million worth of drugs a week. But police were onto it and a month after Tony vanished, on Anzac Day 2006, Purana swooped in raids, grabbing Milad, two others, the lab equipment, drugs and $80,000 in cash. The operation's cook had turned snitch for Purana and recorded the delivery of a parcel of drugs, switched for harmless powder, to Milad's mansion. The drugs were fake but Milad sniffed the package and exclaimed 'beautiful'. Milad paid $88,750 for the drugs and boasted he had enough chemicals to make himself $1 million in two months.

Officers arrested Milad in his driveway. He was also in the gun for charges relating to the Rye lab that had led police to bump into Kabalan years earlier. Milad's property was already spoken for as Tony's bail security but Milad's silk said Ma Mokbel was willing to put up the family home as surety. This time, though, there would be no bail. Milad was still fighting but he was doing so from jail. For police it was one down. The first brother was behind bars.

'The overall plan was the whole organisation and that included the brothers and their extended family,' O'Brien said. 'A lot of the assets were concealed. It was fairly widespread. There were wives and relatives and distant relatives but that's the nature of organised crime. We had all those either concealing, aiding in the concealment of assets by brokering or organising dodgy loans to hide or conceal the assets – creating camouflage.'

Authorities said that over the past twenty years the brothers had earnt their living from the drug trade, and with court approval they gleefully set about restraining Milad and Renate's assets.

Among the seized booty were two Mercedes-Benz cars, gold jewellery, Ducati and Harley-Davidson motorcycles, real estate including Milad and Renate's Brunswick mansion, large-screen televisions and $116,000 in cash. The big freeze of dodgy Mokbel assets exceeded $50 million and came to include an additional $15 million worth of mining shares allegedly belonging to Horty.

The Mokbel wives, who had kept many assets in their names and out of the hands of prosecutors, also came under scrutiny. 'We had the sisters-in-law all party to it, living off it. They were having cosmetic surgery done. All paid for by drug money,' O'Brien said.

In November 2006 Horty's wife, Zaharoula, was arrested for fraudulently obtaining more than $2 million worth of loans and credit lines, including from Westpac and the National Australia Bank. With bright red hair and a vivacious fashion sense 'Roula' cut a flamboyant figure at the city courts. The mother of three had duped the banks, posing as a petrol station owner, oil company manager and freight company employee who was single, with no dependants and on a $250,000 annual salary. Roula's lawyer argued: 'The only reason she has been charged is her name is Mokbel. It is a penalty for the sins of others.' Roula was bailed with reporting obligations including a perhaps Tony-inspired condition that she stay away from airports.

Just hours after Horty had supported his wife of twenty years at court, police arrested him in Sydney Road, Coburg, raided his Preston home and took him in for questioning. He was charged with a series of offences for his role in the drug ring that had already got Milad jailed. Horty was accused of regularly meeting a drug cook in a Coburg cafe to exchange drugs and money. Horty supplied the cook with chemicals to make twenty kilograms of drugs which he bought back for $40,000 per half kilo, police said. The cook turned informer taped Horty saying: 'Have you got any gear? Can you put any aside for me or not? I'll take whatever.'

Horty followed younger brother Milad into custody and, after prosecutors warned that he could use Tony's escape route and unexplained riches to flee, he was refused bail. Already in custody when sentenced, Milad would get eleven years with an eight-year minimum for drug trafficking, stashing profits from crime, and blackmail.

When Kabalan's case eventually got back to court in November 2007 he would put his hand up to a charge of trafficking. He would also admit to delivering ten litres of sulphuric acid to a drug cook, and aiding and abetting the drug-producing syndicate. 'He is not a person who is a leader,' his silk said. 'He is a follower. He is introverted. He is a soft, gentle man still living at home caring for his mum.'

While still in Australia Tony had tried to help his big bro by pressuring the man who delivered Kabalan's box of amphetamines to change his story. But the ploy simply backfired into a new charge on Tony's slate – attempt to pervert the course of justice. Kabalan was jailed for a minimum of two years after the judge accepted he was guilt-stricken over devastating his wife, Anita, his three teenage kids, and Ma.

It seems the police were not the only ones who thought Tony was responsible for Kabalan's demise. Kabalan said: 'I mean, I've paid for me because of my brother but that's another story. You understand? Because people have got their own opinion. That's enough. I don't need to go into it anymore.'

Whoever was at fault, the three Mokbel men were all stuck behind bars of Victorian prisons. They were now all in their forties, losing hair and fighting hard the paunchy ravages of middle age. But just like decades earlier when they were boys on the football field, the Mokbel brothers were still making an impression. When all three were locked up Milad and Kabalan were still being called to court, and appearing by video-link, on fresh trafficking charges. Purana meanwhile was getting court permission to grab more Mokbel-linked properties.

Police were happy to have caged the bruvvers. But one more was needed to complete the set.

21
Greek unorthodox

You can never go home again.

– James Agee

Detectives say the first two days in a homicide investigation are vital. If police don't have a solid lead after forty-eight hours the chance of the case ever getting solved is slashed in half. The statistical folklore about capturing fugitives is less developed, but after hunting the missing Mokbel for a whole year with no success, the pursuing officers knew their case was looking very grim. Federal agents followed dozens of trails only to have them end in dispiriting dead ends. Tony's vanishing act was a criminal embarrassment for the police and the courts. If it turned into a permanent disappearance Mokbel would go from drug-dealing killer to immortal outlaw legend and the authorities' shame would be made permanent.

The day Mokbel failed to appear Agent Jarrod Ragg noticed that the little diary Mokbel had been scrawling in throughout his trial was still sitting in the dock. 'We were all filing out of court ... so I've hung back until everyone moved out of court and the clerk of courts has required me to surrender it to the court, probably correctly so,' Agent Ragg said. 'There was some discussion and it was ultimately decided that if I wanted it I would have to get a search warrant for the court. I don't think it's ever been done before. I had a Crimes Act 1914 section-three search warrant issued for the Supreme Court of Victoria authorised by the Magistrates Court of Victoria.'

Justice Gillard allowed the warrant to be executed on his court. And he scanned the diary to ensure releasing it would not breach the legal professional privilege existing between Tony and his lawyers. 'As he handed it to me he said, "I'm not sure this is going to advance your causes very far, Mr Ragg."'

The diary had very little in it – a vague mention of the Stooge, some doodles and a reference to the car Milad had returned. 'What it did do is it led us to his BMW, which we took back under a warrant from the dealers,' Ragg said. 'We were interested in the GPS in it to see where he'd been.' Unfortunately for the federal investigators it was a tinny GPS with absolutely no memory. 'He had a half-million dollar car or something ridiculous like that and the cheapest, nastiest GPS you could buy.'

'We conducted a fairly significant investigation,' said Agent Ragg, 'but ultimately you run out of legitimate inquiries, you've got to wind things back ... We couldn't take it any further.' As police asked themselves, 'Where in the world is Fat Tony?' the rotund renegade was cutting his way across the Indian Ocean.

With the court in possession of his passport, Mokbel was travelling with no papers, officially stateless. If they sailed into someone's national waters or passed a coastguard his only option was to stick to his hidey hole and officially not exist. If spotted and questioned he would have had to resort to his other more persuasive papers – the bags of cash he carried with him.

There were creature comforts on the multi-cabin 17-metre yacht, including hot water, a deck shower, and cooking facilities. But Mokbel's bed was set up in the front of the vessel which had the greatest vertical movement as it bumped over the swells of the Indian Ocean. Mokbel spent most of the trip seriously seasick and vomiting. With the ceaseless rocking and nausea, the possibility of a jail cell on terra firma must have been growing on Tony. But life on the high seas soon got even more dramatic as Mokbel's escape plan hit its first hitch.

The vessel's 'automatic pilot' broke down and started gushing hydraulic oil. The *Edwena*'s crew had to take turns working shifts manually steering the vessel on course across the heaving ocean. The crew kept the yacht running on cooking oil – further dampening Tony's culinary expectations – before making it safely to the Maldives, 6000 kilometres from Fremantle, for repairs.

As Mokbel grew his sea legs Danielle McGuire continued to lead police through a variety of countries on a merry chase around the northern hemisphere. Her beauty salon, run with Renate, closed five months after she left Australia. Growing more visibly pregnant and with her primary-school-age daughter in tow, Mokbel's girlfriend spent time in Rome, Paris, EuroDisney and at beach resorts in the south of France. A source said McGuire also spent time in Dubai. An expert at counter-surveillance, she would disarm the various Euro-spooks on her trail by smiling at them, waving, or confronting them in a less friendly manner.

'She was too good,' said one overseas source. 'She was quite brazen. She would approach them and tell them to fuck off and stop following her.' She outran the French gendarmes and made for Italy where she eventually slipped her polizia pursuers in Rome. Headlines back in Australia screamed 'INTERPLOD' as, against the odds, she outsmarted overseas police and jumped countries once more. Police had begun to suspect McGuire was leading them not to Mokbel but on a wild goose chase. Now that she too had fallen off the radar authorities had a nasty feeling they had been double duped, that she was now living it up with the country's most notorious criminal in a love nest somewhere on the other side of the planet.

Danielle somehow magically materialised in Greece with no entry stamp in her passport. After shaking the polizia in the Italian capital she is believed to have travelled halfway down the boot-shaped country's heel to Brindisi. From that ancient coastal city a traveller can catch a ferry direct to Greece. They can even take their car. All they have to do is buy a one-way ticket.

Once the *Edwena* was repaired it sailed north-west from the Maldives. It crept through pirate-infested waters around the Horn of Africa, into the Gulf of Aden, then up the Red Sea between Africa and Saudi Arabia. The sloop then sailed through Egypt along the man-made Suez Canal, with bribes slung to appropriate officials, and out the other side to the Mediterranean Sea. From there it was a picturesque sail past white stone islets emerging out of turquoise seas before the *Edwena* came to rest at the Greek Island of Syros. There, after more than forty days and nights on the choppy seas, the Australian fugitive stepped off his yacht and onto Greek land.

For Tony the 10,000-kilometre journey had seen high drama, some laughs and a lot of vomiting. But on the island of Syros police believe Mokbel farewelled his crew and left the three Greek sailors, now home, checking in the yacht and displaying any necessary paperwork. From Syros Tony only had to jump on a ferry full of tourists for a short ride to Pireas, the main port of Athens, and on to the Greek mainland. No passport required.

On 24 December 2006 – just as on every Christmas Eve – wide-eyed Greek children lay sleepless in bed waiting for a bearded portly stranger to visit their country from a faraway land. And on that date something fitting that description but decidedly dodgier and minus any gifts – a swarthy wig-wearing Tony – floated silently into their harbour.

The Greeks call Athens the largest village in the country. It is a metropolis that blends bazaars, bouzouki music, chain outlets, wild chickens, traffic jams and smog. Perched on top of the limestone rock of the Acropolis are the majestic marble columns of the Parthenon which tower over the city. In the shadow of the columns the suburbs of the ancient city stretch to a southern coastal tip where the aqua sea is clean and clear. It was here in the upmarket suburb of Elliniko that Tony, Danielle and Brittany made their home. Greece was the last place authorities expected Mokbel to flee to because it has an extradition agreement with Australia. But once Mokbel arrived in the land of Virgil, Sophocles, Plato, the real Yanni and the fictional Zorba, he and Danielle embraced their new Athenian life with gusto.

Elliniko, near Glyfada, is a summertime playground for rich Athenians and rich international visitors alike. It is a place where the most beautiful people primp and preen on the most beautiful pay beaches. The inhabitants indulge in the best shopping and best seafood. Tony and Danielle's base was a luxury triple-storey villa with ocean views. As the new year drew the curtains on what had been a very large 2006 for both parties, their celebrations were this time unhindered by any pesky curfews.

In February McGuire gave birth to her baby girl in an Athens hospital and managed to avoid having the birth registered. There seemed little question of the paternity of Danielle's baby. A cute pudding-headed butterball, she had dark eyes and flashes of surly and sly looks that were pure Tony. The expanding fugitive family made themselves at home in their street of exclusive addresses guarded by watchdogs and cameras.

Danielle left the apartment much less often than Tony and spent the bulk of her time indoors. She even had a private teacher make a house visit for three hours a day to educate Brittany. Tony, on the other hand, shunned a beans-by-candlelight fugitive existence for a more active and outgoing life, sunning himself by the sea. He would wander the exclusive seaside promenade, suntanned, bearded and in his moptop wig.

The Company delivered Mokbel a doctored Australian passport and driver's licence, which showed him as fictitious Sydney businessman Stephen Papas from Bondi. It was apparently the fake name his old footy team used for dodgy ring-in players. The pictures on his identity documents matched his born-again status as a man with a full head of hair. Locals would see a nicely tanned Mokbel taking a daily constitutional around the fashionable Esperidon Square. He would wear bermuda shorts, smoke cigars and order crushed-ice lattes from Starbucks. The Athenians heard the man in the wig and baseball cap speak English, saw him tip big and assumed he was American.

Mokbel would spend time with Theo Angelakis, a friend of Mr Fixit, Byron Pantazis. Angelakis was a silver-haired, pockmarked Greek shipping figure. He had spent time in Australia and Mokbel and he rapidly became friends and coffee companions. Fat Tony was driving a Mercedes-Benz Kompressor until 'Thin Theo' got him a shiny new Volkswagen four-wheel-drive to replace it. Mokbel would do supermarket runs for nappies and milk in the flashy vehicle and take Danielle to 'aqua baby' swim classes.

As their newborn grew to six months old, her parents got comfortable in their Grecian groove. Once a week the family ate at a trendy deli, To Bakaliko, at a table obscured by plants, always finishing within half an hour. Mokbel's joy at his audacious plot turning out so well was palpable. 'He was very relaxed and friendly, always smiling,' said waiter Yiorgos Angelou. In the land of glowing white walls baked by the sun, kalamata olives, rice puddings, spinach pies, stuffed vine leaves, souvlaki, tavernas, late lunches and 11 pm suppers, it was hard for Mokbel not to be happy.

Back home Carl Williams pled guilty to the murders of Jason and Lewis Moran and Mark Mallia. In late February 2007 Mokbel was charged in his absence with being the money man in Lewis's execution, but there was little chance of Tony going back to face the music and keep Carl company in the clink. Eating dolmadikia in the Athens sun for the rest of his life was a far more attractive prospect than being locked up on the cold barren plains near Geelong waiting to be stabbed with a sharpened toothbrush.

For Tony, Elliniko even held a small reminder of the sounds of home he had heard as a boy in Brunswick and in his more recent life in Port Melbourne. When Mokbel lay down his head at the end of another day in paradise he could hear trams rattling up and down the coast.

22
Paradise and porridge

To be alive is to undo your belt and look for trouble.

– Zorba the Greek

Life in sunny Athens was good for the first couple of Australian crime. But it was not a victimless existence for the expat duo. Back in Melbourne their freedom was being paid for with the freedom of a Mokbel by marriage. Fine-featured, mouselike Renate was married to Tony's punchy younger brother, Milad. She had gone into business with Tony's girlfriend, Danielle. The two women, both thin, chic, bottle blondes of similar height, together ran the hair extension and beauty salon.

When Tony had applied for bail years earlier, the court had demanded a million-dollar surety to ensure the cherub-faced charmer would not do a runner. To prove she was good for the bail amount Renate had sworn on oath she was the owner of the massive Mokbel mansion where she and Milad lived in Downs Street, Brunswick, then worth about $1.1 million. When Mokbel vanished the justice machine started churning to recoup the pledged million-dollar bail from Renate. It then emerged the Brunswick property was owned not by Renate but by a Mokbel family corporate trust and had in any case also been frozen by court order.

The Supreme Court warned Renate she would go directly to jail if she did not come up with the $1 million. Renate couldn't and in March 2007, while Tony and Danielle were soaking up the Athenian sun, Renate was given a blue tracksuit and locked up to serve two years in Victoria's highest security female jail. Graduates of Renate's new home, the Dame Phyllis Frost women's jail in Deer Park in Melbourne's north-west, have told horror stories about the place. Butch convicts carry drug-filled syringes in body cavities, dispense bashings as 'verdicts' of prisoner courts, and stand over epileptic inmates for their medicine. Renate mentally struggled in jail and her three children struggled outside without her. She was ultimately allowed to have her and Milad's pre-school son with her in jail for extended periods. The boy became the youngest Mokbel behind bars.

There were bitter recriminations that Tony's escape had led to the jailing of Milad's wife even in the close-knit Mokbel family where Tony was usually regarded as incapable of doing wrong. Tony and Danielle tried to make some amends, calling their Athens baby Renate. But a mini-namesake was a poor consolation prize for the mother of three locked up with the state's worst female prisoners for two years.

Renate tried to get the court order that demanded she repay the pledged million dollars revoked, but her legal ploy ultimately backfired. As part of her bid Renate had filed an affidavit detailing her assets and financial position. But she failed to disclose the half-million in cash and jewellery she and Milad had buried in her uncle's garden. When police unearthed the booty, prosecutors returned to court and the incarcerated mum copped perjury charges and an additional six-month jail whack.

Renate said she believed Tony would have done the right thing by her, husband Milad, and their three children, aged between three and fourteen. 'I have absolutely no idea where Tony presently is. By absconding, Tony has essentially destroyed my family,' she said. But the prosecution said Tony chose Renate because she was 'most able to play the role of the dumb wife' after he fled.

Renate's mother pleaded with Tony to turn himself in to save her daughter. 'Renate is appealing to Tony to do the right thing and set her free,' she said. Her daughter, she said, had no idea her brother-in-law was a criminal mastermind when she had gone guarantor for him. But, she said, Renate had certainly changed her mind now.

Renate's brother said even Ma Mokbel was none too chuffed with the latest actions of her little cherub. 'Even his mother thinks he should do something to get Renate freed,' the brother said. 'She doesn't speak much English but I get the distinct impression she thinks Tony should face the music. It's not right that Renate should be in jail because of something Tony did.'

Publicly Mokbel matriarch, Lora, was still backing Tony and blaming police for Renate's treatment and the circumstances of her arrest. 'Swear on the life of your own children, do you think these people have any conscience?' she said. 'If they had any conscience would they take a woman from her home and leave [a teenage girl] there?'

But even from sunny Greece Tony was still funnelling cash to Renate and, like many Mokbel matters, it seems the performance was mostly for show. From Athens Tony would speak to his mum and other relatives and associates over the phone. He would get Company members to front at their homes, secure mobile in hand, with Tony already on the line. Mokbel made 2000 phone calls from Greece using a bundle of phones and a collection of codenames. Milad was Baldy, Horty was the Greek, Roula the Greek's wife, and Renate lingering in jail was Blondie.

Mokbel devised a serious but later-abandoned plan to raise $1 million through The Company and other debt-owing associates to bail Renate out. Even had it happened police would have regarded the money as an asset of Tony's and seized it. It never happened anyway and it was unlikely Mokbel was letting Renate's plight ruin his holiday. On a good day he might be his brothers' keeper but surely that didn't extend to their wives as well.

'He didn't care what happened to her even though he made out that he did,' Detective Sergeant Coghlan said. 'He's self-centred. The world revolves around Tony Mokbel and what he can get out of it.' In Tonyworld, police observers have said, even lovers, partners and kin come a distant second to numero uno. 'Obviously he loves his child but when the crunch comes – it's Tony Mokbel,' Coghlan said.

Another Tony plan was to resurrect 'the Uncle' – Renate's uncle Garry, whose garden once had the richest soil in Australia – to buy the Brunswick mansion back after it was forfeited. But that plot, too, ultimately came to nought. Still, Tony was cognisant that the motherless residents of the Downs Street property might not be feeling the most pro-Tony sentiments. From Greece he phoned

Renate Mokbel's then fourteen-year-old daughter, Jade, had a chat, and then sent her $4000 for good measure.

While Renate was in Deer Park jail in her blue tracksuit, and Mokbel was walking a Grecian marina in bermuda shorts, the spotty misfits behind The Company continued pumping out speed and raking in millions. Their efforts paid for his escape, sustained his life on the run and bankrolled his existence in Greece. The Company sent at least $400,000 overseas to finance Mokbel's fugitive lifestyle. They would wire some of it to Greek bank accounts and convert other bundles to euros then have peripheral members of The Company hand-deliver them to Tony. Few weeks would pass without Tony being wired at least another $40,000 or $50,000.

The Company accounts also gave Tony the means to pay friends and family and buy the continued loyalty of those tempted to turn snitch. Tony knew there were a lot of loose lips in the ganglands. Mid-ranking crims who know things talk a lot of bollocks but police can find helpful nuggets of truth among the white noise. Tony also knew persuasive women and men in suits would be doorknocking old associates, planting seeds, and whispering sweet nothings in the ears of the disaffected.

By the first anniversary of his failure to show at court Mokbel had used The Company to get $40,000 to Milad to be spent on lawyers for Renate. A month later The Company gave Horty another $10,000 for legal fees. Despite her family's protests over what a surprise bounder Tony had turned out to be, Renate herself was kept sweet with two direct payments of $20,000 and another of $3000.

When he was still hunkered down in Bonnie Doon Mokbel had sent $2000 to his ex-wife, Carmel. And when he arrived in Greece on Christmas Eve he sent the mother of his earlier children a more substantial yuletide gift of $50,000. On Christmas Day the dutiful son sent his mother, Lora, $10,000. Horty's wife, Zaharoula, who also needed a good lawyer after being charged over the $2 million in fraudulent loans – got $19,500. And a variety of aunts and relatives were also made to feel more positive about the wayward Tony with the arrival of their Company-delivered, tax-free packages.

Mokbel even arranged a special treat for his would-be mother-in-law, Danielle's mum, Joan Madin, although her gift did not materialise until after the fugitive lovers reunited in Greece, so it is possible Danielle was the driving force behind the gesture. On Ms Madin's birthday Company honchos Bart Rizzo and Joseph Mansour journeyed out west to the badlands of the Sunshine shopping plaza to meet their absent boss's would-be mother-in-law. Big Bart handed over photos of Madin's months-old new Grecian granddaughter. Rizzo referred to the baby as the 'heir to the throne' and also gave Ms Madin $2000 cash in an envelope. No stranger to shady characters, Madin lived with the Duke, the alleged shooter of the Hodsons. But the transaction nevertheless left her feeling more positive about her notorious would-be son-in-law. 'That was a good man to my granddaughter,' she said of Mokbel. 'That was her father and that was his daughter.'

Two days after the Sunshine plaza meeting The Company shuttled another $1000 to Madin.

* * *

Tony's friend in Athens, Theo Angelakis, owned his own shipping company and agreed to set up a similar business for Mokbel. The resulting entity was a shelf company with one asset – Mokbel's car. Police believe the company was a front to help 'rinse' money and to help Tony get the *Edwena* registered locally in Greece. It is also possible that in sanctuary Mokbel's global drug ambitions had been reborn and the shipping initiative fitted with his plans for a mass export of drugs in drums by sea.

'They were setting up a new life. They were definitely there to set up a new life,' a police source said. 'He was doing everything to set up a new lifestyle in Greece – including *everything*. He is not a carpenter or a plumber. He hasn't got a trade.' As for the fugitive potentially alerting local authorities to his existence by re-embarking on a drug career, police said Mokbel would not have worried. 'Tony is a very confident man. He doesn't care. He thinks he can get out of it and do anything he wants. Money speaks all languages,' a detective said.

23

Manhunt

There are only the pursued, the pursuing, the busy and the tired.

– F Scott Fitzgerald, *The Great Gatsby*

Mokbel had been flagged with a global red notice. Police forces from Interpol's 184 member countries had been sent photos of him. Federal officers scoured flight passenger lists around the world, put airports on alert and checked the nation's ports.

Officers followed Fat Tony trails to Lebanon until the Israelis started shelling. There were rumours Tony had been tracked by global positioning technology to the Ural Mountains in Russia. Before that it was Lebanon then Dubai. Assistant Commissioner Simon Overland said his whereabouts were anyone's guess. Hopeless Tony trails also led to Turkey, Brazil and even literally underground. Police were tipped Mokbel had been whacked in a revenge hit for his suspected involvement in the death of Mario Condello. The tip said Mokbel's corpse had been thrown into a grave in regional Victoria. Investigating the information police poked torches down cracked country graves looking for a murdered Mokbel.

'I was at that. I didn't believe it for a bleeding moment,' Agent Ragg said. 'I did it because Renate Mokbel was in jail and if

Mokbel was dead in a grave there was a fair case for her to be let out of jail. It was following up every possible lead and making sure every consideration was given to Renate Mokbel if indeed he was dead.'

Tony was, of course, in the land of the living and, police suspect, was probably behind the cemetery ruse. Meanwhile the nation's largest manhunt kept terminating in a series of disheartening cul-de-sacs. The Australian Federal Police had urged the public to help find Mr Mokbel, describing him as 'approximately 175 centimetres tall, solid build with an olive complexion and short, brown coloured, receding hair'. Police had been sweet-talking plebs, doorknocking docketheads and raising the dead but it was getting them no closer to finding their frustrating fugitive.

Tony's 'filthy-lucre FedEx' was keeping would-be weak links staunch. And whether Mokbel had escaped by hovercraft or was hunkered down in Honiara, police knew they were not getting answers doing what they were doing. Mokbel was winning and police needed something new, a circuit breaker, a game changer, anything to reverse the dynamic. It was time to throw a great big rock in the pond and see what floated up. Mokbel had been gone more than a year when two things happened. First: the Victorian government offered a $1 million reward, unprecedented for a fugitive, for anyone giving information leading to Fat Tony's whereabouts. The government reward was announced just weeks after a Melbourne newspaper chief of staff had proposed the idea as a great story to the head of the premier's media unit. Second: the Purana anti-gangland taskforce of Victoria Police, which had been deferring to the federal-led escape probe, decided to embark on their own Get Tony mission.

A constant and important underlying factor in the hunt for Mokbel was the highly fraught relationship between the Victorian and federal authorities. It is a Hollywood staple to have the macho local sheriff and the arrogant federal agent standing at a crime scene in the driving rain shouting at each other over who has carriage of the case. The reality of tensions in Australian policing is similar to this cliché but less friendly. The relationship between the AFP and Victoria Police has soured over a number of joint ventures. There are many instances of unhappiness, and new fights continue today. Generally speaking the feds regard the staties as cowboys mired in corruption, while the staties regard the plastics as wealthy bunglers whose bacon they have to keep saving. Whatever the reality, a drug import destined for Tony Mokbel threatened to create a war between the staties and the plastics.

It is legal to import phenylacetic acid into Australia under licence for legitimate uses. The naturally occurring honey-scented compound is commonly used in perfume production. However, a two-step process can turn mundane phenylacetic acid into amphetamines. Mokbel associates had a cunning plan to come through the front door and use the legal structure to brazenly funnel large amounts of the lucrative drug precursor into Tony's waiting clan labs for conversion.

Mokbel mates involved in the scheme used a chemical-company front to import phenylacetic acid under licence. Even legitimate industry importers like corporate perfumers only ever import the substance in very small amounts, so for the crims' test run they brought in just a trifling eighty-nine grams. When that worked they made their next import bigger – over 2300 times bigger: 205 kilograms. It was a staggering amount to attempt to bring in declared and would have made ninety kilograms of speed worth more than $10 million on the street, but sources said the Therapeutic Goods Administration saw nothing fishy and issued a permit for the import.

Things hit a snag for the villains involved in the perfect crime when police stumbled over the front company while investigating a suspect in a separate plot. That suspect was then linked to the importer in the phenylacetic acid scheme – a man who was a known chemical supplier to a Mokbel drug cook. But watching detectives could not immediately pounce. 'Of course there was no offence committed at that stage,' said Jim O'Brien. 'So really, until we could prove that they intended to deal with it inappropriately [by] diverting it into drug production we had no evidence to charge them with anything,' he said. 'Everything was going on swimmingly well with customs and us [Victoria Police] having signed a joint agency agreement, working hand in hand. But at the last minute they had a bit of a heart attack and had to tell the AFP about it and the AFP got involved. We explained. They said: "We're prepared to let it run."'

Police knew from surveillance that seventy-five kilograms of drugs had been made from the import but had lost track of exactly where they were. What they did have was a time and place the drugs and cash were going to change hands with direct involvement by the Mokbels. O'Brien said that because the location of the drugs was not known, the AFP turned around and accused the Victorians of corruption and swooped on the crooks involved. 'They went and executed all the warrants and arrested all the targets and didn't even tell us they were doing it,' he said. 'They arrested the two. They were remanded in custody and basically didn't have a case against them,' he said.

Had the prisoners given a no-comment interview everyone, particularly the Mokbels, who were not then able to be linked, would have got away with the massive import scot-free. But it wasn't to be. O'Brien commented: 'We decided to turn a negative into a positive and sent people out to interview them. Managed to recruit these two offenders and got them to give evidence against the main offenders and turned what was an abject failure into an overwhelming success. We then charged Horty Mokbel with importation as well because we had direct evidence then linking him.

'Of course the AFP were then running around with faces like smacked arses that we didn't communicate with them according to the joint agency agreement. What goes around comes around.'

Amid these simmering tensions the feds and Victoria Police would again be thrown together in the hunt for Mokbel. 'The AFP were the taskforce set up to locate Mokbel. We weren't involved. They took all the responsibility to locate where he was,' Purana's Detective Sergeant Jim Coghlan said. The fact that the feds had been working for a year and not yet found Mokbel had prompted

Purana to conclude that Mokbel could still be in Australia. Operation Magnum, the Purana taskforce scheme to find Mokbel, started at the St Kilda Road police complex with just eight officers. 'We sat in the kitchen one day and we thought, why don't we have a red hot go at looking for Tony Mokbel? That's how it started,' Detective Sergeant Coghlan said. 'We'd been looking at the Mokbel criminal enterprise for eight years and tasked for the previous eighteen months to take them on and we had done that in relation to Horty and all the rest of them. And then we decided: where's Tony? We had the capabilities to find him – especially if he was still in Australia. We had no indication to believe he was overseas.'

Purana were half right. When Danielle was being chased around the Trevi fountain Tony was still living locally. But by the time Operation Magnum was launched he was practically speaking Greek. It was Tony's bad luck that despite getting involved on a correct but dated assumption, Purana would break through to his whereabouts.

After the reward was offered the phones rang hot. One caller made all the difference. Authorities had hoped the reward bait might net them a useful lead from a peripheral Mokbel crony but it landed them a much bigger fish altogether. 'When VicPol offered the reward which prompted their informant to come forward – that was the break that everyone needed and good on VicPol for getting that break,' said Agent Ragg.

The month the reward was announced a member of Mokbel's Company contacted police. The man dubbed here 'the Reckoner', as his real name cannot be used, had lost a brother to a heroin overdose months earlier. He denied crossing over for the money, saying he only wanted to keep from going to jail. The Reckoner told police: 'I'm mucking around with these guys and they know Tony Mokbel but I don't know where he is.'

Police said the Reckoner's motivation was 'probably a mixture of "I'm in the wrong crew here, I'm in deep," and the fact that I'm bankrupt and a million dollars is a lot of money.' Whether it was dead kin, a fear of prison, or the cash prize, the Reckoner had his choice of a million and two reasons to help police catch their absent amphetamines czar.

The Reckoner was a trusted friend of Rizzo and had got involved in The Company in late 2005 when Rizzo asked if he could use his spare room for mixing amphetamines. The Reckoner had given Rizzo his expired and current Australian passports, which had been doctored into Tony's new identity – the hirsute Stephen Papas. And he had been granted access to the upper echelons of The Company. From the Reckoner police learnt not only about the existence of The Company but the identities of its individual members. Shocked detectives learnt how Tony, even on the run, had brazenly remained the local Mr Big using his drug trade to fund his international exploits.

The Reckoner's account also gave authorities some alleged crimes on which to apply for phone and other warrants. Police promptly moved to bug the cars, houses and intercept the many, many mobiles of The Company men. Most importantly, the Reckoner helped two undercover officers infiltrate the fringes of

The Company's business. The flipping of the Reckoner and the police infiltration was a turning point. Suddenly Tony's Australian ties were no longer a lifeline. They were a massive liability.

The Octopus might have been in a mystery location on the other side of the world, but desperate authorities had finally got a grip on one of his outer tentacles, and they would hold on for dear life. The challenge for the hunters would be clawing their way to where the main body of the beast really lay without alerting their prey to their presence. Mokbel would walk around Athens, as he did in Melbourne, with a big bag of mixed mobiles. He was still regularly in contact with his crew, checking who they were dealing with, that nothing out of the ordinary was happening, that there was nothing on the nose.

The Reckoner continued his business as usual with his Company cronies. He cut, weighed and parcelled drugs in rented hotel rooms. With Rizzo he ran cash and pounds of methamphetamine to Mokbel connections in Lygon Street. Mokbel's justifiably paranoid appetite for new mobiles and SIM cards soon saw the Reckoner asked to get a new phone for the fugitive. It was a golden opportunity for authorities. Police immediately intercepted the number for a direct line to their prime target. But with Tony rotating his brief conversations across numerous handsets, the wiretap was not a final blow but a keyhole peek into Mokbel's new world.

Using information from the Reckoner, police were able to disrupt Mokbel's cash supply. In early May Company members, including Mansour and Issa, conspired to funnel nearly half a million dollars to their boss in Athens. The booty was spirited by Company men through Collingwood, Box Hill and Burwood while police watched on. When the nervous courier saw a marked car in his rear vision and ran a red light, the uniforms had their excuse to pounce without raising suspicions. After a routine search of the vehicle they seized a shopping bag containing $499,950. When Mokbel got the bad news he was not too bothered. He told his crew to get back to work and replace the lost loot within a week. But the dynamic in the hunt had changed. Now it was the police upsetting Mokbel's plans.

In Melbourne Purana detectives pursuing Tony through Operation Magnum were inflicting a series of flesh wounds on Mokbel's body corporate. The Operation Magnum officers used their new mole to set about identifying who was who in The Company and tracing the movement of cash. They had noticed a Company transaction wiring funds to a Stephen Papas in Athens and for the first time were considering Greece as a possible location for Mokbel. Purana were wary of making assumptions. All they had was a Greek connection to Mokbel's crew. And the Mediterranean nation was not yet a big red flashing light on their map of where Tony might be. 'The money was going to Greece. But Tony might have been travelling to Greece to collect money but living somewhere else,' Detective Sergeant Coghlan said. 'With the European Union open he could have been living in Serbia or Italy. Or the money could have been going to a contact or being re-transferred on to other destinations in Europe. All it meant to us was that money was going through certain banks in

Greece.' Nevertheless Melbourne police adjusted some of their shifts to correspond with Athens business hours.

Finding Tony was the biggest game in town for police. But The Company's massive drug conspiracy and its constituent crooks presented an additional stand-alone case that itself had to be catalogued for eventual prosecution. The Reckoner was given The Company's wish list of drug-making equipment and specialist glassware. Police obtained the items and introduced two of their moles into The Company, one posing as a glassware seller interested in buying large amounts of drugs. With the Reckoner vouching for them the two undercovers also made a number of large drug buys which went into the police vault. The Reckoner bought an ounce of cocaine from The Company with police money and also passed it into evidence.

Police now had three moles, a wire on one of Mokbel's lines and a connected country. But despite the breakthroughs there was nervousness in the squad that Mokbel, on the other side of the globe, could slip through their fingers. If the identities of the two officers in The Company or the Reckoner's real game emerged, the whole operation would have been blown. One warning call to Tony that The Company had been penetrated, that the heat was closing in, and Mokbel could again vanish into thin air. Officers had a recurring nightmare of storming European lofts to find them vacant and their pursuit extended for additional years of humiliation and misery. Aside from nabbing Tony, if the undercover officers were discovered by The Company's drug dealers, the consequences could be dire. And just as officers were on the verge of getting their hands on Australia's biggest drug dealer, most wanted fugitive and gangland player, there was a terrifying hitch.

Maybe it was the ease with which the Reckoner's 'friend' was able to obtain specialist drug glassware. Maybe it was the way he had popped up out of nowhere with little backstory and unknown to the other Whitefriars boys. Or perhaps it was just instinct honed on decades of first-hand criminal deception. Whatever triggered his doubts, something about the undercover cop did not gel. Fat Tony smelt a rat. And at one deal everything could have gone wrong.

Big Bart Rizzo trusted his mate the Reckoner inherently but Rizzo's role was also to update Mokbel on the operations of their multimillion-dollar business. In the course of doing this Mokbel told Rizzo he was suspicious about the Reckoner's mate, who was one of the undercover officers. The sage older drug crim gave Rizzo three orders in case his instincts were right. One: keep up your anti-surveillance tactics. Two: never sell the Reckoner's mate more drugs than what the law says is a commercial amount. That way even if it all goes bad you will get to keep your house. And three: strip search the Reckoner's mate.

To make the situation even more precarious Mokbel apparently had a break-in-case-of-emergency scheme to again rapidly disappear. If Greece had been the Plan B to staying in Australia, it seems Mokbel had a Plan C. Mokbel wanted the *Edwena* parked around the corner as a getaway vehicle, police later came to believe. The trusty vessel had saved his bacon once, and, if it became necessary, he would back it for the encore. If Mokbel sensed the heat around the corner he could have quickly sailed from Athens to Cyprus. The north of Cyprus is Turkey-controlled, and under no international obligation to help authorities in Australia.

'I believe [the yacht] was always there to be used,' said Detective Sergeant Jim Coghlan. 'Because he couldn't fly out. Can't walk out. The only other option is [by] boat, which could take him to anywhere there was no extradition treaty.'

Rizzo met with the Reckoner's mate, the police mole, on purported drug business. Rizzo undressed until he was naked as the day he was born. He then demanded, as a show of trust, that the officer do the same. If the police mole refused things would start to get very serious indeed for both the Mokbel hunt and the safety of the undercover officer and the Reckoner.

At that moment, as the officer cast his eye over the unappealing sight of the fat naked felon standing before him, everything hung by a thread. He swallowed his pride and stripped bare in front of Rizzo. Fortunately that day the officer was not wearing a wire. He was clean. Rizzo and Mokbel's immediate concerns were allayed. The hitch was smoothed over. The fugitive remained in Athens and the noose tightened around him.

Purana continued monitoring Mokbel's bugged phone, and then one day as Tony was talking on the wired line the breakthrough came. Mokbel, who was partial to a crushed-ice latte, said: 'I'm having coffee at Starbucks in Glyfada.'

Detective Coghlan's ears pricked up. Having been to Greece, he was the only one in the room who recognised the name of the Athenian suburb. It gelled with the money trail to the Greek capital they had established earlier. 'It wasn't until that day we thought, shit, he's there,' a detective said. 'It meant all right, we have a suburb. It still didn't mean he was living there. The fact he's having coffee could mean doing business with banks and not living there.'

Coghlan asked a Greek friend of his to take photos of the Glyfada coffee precinct so he could show the team the layout of the area. On a Monday morning in late May the photos arrived in Coghlan's inbox. His friend had taken snaps of the Starbucks and then an ice-cream parlour directly opposite.

As Coghlan perused the pictures he heard on a live broadcast of a phone intercept that Danielle was going to meet someone at Haagen Daaz. He zoomed in on the ice-cream shop in the picture. The quality broke down but it was still readable: Haagen Daaz. 'We were all sitting there and I said, "She's going to this place where I'm looking at the picture of it right now,"' he said. The pictures were printed up and the team quietly stared at them, soaking in the details.

Coghlan recalled: 'I said, "There's no way known that she would risk driving in Greece on the wrong side of the road and the potential of getting involved in an accident. I know Danielle and she wouldn't risk doing it."' That meant for Danielle to go to the Haagen Daaz ice-cream parlour she would have to go on foot. Which meant the likelihood of Danielle and Tony both living in or near Glyfada was pretty high. 'That was Monday morning. I was gone by Wednesday,' Jim Coghlan said.

Based on the new information, authorities were confident enough to send a local team to Greece to liaise with the Hellenic authorities. In May 2007 a Purana detective and a federal agent got the two most prized plane tickets in Australian policing – return to Athens to catch Tony Mokbel. Jim Coghlan went for Victoria Police and Agent Jarrod Ragg for the feds. Ragg could not tell loved ones where he was going. He had to ditch his usual mobile phone because callers would be able to tell he was overseas. The pair flew out of Melbourne hoping that within days they could end the global hunt for Tony Mokbel and return with the biggest fish of all.

'I'd been running the Mokbel job since October 2000. It had been a very difficult prosecution. I'd managed to turn two very difficult crooks into witnesses,' Agent Ragg said. 'There'd been an incredible number of issues that we'd overcome. I was just really hoping to get hold of him.' Coghlan and Ragg met with the AFP's man in Greece, David Dalton, who worked the bureaucracy to speed things up. The Australians received an elite team of Greek investigators who, among other things, were incorruptible. Upon landing they still did not have an address and had to energise the occasionally overly relaxed Greek police to get out and look for Mokbel. Only the Greek police would have the immediate authority to arrest and hold him on a domestic charge.

As well as observing the local legal niceties to make any arrest valid, the Australians had to keep out of the frontline lest Tony spot them around town and once again vanish with the wind. 'On a day-to-day basis we were highly aware he would recognise me in a heartbeat because I've spent years sitting in court with him,' Agent Ragg said. 'McGuire would have spotted me in a heartbeat as well.' The Australians kept a low profile, moving between their hotel, the Australian embassy and Greek police headquarters.

'At the time, he was Australia's number one fugitive. When I went to Greece they didn't know who Tony Mokbel was,' Coghlan said. 'But when they brought up his Interpol file he made the top 100 in the world. Which meant the other people on that list were Osama bin Laden and all these other characters. So we've got a bloke from Coburg who's on the top 100 wanted people in the world and that's when they took real notice that he does mean something.'

The Australians gave Greek police twenty photos of Mokbel in various guises and a list of his likely haunts, and shared their belief that he was living in or near Glyfada. 'If he is here, we will find him,' the Greeks proclaimed, and deployed plain-clothes officers to walk past harbourside cafes.

Every day the Australians would check in and give the local police any new tips they had on Mokbel. 'We were turning things that came across the wires from VicPol into intelligence for Greek police,' Ragg said.

Days became a week as the duo tried to identify Glyfada locales that would fit Tony's lifestyle, schools where they may have sent Brittany, and hospitals where Renate may have been born. 'From the wires we were trying to get together a pattern of movement on a week-to-week, day-to-day basis that might enable us to trip over him if we could put him into a routine,' Ragg said.

In early June police crashed a baby swim meeting at a local pool but just missed Tony and Renate by minutes. Frustratingly, even with a baby in tow the super-crim would follow his instincts or be rescued by his luck and become a phantom just moments before the cavalry would arrive.

'By the time we received information, reported through Greek police and they responded, we were just missing him,' Ragg said. 'When we were missing him by half an hour, an hour, you could almost taste it,' he said. 'You just knew you were so close. You could feel there was just something in the air. You're just so close to getting hold of it all.'

Without immediate success, the Greek unit assisting the Australians full-time had to drop the case to get on with their other tasks. 'We started all this with the Greeks on 29 May. They worked solidly with us for the next five or six days but we weren't getting anywhere. We were just too far behind,' Ragg said. 'This was a very busy tactical unit. So they gave us some advice on some official requests we should make.'

Momentum was being lost. Things were again sliding from hopeful to grim. Tony's luck was again on the rise. And then, less than a fortnight after the Australians' arrival, a phone call and a manila folder intervened to change the fortunes of everyone.

It was just like any other Tuesday in Athens for Tony. On 5 June 2007 he woke up in his luxury apartment next to Danielle as the sun broke in and woke the girls.

Mokbel was a fervent enough believer in his own mythology to imagine a lifetime of liberty and Greek sunsets. He and Danielle had been buying furniture and, according to local real estate agents, had planned to buy a house. Mokbel was even making moves to establish himself as a Greek drug kingpin. But Tony was also canny enough to realise each day of freedom could be the last. On that Tuesday he would spend time with the girls, don his wig and cap before visiting friends, warm the blood in the Athenian sun and have a business meeting at an exclusive harbourside eatery. Even if his days in the sun were numbered it would be la dolce vita to the last.

That morning Mokbel was on a call to Australia when he broke away from the chat to tell someone in the background: 'I'll see you at the Delfinia at eleven.' It was an uncharacteristic slip-up for Tony, who usually tried to maintain a professional criminal phone manner. Purana's surveillance picked up the comment.

Coghlan and Ragg leapt to the Greek phonebooks. The Delfinia's number was 005. That meant it was in Glyfada. At 9.45 am the Greeks were forwarded the Delfinia intelligence and dispatched officers almost immediately. The first crew were deployed on mopeds to try to cut their way through the horrendous Athens traffic and get to Tony.

'We were asked to make a decision on what we wanted the Greek police to do. Whether we wanted him followed or wanted him arrested on site. Given the circumstances we all agreed he should be arrested on site,' Agent Ragg said. Under Greek law the Interpol red notice would allow them to arrest Mokbel. Authorities had also taken out a diplomatic document, a provisional arrest order, requesting Hellenic police to make an arrest.

Mokbel visited Foula Pantazis, the wife of his escape mastermind, Byron, in her room at the Hotel Fenix in Glyfada. There he unexpectedly bumped into her daughter, Yvonne Warfe, his co-traveller and baby provider from the surreal road trip across the Nullarbor. Tony was back in his 'Yanni' wig so the reunion, while a surprise, would not have been completely out of context for Yvonne. They had a short exchange of pleasantries then moved on. Mokbel went to meet his shipping-industry friend Theo Angelakis at the Delfinia – an expensive cafe overlooking a marina full of expensive yachts. Fat Tony nonchalantly sipped a short black and talked shop with Thin Theo in what would be their last rendezvous.

Tony and Theo were taking in the ambience of trams and sea and the sound of sail toggles clinking against masts when Greek police arrived. The officers cast their eyes about, but the paunchy pale Tony from the photos with signature exposed pate was nowhere to be seen. Members of the Greek team went through the cafe but they could not find their target. They saw Angelakis and his colleague with the moptop hairstyle but did not recognise the latter as Mokbel.

The officers had, however, been told Mokbel was to be at the Delfinia for a business meeting. One of the younger Greek officers again looked at the short, tanned man with the biker moustache, sunglasses, cap and Beatlesque wig. He then noticed the older pockmarked Greek he was chatting with was holding a manila folder. 'He thought, stuff it, they're the only two looking like they're at a business meeting. So he's gone over and fronted them,' Agent Ragg said.

The officers worked their way through the exclusive cafe crowd as if on a routine identity check. The Delfinia's menu touted $32 caesar salads replete with anchovies, and fresh red snapper at $96 a kilo, but the only catch the Greek police were interested in was the heavily disguised Octopus on the terrace.

Mokbel was asked for his ID. He showed them his Stephen Papas passport and said: 'Why are you asking?'

The police perused Mokbel's documents and asked the two men to accompany them to the station. The Greeks, who had been told by the Australians that Mokbel had been using the name Stephen Papas, were confident they had their man. At 11.15 they called the Australians and told them so.

Greece is the fifth most corrupt country in the world, according to Transparency International, and has been labelled 'the EU champ of corruption' for kickbacks to public officials. Mokbel – the Australian champ of corruption – allegedly offered his accompanying officers a $1.6 million bribe to let him go. Tony was good for the amount. But the arresting officers refused. Unrebuffed by the rejection Mokbel was optimistic he could talk his way out of the squeeze. He thought the local fuzz were just interested in his bodgy passport. He was still insisting he was Stephen Papas of Bondi and he was still confident that diplomacy and cash could conquer the small misunderstanding of his arrest.

Coghlan and Ragg made their way to the Athens police station. By the time they got there silver-tongued Mokbel had been making some progress with his captors. 'Tony had been talking to them for quite a while by now and he had been denying who he was,' Ragg said. Mokbel had been maintaining he was Stephen Papas and offering explanations which to the Greeks were plausible. The Australians outside Mokbel's interview room were shown Mokbel's hybrid Victoria–New South Wales fake licence and pointed out the flaws to the Greeks, stating it justified arrest. 'They said, "Well, look, we're happy with that but we want you guys to go in and do a physical indentification,"' Ragg said.

Tony was sitting in handcuffs with two Greek police when Ragg and Coghlan entered the room. His face fell when he saw the federal agent and the Purana detective. 'I walk in. His eyes went wide and he went, "Jarrod!"' Ragg said. 'I said, "How are you, Tony?" and he shook my hand. He looked genuinely pleased to see me for about five seconds. He then got pretty angry. He got very angry. And he had quite a bit to say about a number of issues.'

Mokbel unleashed a wide-ranging spray threatening Ragg. He told the agent he was prepared to do the jail time over the cocaine charges, but he said when he was provided with the witness statements against him on the Saturday before he left, he had to go. Mokbel told Ragg: 'I won't contest the extradition if Simon Overland agrees to drop the murder charges but otherwise I'll tie things up in Greece for ten years.'

Mokbel was never going to stop trying his luck. He would never stop playing courts and legal systems like lotto machines. He would never stop offering bribes and trying to cut impossible deals. It was just not in his nature. But from the moment Tony saw the Australians he knew it was curtains. He knew the great escape was over.

Mokbel told Coghlan: 'I don't know how you did it, but you've done a brilliant job.'

24

House wins

> Well you wake up in the morning, hear the ding dong ring
> You go a-marching to the table, see the same damn thing
> Knife and fork are on the table, there's nothing in my pan,
> And if you say anything about it, you're in trouble with the man.
>
> – Huddie Ledbetter, 'Midnight Special'

Inside Athens police headquarters a sullen Mokbel confirmed his true identity. Tony took his cap and sunglasses off and the Hellenic police took his fingerprints and mugshots. The iconic picture of the famously balding Mokbel with a face like thunder in an embarrassingly askew wig was beamed around the world.

The authorities' sense of joy and relief at grabbing Fat Tony was made even headier by an opportunity to mock the villain. For Mokbel, his cronies and various lawyers, it left a bitter taste. A cartoonist depicted Tony's rug as a furry woodland animal that – when police arrived pointing pistols – stood up with its paws in the air. 'Nice try,' said Assistant Police Commissioner Simon Overland, getting in on the carnival atmosphere. Editors published those words across the swizzled rug image for maximum effect.

Judge Betty King was on holidays overseas when she learnt Mokbel – and his toupee – had been apprehended. 'I was sitting on a beach in Mexico and I got the text that Mokbel had been arrested but I couldn't get the vision,' she said. 'So I didn't get to see the really bad ferret – like a squashed cat.'

Back in Greece Mokbel's initial sporting recognition of a job well done soured into threats against the Australian detective's family. He was no longer happy to see Coghlan and was equally unimpressed with Ragg, who had been pursuing Mokbel since 2000 and was behind his cocaine conviction. 'When [Ragg] couldn't get at me he went after all my friends and associates, threatening them and trying to get them to give him stuff on me,' Mokbel said. 'It really pissed me off that he was going around pressuring people and putting the screws on them to roll over when we could have just worked things out and come to some sort of plea bargain.'

Ragg did not see it that way. 'This is where Tony's got a warped perspective. I investigated Mokbel hard. My personal opinion is everyone's got a right to a fair trial but the public have a right to expect a vigorous, professional and competent investigation and that's what I tried to deliver,' he said. 'If he took personal offence at that, well, the game he's involved in is a game of criminal activity.'

Coghlan rang Melbourne with the good news: we've got Tony. Shut down The Company. Police had lanced the head of the beast and the green light was given to start lopping the tentacles. If they had reversed the order and gone after Company members first, Mokbel would have been notified and vanished into thin air. 'If we had not got him first then arrested everybody here we'd never get him,' Coghlan said. Instead they got one with the lot.

There were rude awakenings throughout Melbourne on Wednesday 6 June 2007 as more than 120 Victoria Police officers raided twenty-two homes across the city and reduced The Company to rubble. Fourteen Mokbel soldiers were arrested, including Mokbel's amphetamines lieutenants Mansour and Rizzo and speed siblings Issa and Elias, who had helped Tony escape. Tricarico was picked up for following his dead dad into the drug business, and so were Company helpers Benedetti, Ferraro and Ryan. Discoveries made during The Company raids gave rise to dozens of new charges. Raiding officers netted half a kilogram of MDMA, more than $790,000 in cash, and a fortune in other drugs, scales, glassware, jewellery, mobiles, motorbikes, and framed memorabilia from the Al Pacino gangster film *Scarface*.

Greek police interviewed Mokbel and held him on document fraud charges. That afternoon police took him back to his Elliniko apartment for a search. There Danielle and Brittany also learnt it was curtains. Theo Angelakis was interviewed and let go without charge.

The Australians remained for a week, monitoring the media and Mokbel's custody. 'There was an absolute media frenzy. We warned the Greek cops and said there will be a fair bit of media attention. They couldn't believe it,' Agent Ragg said. 'They truly didn't understand the importance of Mokbel's arrest until the media started.'

The then AFP Commissioner Mick Keelty jetted into Athens. It was reported Keelty had been at a conference of South-East Asian police chiefs in Singapore when Greek police arrested Mokbel. Agent Ragg said Keelty was either in Cyprus or on his way to Cyprus. 'He went to Athens to formally thank the commissioner of the Greek police,' Ragg said. 'It was a coincidence. He wasn't flown to this part of the world for that event.'

Others were more sceptical and viewed it as showboating by the plastics. 'The feds are very quick to go around and claim somebody else's work, as they attempted to do when we picked up Tony in Greece,' ex-Purana chief Jim O'Brien said. 'You couldn't get Mick Keelty off the phone quick enough to get over there. Just happened to be in Singapore at the time. Apparently it's a bit close to Greece.'

Danielle said she had known for months, even when still pregnant with Renate, that the police were closing in but she and Tony refused to leave because she was about to give birth. She claimed that while heavily pregnant she had spotted international surveillance teams in Athens just as she had in France and Italy. But her version fails to explain why they did not flee in the time between Renate's birth and Tony's arrest. 'I saw them all through Europe ... and I saw them here too,' she said. 'I was pregnant and about to give birth.'

Once caught Mokbel claimed he had been calling Australia laying the groundwork for a deal to return. 'I don't know how they did it, if it was an informer rolling over, but you've got to give it to them, they found me and got me,' he said. 'I knew I couldn't last forever or even for ten years on the run. I've got Danielle and the kids to think about, and I had already decided to try to do a deal to come back and do some time. I know the police would have been bugging my phone here, and those tapes will show I was already talking to people back in Australia about sending Danielle back to represent me and try to come to an arrangement for me to come back.' But Mokbel also said his plans were to open a restaurant in Greece and work an honest life in the kitchen.

Australian authorities would still face a nearly year-long tooth-and-nail fight trying to lawfully extract a recalcitrant Mokbel from Greece. 'It's a two-step thing. The big success was locating him and arresting him and getting him before a competent court's jurisdiction,' Agent Ragg said. 'That was the big breakthrough. That was the big success. Then we were prepared for what could be years of delay.'

There would still be cause for nerves that Tony could revive his vanishing trick even from custody. But all said it was a famous victory for police. They had caught Australia's biggest drug dealer and most wanted fugitive. There were a few more hoops to jump through but if everything went well the end for Mokbel was nigh.

Tony Mokbel, fallen from the Athenian high life to the slums of a seedy foreign prison cell, recognised the magnitude of the setback. But, delusionally optimistic, his spirit had still not been broken. Tony sincerely believed he would get bail in Greece. When that happened his plan was to reunite with the woman to whom he felt the greatest debt of obligation – *Edwena*, his sloop.

Now he was caught Mokbel could finally tell why, how and where he fled. But instead of a straight, unapologetic rollicking tale he kept silent on the details of his escape and claimed he fled because a fair trial was impossible on his upcoming murder charge. Mokbel claimed the very next month he was planning to contact Ragg to negotiate his return because he was missing his family in Australia 'and life in Greece with McGuire was difficult'.

Mokbel claimed it was McGuire's surprise conception that brought her to Greece. 'He said to me the only reason she's over there is she got pregnant,' Agent Ragg said. 'Knowing her she's visited him in Bonnie Doon, got up the duff, then he's done a runner. She's worked out she's up the duff and then she's joined him,' he said.

Mokbel spent six days in the cells of the Athens police station as a steady stream of drug addicts and sex workers passed through. He hired a local lawyer, Yiannis Vlachos, and sauntered into the central Athens court in jeans, T-shirt and thongs to face false document charges. He insisted Danielle retrieve his infamous wig, as well as his sunglasses, six mobiles, and $2700 in euros, from police custody.

Asked in court whether he had any objections to the extradition warrant he avoided torturous legal arguments. 'Yes,' Mokbel said. 'I don't want to be extradited.' When Australian authorities refused to negotiate, Mokbel instructed his lawyer to use every available option to fight extradition and delay the case as long as possible. Mokbel said he would not have fought extradition had it just been the drugs charges, but he objected to the Lewis Moran murder charge. 'I had nothing to do with any murders and morally it would just be wrong to go to jail for that,' he said. 'I didn't do anything. Why would I be so stupid?'

Asked if he had ever killed anyone, Mokbel insisted: 'No, a million per cent, no.' His denials later assumed a DIY ethos. 'I've never killed anyone, I never had any involvement with killing anyone,' Mokbel said. 'If I was going to kill someone I'd do it myself. I've always been a man like that. I wouldn't get someone to do it for me. It's embarrassing.'

After denying any blood on his hands Tony tried to spin the truly indefensible – his wonky wig of infamy. 'When I took the cap off, it moved,' Mokbel said. 'It doesn't look so bad.' But the photo on his dodgy Stephen Papas driver's licence showed the wig, even on straight, looked jarringly odd – like Tony was attempting to play the thirteen-year-old version of himself in a bad telemovie of his life, although the wig did attract some support from an unexpected quarter – Agent Ragg: 'He copped a lot of flak over that wig. The wig is obviously going to look a bit rough when it's taken off his head, looked at by half a dozen Greek cops and then stuck back on his head sideways.

'You've got to have a bit of empathy for him. It was good enough that they couldn't spot him in it. I feel a bit sorry for him. Danielle was caned for letting him go out with such a monstrosity on him considering her profession [as a hairdresser]. It was a relatively good quality wig if worn correctly and not just banged on his head by cops for a photo.'

Simon Overland also speculated that the terribleness of the wig was part of its criminal genius – it was so bad it drew the eye away from the wearer's face.

Mokbel tired of the squalid conditions of the Athens police cells and the passing parade of prostitutes, pushers and trannies. He complained and asked to be moved. His request was met with a gruff 'This is not a hotel.' Mokbel should have been careful what he wished for. He was soon moved from the cells to one of the worst jails in Europe.

Korydallos prison is a crowded hellhole that houses three times its actual capacity of feral inmates. Mokbel's living conditions were terrible. He routinely complained about nights spent wiping cockroaches off his face. He also grumpily eyeballed Michelin-free vegetable dinners.

Korydallos was also home to some very vicious characters, including members of Greek Marxist terror group 17 November, who were linked to twenty-three assassinations. But the squalid existence was not so bad that Mokbel surrendered his extradition fight, which would have guaranteed an instant ticket back to a Victorian jail. He was, for a time, in one of the cleaner, quieter wings with just one cell mate who was a fellow drug trafficker. Some former inmates said Korydallos was so horrific Mokbel would be begging to come home within weeks. They didn't know Tony.

Mokbel had a multi-pronged legal strategy. His lawyer back home would argue in an Australian court action that the extradition order was invalid because it was signed by the Justice Minister not the Attorney General. In Greece he would seek asylum on the basis that he could never get a fair trial in Australia. More bizarrely, Mokbel had also pulled strings to get Lebanese authorities to apply to extradite him there rather than Australia.

While his hired guns fought the legal battle Mokbel deployed his famous charm during his perp walks to wage the battle for hearts and minds. According to Tony's new script the Athenian waiters who daily noted Mokbel's beaming smile had been mistaken. Mokbel now said his fugitive months were miserable. He had not been living the high life but pining for his barbecue, Hills hoist, thirty-two godchildren and the Aussie fair go. Life on the run was terrible. It was not something he'd wish on anyone, Mokbel said. 'You miss your family and friends. It's not a life,' he said.

After six months living together in Athens the lovers were forced apart. Outside the court a downbeat Danielle breastfed her baby alone in a courtyard. A melancholy Brittany, who had grown fond of her father figure, sat patiently, paying in blues for her mother's latest unorthodox choice of suitor. 'Whether he is guilty or innocent, whatever, we have to think of the kids,' McGuire said. 'I've got to think of the kids. The kids come first. The children are innocent. Leave them alone. I'm sick of my life being portrayed as some kind of bullshit TV drama,' she said. Earlier she had grabbed a female photographer's wrist in a fevered attack. She was angry, she said, at her portrayal in the Australian media as 'some kind of gangster's moll'.

Unable to get a visit from his girlfriend, Brittany, and his lookalike baby girl, Renate, Mokbel started to contemplate making an honest woman of Danielle, or at least marrying her. 'I would marry her and hopefully it would last until the day I die,' Mokbel said. 'I believe every woman in the world deserves a beautiful wedding. If I ever get that chance, I will make it up to her.'

But Mokbel's Greek lawyer let slip that the wedding plans were to get improved visiting rights for Danielle, who had not been allowed to visit him at Korydallos. 'That's probably the biggest killer at the moment – not seeing Danielle and our beautiful daughter and my beautiful Brittany,' Mokbel said. 'It's heartbreaking.' The notorious couple scotched their plans for a jailhouse wedding after they became bogged down in Greek bureaucracy. Mokbel was unable to get documents from Australia proving he was single and therefore free to get married, as demanded by Greek law. He was also facing some resistance from Greek authorities over the planned prison wedding.

When Tony got a chance to address a Greek court he did so in a loud voice, speaking through an interpreter. He admitted fleeing Australia but claimed it was because the authorities there had waged a vendetta against him. He brought to bear some chequered character witnesses, saying quadruple killer Carl Williams had vouched for him.

At the jail Mokbel was permitted exercise in a congested yard for a few hours each day. His lawyer said he was depressed. But on the regular perp walks into and out of court, Mokbel maintained a constantly cool, even cheerful demeanour, winning over his guards and many in the press gang. Waiting in the back row of the chaotic courtroom for his case to come up, Mokbel would laugh and joke with his captors. One day dozens of prostitutes came before the magistrate. 'This is the biggest brothel I've ever seen,' Mokbel joked. But it wasn't.

Tony's affection for Greece remained undimmed despite the dramatic change in his circumstances. Sometimes he was too laidback even for his hosts. Mokbel angered a magistrate by failing to front on a day the mercury edged towards 40°C, the prisoner declaring it too hot to go out. On another no-show his lawyer said his absent client's kidneys were playing up.

When his hearing over the fake document charges was adjourned due to a national interpreters' strike, Tony said he was worried it would make him look like he was trying to hold things up. 'What it does is it makes me look like a monster,' he said.

Mokbel was occasionally moved between Korydallos and the 'softer' Larissa prison out of the city. But by late 2007 nervousness that the important inmate could either escape or become a target saw him consigned to solitary at Korydallos with no view of the sky. Details are sketchy and today police are dismissive that there was a serious escape plan being hatched. But at the time Mokbel's lawyer said: 'There was information from the Australian police that he might try an escape, but also there was information that his life was in danger.' Perhaps it was an Australian ruse to ensure the Greeks gave Mokbel the attention he required. Whatever the case they were keeping their quarry guessing.

'It has not been easy. I've had a tough time,' a haggard Mokbel, flanked by seven armed policemen, said at court. 'I'm OK, though. I'm holding my head up – always. At the moment they've got me in solitary confinement. I don't know why, but, yes, it is very tough.'

Strangely enough Mokbel was not the only Melburnian amphetamines kingpin in Korydallos. Dimitros 'Jimmy' Samsonidis had been busted in Athens in May 2006 by an international sting involving the AFP. He was caught trying to send a tonne of ephedrine to Melbourne for processing into 80 million speed tablets. Samsonidis had done jail time in Victoria in the 1970s when he was convicted of manslaughter, and in the late eighties had become one of Australia's biggest heroin dealers. Samsonidis had been involved with the Moran clan's drug operations as Tony was coming up in the underworld. And police believe Samsonidis had been one of the young Mokbel's 'mentors' who taught him the burgeoning arts of speed cooking and tablet pressing. In November 2007 Samsonidis was sentenced to life in Korydallos.

By late 2007 Mokbel had bounced back and was jogging eight kilometres a day in laps of his jail compound. In the heart of one of the world's most brutal prisons in a foreign country with a foreign tongue, the charismatic Australian managed to get a group of hardened convicts to join his let's-get-physical program. Prison authorities also noted Mokbel's contagious humour but remained guarded lest it was an attempt to lull them into a false sense of security.

'He's got about a dozen other prisoners getting into his routine and the guards are very pleased because they've never behaved better,' his Australian lawyer, Mirko Bagaric, said. 'Next time you see him he'll be as chiselled as Ben Cousins.' The lawyer and academic then slammed as 'scurrilous' police speculation that Tony was getting in shape for a daring escape bid. 'The Greek prisons are some of the best in the world in terms of security,' he said. Others were not so confident.

While Mokbel was in Greek custody Purana detectives in Melbourne charged him with the murder of Michael Marshall.

Tony said the cops were just loading him up to help the extradition attempt. He was partly right. Assuming they could bring Mokbel before an Australian court, prosecutors would only be able to pursue him for charges on which he was extradited. They were taking no chances on leaving any out they may have later wanted to pursue. 'If anyone looks at the brief they'd laugh,' Mokbel said. 'They want to look good.'

What Purana really wanted was to stop Mokbel's legal eagles dodging a prosecution down the line on a technicality of international law. 'Prior to him going to Greece if you hadn't charged him with certain charges you can't then bring him back on three and hit him with another three,' Purana Chief Inspector Bernie Edwards said. 'Everything you think he has done they needed to charge him with those,' he said. 'So if you've got a particular charge – say the murder of Marshall – you would be more inclined to charge. If you don't charge and bring him back and then the case gets really strong, you won't have that option.'

Australian authorities were also nervous that Mokbel could put more egg on their face by slipping away from the laidback and corruptible Greeks. Their anxiety over whether Korydallos could hold Mokbel was not without foundation. Costas Passaris was a gang leader jailed over a litany of assaults and violent robberies. Passaris escaped Korydallos in 2001 while being transferred to hospital. Two police were killed in the process and the local force swarmed on his suspected location. Athens police thought they had him surrounded in his apartment, but somehow, even though he had been shot in the hand, Passaris managed to evade fifty officers waiting for him. The wig method had done little for Mokbel but it worked wonders for Passaris, who, wearing a rug and glasses, walked through a police cordon to freedom. He was eventually caught in Romania.

That was not the only Korydallos cock-up keeping Australian authorities awake at night. In 2006 the Greek Robin Hood – serial armed robber and kidnapper Vassilis Paleokostas, who shared his loot with poor farmers – mounted a spectacular airborne jail break from the fortress prison. A hijacked helicopter had landed in the jail courtyard spiriting away Vassilis and his Albanian sidekick, alleged hitman Alket Rizaj, taking guards by surprise. Guards said they did not react immediately because they thought the blue and white chopper belonged to police. Making matters worse, the plot's mastermind was Vassilis's brother Nikos 'the Phantom' Paleokostas, himself a wanted man who had managed to remain at large for a decade. The escapees deployed smoke flares to cause confusion as the helicopter took off with the two inmates on board. The crooks forced the pilot to land in a nearby cemetery where they fanged it to freedom on waiting motorbikes.

If knowing all this made Australian authorities a little edgy about their prized catch, it was fortunate they could not see into the future. After Paleokostas had been at large for two years, hiding out with his conspirators in mountains outside Athens, he returned to his old tricks. A Greek aluminium tycoon was kidnapped for a twelve million euro ransom and Paleokostas was the prime suspect. Police managed to arrest him two months later and he was returned to Korydallos.

This time the prison was taking no chances. Paleokostas and Rizaj were thrown into solitary confinement. They were removed from solitary only for their trial over their 2006 jailbreak. A day before the court case was to commence another rented helicopter appeared on the horizon. Less than three years after the first escape it all happened again using nearly the exact same method. This time a female passenger in the helicopter threw a rope ladder to Vassilis and Alket in the prison courtyard. The whole thing took four minutes. Guards managed to puncture the fuel tank but not stall its escape as the femme fatale in the chopper returned fire. As inmates cheered, a sinking feeling enveloped the guards, who fired hopelessly into the air and tried to figure out the Greek for déjà vu.

While locked up Mokbel was able to get his hands on several mobile phones. Eternally optimistic, egomaniacal and convinced of his prowess as a deal maker, he phoned the Purana taskforce from his Greek jail. He asked for the officer in command at the time, Detective Jim O'Brien, but was not patched through on his first attempt. O'Brien got a message Tony had called. He instructed that if Tony rang back he was to be put through. Mokbel phoned again and his attempt at getting a deal went something like the following.

O'Brien: 'Hello, Tony.'

Mokbel: 'Jim, let's work this out. Con will speak to Paul when he gets back from overseas on Monday. They'll talk and they'll work out something. We're all prepared to do a little bit of jail but not too much.'

O'Brien: 'Look, come back and we'll have a talk about this.'

Mokbel: 'I'm a drug dealer but I'm not a killer.'

O'Brien: 'Well, come back. All things are possible. Come back and we'll have a talk.'

Con was Con Heliotis, QC, Tony's reliable barrister. Paul was Paul Coghlan, the Director of Public Prosecutions. Tony not only knew the name of the DPP, he knew Mr Coghlan was overseas and he knew when he was getting back. O'Brien's reasonable-sounding offer – 'come back' – was the last thing Tony wanted. 'He was highly against coming back. At that stage the empire was crumbling around him. We never got to have the talk,' Jim O'Brien said.

In Australia Mokbel's legal team sought leave to appeal their flagging wrong-signature-on-the-extradition-order argument to the High Court. Leave was denied. Asked on his regular perp walk outside court by a fellow Australian if he would be home by Christmas, Tony wryly responded: 'I hope not.' The Greek Supreme Court stayed his extradition until his appeal to the Australian High Court was completed. Tony's prize was getting to spend a cruel Yule and new year in a subterranean dungeon-like cell under the floor of Korydallos prison.

As Mokbel's defensive legal actions floundered the jailbird reacted by expanding his coterie of lawyers. He hired a former Greek MP and high-profile celebrity criminal lawyer, Alexandros Lykourezos. The mouthpiece had previously advised accused war criminal Ratko Mladic, the so-called 'Butcher of Bosnia'. 'When you have Lykourezos by your side the other team normally go home – it's over, he will win,' a court observer said.

But in early 2008 Mokbel's stalling tactics ran out. The Greek Supreme Court took just three minutes to order the fugitive back to Australia to face the music on his litany of drug and murder charges. Judge Konstantinos Sarandinos directed four words at Tony which the fugitive did not want to hear: 'You will be extradicted.' Tony's wildcard also failed – a Lebanese warrant arrived just minutes before the decision, but was overruled.

Despite his inherent optimism Mokbel could recognise the dying of the light, and the bigwig wigged out. 'I ran away when I realised I wasn't going to get a fair trial, but there is absolutely no way in a million years I'm going to get a fair go now,' Mokbel said. 'You've had the prime minister and everyone getting stuck into me, so I won't get a fair trial even if I die and come back again and appear in court. You would probably get a fairer trial for me in bloody Indonesia,' he said.

Tony and Danielle exchanged 'I love you darls' across the courtroom as the prisoner was taken away. All that was left was for the Greek government to rubberstamp the decision. But Mokbel refused to concede defeat. He got a new Greek human rights lawyer, Vasillis Hirdaris, and appealed to the European Court of Human Rights.

'Tony was a great believer that he would have got bail in Greece,' said Purana chief Bernie Edwards. 'His plan was he could extend his appeal to the European Court of Human Rights over a number of years, then the court would have to give him bail until that process ended,' he said. 'The way he saw things he had a chance to beat the lot. He believed he could get bail. He's an eternal optimist.'

But before Tony's human rights application got anywhere the Greek Justice Minister signed off on the court's decision. It meant Australian authorities could extradite Mokbel back home to serve out his existing prison sentence and face the new charges.

Some had beaten the system. Christopher Skase and Robert Trimbole remained out of reach of authorities in Spain, which has no extradition agreement with Australia. But after an eleven-month legal fight fraught with fears that Mokbel would once more escape, it was over. Mokbel the uber-gambler had played a near-faultless hand but the house had still won. Fat Tony was coming home.

25

Homecoming

Oh, sinnerman, where you gonna run to?
Oh, sinnerman, where you gonna run to?
Oh, sinnerman, where you gonna run to?
All on that day.

– 'Sinnerman', traditional

For a day and a half the 27-seater Australian jet sat on the tarmac away from the main passenger terminals, guarded against interference by security cameras and foot patrols. If anyone was a candidate to attempt a brazen escape even this late in the game, Tony Mokbel was. Police were conscious he had accumulated hundreds of criminal contacts over the years and still had millions hidden to pay off any helpers.

In addition to those who would want to see Mokbel free rather than brought back to Australia there were plenty who would have preferred to see him dead. Criminals and bent cops alike who had dealt with Mokbel had everything to fear from a man facing a lengthy jail sentence who could decide to tell tales.

At 10.30 the night before he flew out, Tony had a short phone conversation with Danielle from custody. 'I'm going. I love you,' he told her. The next morning the prisoner was woken early and taken from Korydallos jail in a convoy of vehicles and driven fifty minutes to the airport. Industrial action by Athens air traffic controllers threatened to derail proceedings, but any hopes Mokbel might have harboured of a last-minute delay were dashed when the snap strike ended and normal flight times resumed.

After a final check of the plane's fuselage, eight uniformed state and federal police escorted a casual Mokbel, dressed in a black T-shirt and khaki pants, on board. The jet taxied down the runway and took off, leaving Athens just before 9 am Greek time. Out the window was central Athens, the Parthenon, the mountain range where fellow fugitive Paleokostas had hidden out, and the little tram rattling out to Glyfada near where Danielle, Brittany and Renate remained.

The return voyage of Tony Mokbel was decidedly more luxurious than his furtive rough-seas departure. The fugitive was handcuffed and surrounded by burly men with machine guns. But he was also on a private $40 million Gulfstream IV jet hired just for him. The 'con air' flight cost the public $450,000, although authorities said Tony would later pay the bill with seized assets.

With his hands cuffed in front of him Mokbel spoke little during the 21-hour flight home. There were AFP agents and heavily armed Soggies on the Mokbel jet. But unlike at his arrest, there were few familiar faces from his lifetime of being pursued by the law. Sensitivities to the prisoner's shameless ploys and lawyer-happy ways meant officers with close connections to his cases – such as Purana detectives – were left off the plane. 'So there were no allegations: you unofficially promised me this or you pestered him,' Purana chief Bernie Edwards said. 'They were there straight out for transport.'

As on his departing trip Mokbel stopped between Greece and Australia at the Maldives. This time it was in more comfortable circumstances. Mokbel was not doubled over from seasickness and the stop was for refuelling rather than emergency repairs.

As the nation's most notorious criminal winged his way back home plenty of gangland women who had personally known Mokbel were willing to savour his demise. Judy Moran, for one, had not forgiven him. Mokbel was charged with the murder of her ex-partner, Lewis, and Tony had been rolling with Carl Williams when Carl had arranged the deaths of her sons Mark and Jason. Mokbel's capture had given the crime family matriarch a sudden reverence for the forces of law and order.

'I always knew he'd be back here. The police were very strong in their thoughts of getting him back here,' Judy said. 'We must give all gratitude to them and the government. Why should he be over in Greece living the high life? He has to face justice and justice will be served and he won't be out for the rest of his life. I will [celebrate] when he receives the right sentence – life for each murder, not just concurrent. He put my family and myself in a war zone. Justice will be served,' she said. Capitalising on Mokbel's most embarrassing moment she offered to send some of her blonde hair clippings to Tony's jail so he could make himself a new wig.

Another underworld widow, Wendy Peirce, whose husband, Victor, was gunned down by Veniamin, pulled even fewer punches than Judy Moran about the homeward-bound fugitive. 'Personally

I think he's a disgrace. He's got kids of his own and he's allegedly getting charged with the murder of Lewis Moran and he had a wife and kids,' Peirce said. 'I think he's just an arrogant pig. That's the impression I had when I first met him. People say he's a gentleman in a suit and tie. Whether he's in a monkey suit he's still a pig. He came across as being arrogant, short and fat. A bald-headed fat arrogant person. And I hope justice prevails if he's guilty of the murders,' she said. 'I hope justice is served then directed to life in prison.'

There were kinder words for incoming Tony from his would-be mother-in-law, Joan Madin, who he had kept moneyed from abroad. Danielle's mum said her daughter had always been enamoured of Mokbel and would stand by her man. 'My daughter loves him. She has always loved him and she will always be there for him – always,' she told the author.

Roberta Williams also had kind words for the returning renegade. 'Tony was a great bloke. He doesn't put an act on, he's just a great, kind, caring bloke,' she said. 'A very, very excellent bloke, top bloke, one of the best blokes you could ever meet. He's the best dad you could ask for, the best uncle, brother. You can't fault him. He's honest, he's upfront, he'll just say it how it is – he won't piss in your pocket.'

At 6 am on Saturday 17 May 2008 the jet landed in Australia at Port Hedland on the north-west coast. It cleared customs before beginning the final cross-country leg to Victoria. Tony was retracing in reverse his escape route – flying over the transcontinental road trip he had made seventeen months earlier with the Reservoir dogs. Once Mokbel landed on terra firma it was Victoria Police's job to get him into prison without incident.

Despite the massive interest, the details of Mokbel's return were kept a tightly held secret. There was a series of diversions and false alarms as Mokbel's hometown press scrambled desperately to establish where Fat Tony would land. Speculation was rife that the jet could land at Avalon airport, not far from his ultimate destination of Barwon prison near Geelong. Rumours also circulated that on Saturday morning Soggies had been seen training at Point Cook, which suggested the RAAF base was another possibility. One school of thought predicted Mokbel would land in Adelaide then be taken by road more than seven hours to his cell.

By early afternoon Essendon Airport firmed as a late-breaking smokie after a prison van was spotted pulling out of a hangar. In the end mysterious van sightings were red herrings and all the chatter was just white noise filling the vacuum of a frustratingly well-kept secret.

After 15,000 kilometres and twenty-one hours in the air, Fat Tony finally landed in his hometown in rain on the outskirts of the city's main airport at Tullamarine at 1 pm. It was a bleak, gunmetal-grey, bitter, wet Melbourne day. Six Soggies walked the handcuffed crim from the jet to a waiting helicopter. A second helicopter took off as a decoy. Authorities were nervous that until Mokbel was safely behind bars at Barwon, he might still pull off another dangerous stunt. 'There were concerns about him escaping, people getting at him and the safety of the police involved,' said Edwards.

An armoured van travelled south from New South Wales. In the back was another crew of Special Operations Group officers and Purana chief Bernie Edwards. They met the whirlybird in a paddock near Barwon and Mokbel was escorted from the chopper to the van.

It can be frustrating being a straight cop, following the rules to the letter and restraining your dislike of lawyered-up millionaire criminals. But there are some small pleasures. There was a leak in the roof of the armoured vehicle and the grisly weather was manifesting itself inside the van in a constant cold water drip onto a seat. 'That's where Tony got to sit,' Purana chief Edwards said. 'Because he was the last one in.'

Mokbel was given his paper warrants and told a bail justice would visit him later in prison. 'Documents had to be served on him prior to him being in custody. Everything was planned down to the most minute detail so there wouldn't be an argument – "You should have served documents on him before prison,"' Edwards said. He said the secrecy of the operation was to protect those bringing Mokbel back. 'If I was sitting on that plane and every man and his dog knew every detail, I would be fuming,' he said.

Barwon maximum-security prison rises out of flat paddocks in Lara near Geelong. A nondescript driveway leads into a haphazard carpark in the shadow of a stone building that looks more like a medieval castle than a modern jail. Not long after the helicopters hit the air, the armoured van containing Mokbel followed by a blue four-wheel-drive rolled up the drive and straight into the jail compound. And with that Mokbel's wet, confusing, rumour-filled, anticlimactic homecoming was over, and the fugitive was banged up back home.

A bail justice held an out-of-sessions hearing in the prison to avoid risks associated with taking Mokbel into the inner-city courts. Never one to shy away from an unreasonable request, Mokbel no doubt raised, as he said he would, the prospect of bail. But with the fugitive's excellent adventures still fresh in everyone's memory, the court official remanded the prisoner in custody.

Inside the jail his new neighbours included his long-time friend Carl Williams, a number of their gangland acquaintances whose names are suppressed, and Muslim terror plotters. If the weather was a comedown from Greece it would be hard to describe what Barwon's culinary offerings must have looked like compared to fresh seafood, souvlaki and dolmadikia. The prison kitchen's chicken slop with bun would struggle to keep Fat Tony in the manner to which he had become accustomed.

Tony had lasted two years and two months on the run since failing to show at court. 'Getting him back was great but we knew all the trials were going to follow,' said Jim Coghlan. 'The absolute exhilaration for me was the arrest over there. Going to Greece and those three weeks.' Now that he was back behind bars the police job was over. Officers would still have to give evidence at Tony's trials but the rest was down to the prosecutors.

Inspector Edwards: 'It's a fantastic story for the people involved and the previous management of Purana. Jim O'Brien left before Mokbel was brought back. Pity he wasn't here for that.'

Edwards, O'Brien and Coghlan have all been coppers for about three decades and the bringing to justice of the Mokbels was likely to remain the pinnacle of their careers. 'We've been in the job for what, twenty-eight years, nearly thirty years,' Detective Sergeant Jim Coghlan said. 'Nothing I can do from here on in can compare to this.'

26

Bigwigs

> I spent a lot of my money on booze, birds and fast cars. The rest I just squandered.
>
> – George Best

Towards the twilight of the Mokbels' decades-long crime wave a defence barrister claimed the family's notoriety had reached a point where they compared to noteworthy historical crims Ned Kelly and Squizzy Taylor. Portraying Horty, Milad, Tony and Kabalan by inference as a kind of meth-running Kelly gang for the 2000s is too flattering a comparison. But there are some superficial similarities between bushranger Ned and bigwig Tony.

Mokbel's great escape and ability to remain at large, evading and outsmarting a massive manhunt while his legend grew, echoed Ned's dashing feats. While at large both funnelled ill-gotten gains to ensure the loyalty of insiders who could dob them in. And despite their efforts both were betrayed by a member of their gang turned snitch. But that's where the similarities stop.

Ned Kelly will always be hated in some quarters because police were killed in cold blood. But there are many who regard the Kellys as small-time crooks oppressed, harangued and pushed to breaking point by dodgy members of the local constabulary. Ned never got rich from his criminal efforts, instead distributing his stolen wealth to impoverished settlers. The Mokbels turned to crime out of boredom and greed and kept the riches for themselves. Ned believed in some things bigger than himself – intangible things like unswerving loyalty, and concrete aims like turning north-eastern Victoria into a republic. Tony, on the other hand, believed in Tony.

The Mokbel mouthpiece was much closer to the mark with the Squizzy Taylor comparison. Squizzy was described as a colourful and dapper figure who dressed loudly, and strutted through Melbourne's courts, racecourses and theatres.

The striking similarities between the Depression-era spiv and new millennium crime boss don't end with surface style. Joseph 'Squizzy' Taylor liked to sell cocaine and hang out at the track. He had an unflattering nickname foisted upon him (after a squinty, ulcerated eye). He dabbled in prostitution and profited from selling drugs and fixing horseraces. Like Tony, Squizzy dodged several convictions over serious crimes for which he should have gone down. And he ran a lucrative jury-rigging business and boasted of subverting the justice system.

Like Tony, Squizzy was a principal figure in a Melbourne gangland war that broke out between rival crime clans. Several men were shot in the underworld upheaval but Squizzy emerged at the end unscathed. He also thought nothing of having someone killed if they stood in his way. After being caught by police he was charged but fled, became a fugitive, and eluded police for a year.

It remains to be seen whether there will ever be a pub named in Tony's honour, as there has been for Squizzy. More likely somewhere along the line a still-loyal associate will name a racehorse Fat Tony, as has been done for Tony's old speed contact Kiwi Joe. If authorities object we might see a more cryptic equine tribute like Achache Prince.

Mokbel always had a lot of names to choose from. He had been many things to many people and had a plethora of titles to show for it. He had started life as Antonios, which became Tony once subjected to affectionate Australian abbreviation. That became Fat Tony and, as his tentacles spread, he became in newspaper-speak the Octopus. Occasionally circumstances dictated others give him a different name, like when TV producers had to call him Mr B to disguise the notoriety of his real identity. Sometimes he had to change his name himself – to Yanni or Stephen Papas – to flee the consequences of his actions. But while the label might have changed the substance stayed constant. Whatever his nom du jour Mokbel's criminal instincts and insatiable lust for scams and clams remained diabolically consistent.

From a young age Mokbel had determined his would be a life of opportunism. In fact he routinely asked if things were 'dodgy', using the word – different to most – as a positive adjective. If the response was that the particular person, product or scheme was dodgy, Mokbel would light up and want in. But while he was a natural born crim Mokbel would never have graduated to bigwig had he not, underneath, also been something of a talented businessman. The crime kingpin possessed two traits common to most self-made millionaires: an unwavering self-belief and a fearless gambling streak. But his most marked entrepreneurial trait was his scattergun approach to investment. It earnt Mokbel and those in cahoots with him a secret fortune.

It was not just pills and ponies, although on the latter one informed source said the Mokbels secretly controlled up to eight racehorses, greatly improving their ability to pick winners. Police suspected Mokbel secretly owned more than a dozen pubs and clubs. He and Milad had the run of some of Chapel Street's most colourful after-dark venues despite their names not appearing on any documents. Nightclub insiders said the Mokbels were likely to have had an interest in scores more across Melbourne. Mokbel's property speculation was so rampant that after he was jailed authorities were still untangling assets owned by his extensive network of contacts on his behalf. The extent of his brothel ownership and investment in the sex industry is also still largely unknown and the source of much urban legend.

As well as the big schemes Mokbel would jump into anything else: cheap suits off the back of a truck, business loans to fledgling enterprises, muscling into legitimate ventures, sending heavies to persuade people to transfer their liquor licence to him, loan sharking to hopeless gamblers, or a bet on two flies walking up a wall.

The drug trade is not without its slings and arrows. Police can threaten not just business but liberty. And rivals can threaten not just liberty but life. However, jail and the reaper aside, the ability to turn a large profit from drugs makes it much more of a no-brainer than real business. There is no red tape, no quarterly statements, no tax, no employee entitlements to pay, and the return on investment is incomparable to any legal product. There are also no consumer protection laws to worry about. If Tony had been in the canned-fruit trade and his product started making people as sick as The Company's occasional poisonous yields, he would have been out of business. That said, Mokbel knew his industry and he knew it could make him money wherever, whenever. The high school dropout was also no minnow when it came to knowledge of the various complicated multi-step processes that can be used to create meth from more easily obtained chemicals.

If he spent the early part of his career dodging drug charges and denying he was a drug dealer, Mokbel dropped the facade once he was accused of being a killer. I'm not a killer, I'm a drug dealer, he would tell police. Mokbel was comfortable with the role. He was a drug lord the same way his uncle was a priest. It was what he did. It was his job. And while he waited for the world to catch up he would get on with his lucrative trade. Getting the stuff past objecting authorities just required extra cunning, skills and leadership, which Mokbel reckoned he had in spades.

'He either doesn't realise or doesn't care about the health of the nation,' Detective Inspector Bernie Edwards said. 'I don't think he really, *really* looks at drug trafficking as if "I'm killing all these people, I'm going to stuff the health system." He just knows it's lucrative.'

When Mokbel was living in disguise in Athens he made a phone call outlining a plan for a mass movement of drugs. Tony spoke of using fishing trawlers and making a mid-ocean transfer from one boat to another of drums full of drugs. The high seas plot was outlined by Mokbel just a week before he was arrested. Tony, it seems, was starting to set up business in Greece. It is less clear if he was being helped by Theo Angelakis or even Samsonidis. Whatever the case, the informer who brought him down, the Grifter, had laid a template for this kind of entrepreneurialism at large by establishing a global drug business while AWOL overseas. It is almost certain that had Mokbel not been arrested he would have established a Greek drug operation to run in tandem with his Australian syndicates. While in Australia Mokbel was constantly importing from overseas, but the boldness of going truly global while a wanted fugitive was both breathtaking and typical.

Only Tony Mokbel knows just how much money he made in his career. And perhaps, after all the dud bets, lobsters, loans and ladies, even he might struggle to give an accurate reckoning. Presented with estimates he would likely scoff and beseech 'Turn it up,' sticking to his public version of history that he's a small-time crook. But the known record on Mokbel's family syndicate says different. Fifteen million dollars worth of clean coal technology shares were frozen for allegedly being owned by Horty Mokbel. Milad has fought efforts to seize $5 million of his assets. And digging up Renate's uncle's yard reaped half a million in cash and jewels.

All up an estimated $55 million in assets have been seized from Mokbel and his associates by authorities. But trying to estimate Mokbel's millions is like peering through a keyhole to calculate Aladdin's booty. Purana's taskforce Senior Detective Abigail Hantsis told a court: 'For every dollar we have seized off the defendant and his family, we estimate that there is another $5 buried in someone's backyard.' The one-sixth-seized estimate puts the Mokbel fortune at a third of a billion dollars. This figure likely factors in assets police suspect really belong to the Mokbels but can't prove. It may not include Mokbel assets that authorities have absolutely no idea about – what Donald Rumsfeld would call 'unknown unknowns'.

Associates like the one who estimated that Mokbel made $100 million in the back end of his career were basing it on the operations they knew of. But not even Tony's brothers knew all his investments and businesses. The Company thought that they were it, that they were Mokbel's crew. But detectives said Mokbel did not just have *The* Company – he had Companies. He put individual members of importing, supplying and manufacturing crews together in an arrangement where only he could see the whole ant farm.

For decades Tony ran a number of meth-making syndicates, sometimes simultaneously, and imported almost every other type of illegal substance. Hundreds of millions of dollars would have passed through Fat Tony's hands during his life of crime, sweetened by gambling wins from the tracksuit era onwards. Known drug yields connected to Mokbel cast some light on the scale of his earnings. After it exploded it was found that the Brunswick lab was producing drugs with a potential street value of $78 million. It is not known whether his Coburg and other labs beat that figure. His busted elephantine hash import would have been worth $147 million on the street. The Mexican cocaine import Mokbel considered barely worth it amounted to three-quarters of a million bucks. Police fear they missed a $50-million pill import and claim he took delivery of chemicals that could make $14 million worth of drugs.

We know Mokbel planned an MDMA import and claimed he could make up to $20 million worth of ecstasy pills in a short time. The Company was producing tens of millions of dollars of meth. The Rye lab could earn $560,000 in less than two days. Mokbel boasted at one point that he had chemicals to make him $1 million in less than two months. The Strathmore lab run by Milad was apparently pumping out $1 million of drugs a week. And the marina project the Mokbels tried to crash was worth $200 million. There were others but to continue the roll call makes the colossal funds involved just seem like Monopoly money. As well as these there are the drug imports that got under the radar and the clan labs that kept pumping out speed undetected. Factor in the family network's cash flows that went unseen or got away, and the wealth involved becomes dizzying. Hundreds of millions stacked on hundreds of millions quickly add up to substantial fractions of billions.

The largest deal Mokbel was ever connected with was the ephedrine import. It placed him at the head of a $2,000,000,000 drug ring but the prosecution was ultimately scotched because of police corruption. The whole weird science of trying to quantify an illegal, paperless, deliberately invisible, multi-layered business run over decades can yield some truly terrifying figures for criminal profits. But the drugs and money that passed through Mokbel's hands or control, not just what he managed to keep, must have gone a large chunk of the way towards making him a billion-dollar bigwig.

John William Samuel Higgs was consolidating his operations in the 1980s and by the nineties was reputedly behind the largest amphetamine ring in Victoria. When Higgs was near the height of his powers, as was seen in the taped dealings with Kiwi Joe, Mokbel was making his presence felt and working toward his own grand plan. Higgs went to jail after being busted by fallen drug detective Wayne Strawhorn, who was also close to Mokbel before he had him brought in. Until Mokbel stole both titles Higgs was the nation's speed king and the last drug trafficker banned from the track by racing authorities.

There are plenty of ruthless, amoral, money-hungry criminals in Australia. Some struggle to get a stolen TV past the counter at Cash Converters. Few become multimillionaires. And almost none get to the level of wealth that Mokbel reached. The lubricants of Mokbel's criminal success have been his charm, charisma and gift of the gab. Even now in prison where his sociopathic past is well known, and where he is attempting to harangue officials into better conditions through complaints, jail sources say their most high-profile prisoner is 'renowned for being charming'.

Of course lovable Tony can quickly turn to ugly threats. But these have been an absolute last resort when faced by someone immune to his charm. The Grifter, Mick Gatto, 'weak link' Parisi, the Stooge and Milad's cook turned informant are among those who have got the chilling impression Mokbel might suddenly have them knocked. Before third parties intervened, a female debtor feared for her safety after Horty personally threatened to harm her unless she paid up, an underworld source said. But for ninety-nine per cent of situations Mokbel could charm, spin, beg, lie or cajole his way to what he wanted. The best liars believe what they say. There is no room for self-doubt in this dynamic. Tony was in Tony's corner arguing the case for Tony. And there is not a set of stark unflattering facts in existence that Mokbel would not attempt to spin in his own favour.

A good persuader knows that repetition, like a constant drip on a large stone, can wear the recipient down. It can even make the incredible seem credible. It is remarkable to go over the records of Mokbel's responses at the only point in his life he was interviewed multiple times – during his custody and court walks in Athens. His responses, in the guise of the candour of the moment, such as the 'we were all friends' gangland war line, are almost identical quotes only slightly altered. The unflagging self-serving spin – it was a good wig, it just moved – coupled with his opportunistic criminality meant Mokbel's motives for the most standard human endeavours would remain in doubt even after the Gospel According to Tony had been delivered.

The timing of his wedding plans was certainly suspicious. Tony had dated Danielle as a free man for years. The relationship continued while she served a stretch. But it was only once Tony was banged up in a Greek jail that wedding bells started to ring in our protagonist's ears. Mokbel's lawyer let it slip that the matrimonial plot was to improve his client's visiting rights. But even when Mokbel admits an angle, it's hard not to wonder whether the ostensible candour is not masking a different angle altogether.

For years Mokbel's supporters said he was a property developer not a drug tycoon. Mokbel then said he was a drug dealer not a killer. He later said if he was going to have someone killed he would do it himself and not hire a hitman. When nabbed he said he was making plans to come back to Australia anyway. When nabbed he also said he planned to live out his days making an honest living in a kitchen in Greece. Mokbel said he fled Australia at the eleventh hour in his cocaine case because he was never going to get a fair trial. Once he was nabbed he apologised to Judge Gillard whose bail he breached but said essentially: Now I'm really not going to get a fair trial.

Mokbel told a female reporter he wanted to marry Danielle because every woman deserved that special day. But he then made no applications once moved from a Greek to a Victorian prison to reignite the matrimonial flame. Were the wedding plans a bid for sympathy from Greek authorities? Was the aim to improve their legal status? Was it, as stated, to gain prison visits? Or was it a few steps ahead – for sympathy from potential female Australian jurors?

Danielle getting pregnant when they last saw each other before meeting in Greece would normally be regarded as an endearing quirk of fate. But with Tony you always have to wonder: was it a Ronnie Biggs baby? Was it meant to help their status as Greeks in an emergency? What are the chances after years together that their last dalliance before Mokbel fled led to their first child?

There was some speculation the bub could be used to help the fix her dad was in. Experts said maybe but probably not. 'It would raise the prospect of him making the argument that his removal from Greece would create significant difficulties for his family,' said Australian National University professor Don Rothwell. 'On my understanding ... I wouldn't see [Renate] as sufficient reason to refuse extradition.' It does not clarify anything much but Tony said Renate was unplanned. 'We didn't plan it. It happened,' he said. 'I wasn't aware of it until some months down the track. Danielle wanted to keep her. I'm glad, she's a beautiful baby.'

The strange timing of baby Renate, if not planned, indicates Tony was less of a cunning plotter than the facts of his life would suggest – and more of a reckless chancer who got continually lucky. If planned Renate simply did not turn out to be the emergency magic jail key her old man might have hoped. And then while Mokbel was locked up in Greece, his empire crumbled. 'That's what it was about for us,' Jim O'Brien said. 'It was about pulling it apart brick by brick and just letting it crash around him. It was all planned.'

O'Brien has little sympathy for the adult Renate or the Mokbel women generally who, while their men are in jail, now linger among broader society like the last stragglers at a finished party. 'They're quite happy to [metaphorically] prostitute themselves and live off the back of it and have their kids live off it and all the rest of it,' he said. Mokbel undoubtedly loved his kids, O'Brien said. 'But then he's quite happy to shovel drugs down your kids' throats and mine as long as it's not his own.'

For those who pursued him for years the rise and fall of the insatiable crime boss was down to pure pragmatism. 'He ran a milk bar in Rosanna for a little while and that didn't do anything and he thought, "Shit, there's more to life than doing this,"' Jim Coghlan said. 'When you talk about Tony Mokbel to me, Tony Mokbel isn't just a person. Tony Mokbel is a group. He had a company running for him.'

Agent Ragg was motivated during his seven-year pursuit of Mokbel by the simple thrill of hunting a good crook. 'It's about doing the job. You've got a crook. He's a good crook. You've got a good brief on him. He's a crook that's worth putting the effort into,' Ragg said. 'There's a lot of allegations from him that I made it personal. But it's never been personal for me. He's just a crook. That's all he is. He's a drug importer. And that's as far as it goes.'

It seems every cop who has dealt with Mokbel has a slightly different view. 'You've got to be careful with him because he's not stupid but he's certainly by no means intelligent,' one, who did not want to be named, said. 'He's got a lot of street cunning. But he's done some bloody stupid things.'

For authorities, criminal bigwigs like Mokbel are a clear and present danger not just to the public but to the public purse. According to Jim O'Brien: 'The two greatest fears to any parent in this community today and repeated across Australia are simple. It is that your children will either, one, become killed in a motor vehicle accident or, two, they'll end up using illicit drugs. What is the cost? Illicit drug use costs the state government $845 million a year. Some single aged pensioners would be very happy if they had that amount of money going to settle drug issues. One murder is costed out to the state at $1.6 million a year. We have probably between seventy to a hundred murders a year in Victoria.'

Fat Tony may end up behind bars for a long time, but caging him will not completely address the Mokbel phenomenon. 'I think law enforcement can learn a lot about well-resourced and determined criminal organisations from an examination of the Mokbel organised crime syndicate,' said Agent Ragg. Wealthy, cunning Mr Bigs with cadres of the best lawyers, corporate structures, and a war chest for corruption and extortion pose a serious if not existential threat to the justice system.

It can be striking how much heat and smoke can surround a criminal without ever combusting into actual convictions. Mokbel's mate Lucky is the perfect case in point. His experiences in the crime world also underscore how fleeting life and death can be on the streets Tony inhabited. One of Crown Casino's two hundred biggest gamblers, Lucky shared his friend's passion for a punt and more than a little of Tony's teflon coating when it came to dodging convictions. Police suspected Lucky was involved in Mokbel's hashish and ephedrine imports that led to both of them being picked up in the August 2001 swoop. But Lucky emerged unscathed from his brush with the law. His ephedrine charges were dropped and he was found not guilty over the hash haul.

Lucky, who also had legitimate transport dealings, was regarded in drug importation circles as a very useful man for his little black book of dodgy dock and freight workers. But the danger and ruthlessness of Mokbel's world became more starkly apparent in some of Lucky's alleged later work. Police are still trying to establish whether Tony had any connection to these later drug hauls.

Lucky was arrested by the federal police in 2005 over an import of five million ecstasy tablets – or more than a tonne of the illegal drug. The crime had followed Tony's modus operandi of hiding the drugs in a container of tiles and 'piggybacking' it through in a shipment registered to and bound for a real company. Lucky, unlike two of his colleagues, had not been caught red-handed with the drugs. He was purportedly bankrupt yet had recently lost $726,000 gambling. And while the drug case against him was not strong, the court noted that the bankrupt's outlay of 'astronomic sums' at the Casino did raise questions. Ultimately the two removalists were convicted but Lucky and three others were acquitted and walked from court.

Lucky's involvement with the justice system did not finish there. He was arrested in 2008 over a world-record ecstasy bust with twenty other suspects including Mokbel-predecessor Higgs and alleged members of the local Italian mob. Lucky was later charged over the importation of six tonnes of pseudoephedrine to make speed and ice, hidden in fruit juice cartons and smuggled from Asia.

The danger for bit players in Lucky and Mokbel's drug world bubbled to the surface in the import of the five million ecstasy tablets over which Lucky was acquitted. One of the alleged helpers in that conspiracy was Antonio Sergi. During the trial the prosecutor claimed: 'While Sergi is doing the hands-on work, Mr Lucky is effectively pulling the strings in the background.' It seems some of the criminal bigwigs behind the scheme were concerned by Sergi's arrest and particularly worried he would not keep his mouth shut.

Sergi was lured on false pretences to a Moonee Ponds park in the very early hours of a Sunday morning in November 2005. He was sitting in his vehicle – the favoured gangland trap as the car boxes in the target – when a gunman snuck up and fired three shots through the passenger window. The dispatch from a high-calibre handgun hit Sergi in the chest and both arms. Sergi played dead and when the assassin fled he drove himself, bleeding like a stuck pig, to the nearby police station for help. Miraculously he survived. He ignored police pleas to give evidence against his attackers, but staying staunch proved to be no invisible shield. Sergi became the subject of another bungled attempt on his life three months later.

Hitman Craig Bradley had been seen staking out Sergi's Sydenham home and was suspected of heading there in a stolen car to kill his mark when he crashed into a nearby house. A concerned neighbour who came to the crash scene saw that Bradley had a gun and called police as he fled on foot. Two officers trawling the area recognised a man on foot in a leather jacket who fitted the description on their police radio. One of the cops got out of the squad car and shouted to Bradley: 'Keep your hands where I can see them, I want to talk to you.' But Bradley pulled his gun out and fired five shots at the officer, who dived back into the cop car as two bullets hit his boots and another grazed his shin. The police driver jumped out and trained his weapon on Bradley, who fired a shot at him, missed, and then fled.

Bradley was arrested later in a nearby street having dumped two sets of rubber gloves, a balaclava and the gun. When police searched him they found a piece of paper detailing Sergi's address and number plate and a photo of the intended target with a cross drawn over his right eye.

Lucky's links to matters of mortality did not end there. In March 2009 Purana detectives grabbed Lucky and Francesco Madafferi, his co-accused in the record ecstasy bust, as they left court. Lucky's associates attacked, spat at and cursed journalists after he was arrested outside the court. The pair were questioned over two alleged murder plots due to have occurred in March and July the previous year, both of which were cancelled at the last minute. And Madafferi was charged with conspiracy to commit murder. But it seemed once more Lucky had dodged a bullet.

Most criminals pose little threat to civilised society because they are so easily caught red-handed. They can be found catching taxis to crime scenes, wearing super sheer pantyhose on their head to rob banks, using their credit card to hire trailers to move bodies, or in one case leaving severed fingertips – complete with actual prints – on a broken window at the crime scene.

Then there are the Tony Mokbels. They play the odds, pay top dollar to top lawyers and delay trials until something comes up. It's not that they think they will never get caught, just that they are willing to do a bit of time here and there, spend a lot of their life living it up on bail, and in the meantime make millions from the constant manufacture, import and sale of drugs. They have the kind of criminal corporate memory that used to belong only to mafia-style groups: anti-surveillance techniques, walk and talks, assets in others' names, and trading drugs in quantities just under the limit of what the law regards as a more serious offence.

The individual judicial decisions that helped Mokbel may themselves make perfect sense, but taken as a whole they beggar belief. Given the epic ambitions of drug syndicates like Mokbel's it is reasonable to assume they will, as they have, continue their criminal activities while on bail. According to Jim O'Brien: 'Organised crime is great at succession planning. During the course of Purana we saw that on a number of occasions where they had people they knew were going to jail due for sentence and out on bail who were actually teaching others how to manufacture drugs.

'What's going on with the Magistrates Court at Melbourne? Why are people like [a Mokbel drug manufacturer], who were large commercial quantity cooks, drug traffickers, released on bail? A day after [they're] put in the boot of the car and driven to a major lab in Gisborne by Tony Mokbel to start cooking again. Why are these people on bail?'

Part of the problem appears to be the inability of a list of prior convictions to convey the reality of the danger of particular defendants being released. Mokbel's career shows how a relatively short list of priors can mask a life of crime and a trail of jailed fall guys. Decisions like the one by the magistrate who released Mokbel while the Grifter was out (before a judge later corrected the mistake) also fundamentally jeopardise a working cog in the system – the ability of police to get criminals to feel confident enough to turn witness.

A senior police source who did not wish to be named said courts had been manipulated by lawyers who had forgotten their obligation to be officers of the court: 'The court is utterly abused by barristers representing these people. Tactics of delay do nothing but weaken the prosecution but that's what they're all about. Witnesses against Mokbel were initially quite happy to do their civic duty. And as his notoriety increased and the gangland wars went on people were abjectly terrified giving a minor piece of evidence in a large case. They know the longer they drag things out the harder it is to prosecute. It's all fair but I believe an abuse of process. There needs to be some consideration from the judiciary.'

Mokbel's indefatigable attempts to bribe authority figures, including judges, could be explained as part of his character. Tony was an eternal optimist who thought everyone had their price. When his philosophy was threatened by someone who would not be bought he would change in a flash from charming to chilling. More ominously, Mokbel's incessant bribe attempts could suggest at some point they were a success. Organised crime needs corruption to exist and prosper – and not just in the police force. Mokbel told crime colleagues he once paid a magistrate $20,000 for the right result. Mokbel could be a terrible skite but at least some of the time his big talk was matched by his big actions.

In the trenches at the front line of the war on drugs things are stacked fairly evenly. Savvy drug criminals who have good barristers and don't use their product can make an easy few million without a great risk of doing time. Importers with cronies on the docks and with access to customs have brilliant odds. 'There's never going to be a recession in policing in Victoria or anywhere else. It doesn't suffer a recession,' O'Brien said.

Levelling the field for the good guys are instances of heavy financial investment and police leadership. Victoria Police dropped the ball on the underworld and the drug squad aided rather than suppressed the gangland war. But Purana is an international example of where thoughtful funded policing succeeds.

Also helping the forces of law and order are technological advances such as telephone intercepts – TIs – and the seeming inability of villains to watch what they say on phones they suspect are off. TIs have been like kryptonite to some groups in organised crime. Police are now racing the future to work out new and better ways to intercept email. Many crooks currently in jail around Australia might be enjoying the sunshine had they put down their beloved mobiles and visited an internet cafe instead.

But insiders say the fight against the major drug trade is fundamentally conflicted on two fronts. The first is belief. Drug policy is undermined by the reality that large swathes of society take or have taken illicit drugs like cannabis and ecstasy. In recognition of this police give well-behaved ravers paper fines and diversions when they are caught with ecstasy. It would be deluded to think all police were Elliot Ness-style teetotallers who live separately from the drug culture.

Experts say we need to establish whether there should be a war on drugs, and if so what drugs should be included. There need to be good health reasons to maintain the unenforced illegality of some drugs while legal drugs like alcohol are behind so much damage, and tobacco addicts are free to smoke cigarettes through tracheotomy holes outside public hospitals. But however imperfect our drug policy is, it does not mean jailed kingpins are political prisoners, as some seem to believe. The people at the top of the drug trade are very nasty characters. In poor countries and ghettos they prey on their local communities, rule by fear and kill to get ahead. Sometimes they insert cocaine in women's thighs, sew them up, and force them to catch international flights in half-dead states. The best argument against buying drugs is not the sort we always hear but to personally boycott the monstrous actions behind the trade.

The second thing law enforcement insiders state is hobbling the fight against drugs is will. Once society arrives at a policy it actually believes in and decides where on the supply chain the war should be fought – for instance, heroin importers – then that war should be actually and seriously prosecuted. There is a smug view masquerading as informed worldliness that the war on drugs is unwinnable. That view assumes that a war has already actually been waged and funded with winning in mind, but there is a lot more that could be done.

Australia is an island. It is not like America with the drug cartels of Mexico on its doorstep and a porous border with Canada. Only one in twenty shipping containers are X-rayed by customs. Comprehensive international freight checks rather than rare random ones would make a difference. So would removing the convicted criminals, associates and suspects who bring the drugs and precursors from jobs at airports, wharves and transport companies. The right of suspected criminals to work on the wharves should not be confused with fundamental human rights like life, liberty, freedom of speech and freedom from tyranny. Even further inroads might be made if the system stopped eating itself with delays, granting bail to syndicate drug cooks and giving rich Mr Bigs taxpayers' dollars in Legal Aid.

Ultimately there may be no barriers to kamikaze kingpins as relentless as Tony Mokbel. He was one of the most successful crooks that Australia has ever seen. Government posters warning of the dangers of ice now dot his old Brunswick stamping grounds, a legacy of the dangerous local industry he helped pioneer. Even as authorities clamped down on Mokbel's properties in Noosa and elsewhere, he was seeking to keep them by 'selling' them to cronies who would deny knowing Tony. He survived a gangland war that put dozens to death and then was one of the last survivors to be jailed.

It has taken more than a decade to put the Mokbels behind bars, but for police the Tony Mokbel story has a happy ending. Agent Ragg said he won't forget his years pursuing Mokbel. 'There's a lot of things learnt. Never give up. Professionalism and persistence. Just because it's hard, don't give up. The harder it is probably the more worthwhile it is,' he said. 'Things went on during those eight years that certainly shaped my career and taught me to be a better investigator.'

In the meantime we can only guess how many other little Tonys whose names we don't yet know are working the courts and working their way up to bigwig. For them the romance of crime and the lure of easy money and outsmarting the authorities is probably as seductive as it was to Mokbel. But crims that get the luxury of living to an old age see things differently from the other end.

Billy 'the Texan' Longley was a convicted killer and union hard man in the Painters and Dockers war decades before Mokbel's heyday. Longley and ex-cop Skull Murphy became unlikely mates and do presentations to at-risk students warning them about the grisly reality of a life of crime. The kids won't take it from an ex-copper, but they listen to the spiel by the Texan when he delivers his toe-curling cautionary tale to the teen delinquents who might fancy themselves as the next Mr Bigs:

'Listen, son. I'm an old criminal. If you want to be a criminal I'll tell you how to be a criminal. I'll tell you how to go and get a gun and put it to someone's head, or how to rob a bank or do all these kinds of things. But remember this. You're a good-looking young boy. You're seventeen or eighteen and you're going to go to jail. And when you get out to Pentridge or a place like that, because you're so good-looking they're going to put you down on the ground and they're going to bloody well stick it up your arse. And you will be biting pieces out of the concrete kerbing. That's what's going to happen to you.

'If you want me to tell you how to be a criminal after all that, I'll tell you.'

27

Dead cat bounce

> There will come a day
> And youth will pass away
> Then what will people say about me
> When the end comes I know
> They'll say 'Just a gigolo'
> As life goes on without me.
>
> – Julius Brammer, Irving Caesar and Leonello Casucci,
> 'Just a Gigolo'

The way police had located Mokbel overseas meant they did not instantly know all the details, nor all the people, involved in his escape. After he was arrested detectives were still unravelling Tony's tangled trail. They discovered money being paid to four Greek men and when they investigated further discovered all four recipients were sailors.

'Why are sailors receiving money? Have they ever come to Australia?' Detective Sergeant Jim Coghlan asked. 'We do the checks. All of a sudden we've got four in Sydney,' he said. 'We found cheques made up to a bloke in Sydney who sold a yacht and pieced it all together.'

It must have been a nervous few months for those who had actively or passively helped Mokbel in his escape. They knew Tony had been nabbed in Greece but they did not know how much of the puzzle police had filled in and whether they were even traceable to the plot. Eventually everyone, from the Reservoir dogs to the Zeidans, got a knock at the door and a day in court.

The fortunes of other bit players in the Mokbel saga were also changing. When Mokbel fled Australia he had knocked his old chum the Grifter off the top perch as the nation's most wanted international fugitive. When Mokbel was nabbed the Grifter resumed pole position. And the bizarrely mirroring lives of the duo continued when just months after authorities pounced on Mokbel in Greece they also grabbed the Grifter in Holland.

The Grifter was arrested at Amsterdam airport about to board a flight to Thailand with a fake passport. In late September 2008 he lost his fight against extradition from the Netherlands. He was flown home and formally charged and was back in local custody by New Year 2009.

A month after Tony's stylish but drenched homecoming, Danielle McGuire and her two daughters arrived in Melbourne with less fanfare on a commercial flight from Athens. Federal police arranged special treatment for the fugitive's girlfriend. They snuck her out a side door of the terminal so she would not have to face the waiting press. When the press tracked her to her mother's place an agitated male friend from a neighbouring block threatened to release dogs on them.

Danielle must have grown accustomed to the ocean views in Elliniko. Someone paid for the unemployed former hairdresser to reside in an exclusive Albert Park apartment complex touted as a 'boutique building located on Melbourne's premier beachfront boulevard'. The Mokbel men were all locked up, Renate had been jailed, and Horty's wife, Roula, was being pursued. Police were freezing and seizing any Mokbel asset they could find, but somehow Fat Tony still had funds flowing even once he was locked in the most sterile and monitored square metres in the country. Ms McGuire's home – advertised at $590 rent a week with a $3000 bond – included a gymnasium, steam room and heated outdoor lap pool.

McGuire returned to driving her $40,000 Ford Territory around town, shuttling her older daughter to an exclusive Brighton girls' school. Her lifestyle fuelled speculation that Mokbel had more hidden away than just a few buried jam jars in Bonnie Doon. Purana had said what they managed to seize was probably only a sixth of the fortune. Then, in that context, in October 2008 public body Legal Aid Victoria, in their infinite wisdom, decided they would accept multimillionaire Tony's application for the public to fund his defence. It had been a long relationship between Legal Aid and the Mokbels. Property documents show the public body had placed a caveat, most likely for a debt owed, on Ma Mokbel's Brunswick house near the start of Tony's criminal career.

Mokbel meanwhile was acclimatising to his new digs on the arid plains away from the Athenian sunshine. After crashing to earth in a cold, sterile cell the plucky little pill merchant bounced back, appearing chirpy and dapperly dressed at his court appearances in a series of primary colour ties and expensive suits. This was Tony's strength: convincing people he was a people person, not a killing-people person. If he had been a politician you would have had him out on the hustings pressing flesh around the clock. And when it came to the Lewis Moran murder trial, that's essentially what his defence team did. Instead of hiding their notorious client away they made Mokbel an exhibit.

Mokbel's latest platoon of taxpayer-funded legal eagles set about whittling down their client's lengthy list of charges. Mokbel had a minor legal win in his early court appearances. Three conspiracy charges were dropped because of a quirk of extradition law that required the laws of the fled-to country have the same offence on their books. He then had a much bigger win. In April 2009 prosecutors dropped the Michael Marshall murder charge, primarily based on the Runner's account, due to a lack of evidence. Multiple drug charges aside, that left only the small matter of Lewis Moran getting two bullets in his head in a public bar in the middle of 'Tonytown' – Sydney Road, Brunswick.

The city had been through a decade of gangland killings, colourful characters and their consequent court cases. Art and life had imitated each other to such an extent that courts banned the screening in Victoria of a TV drama, *Underbelly*, about the shootings. The woman behind the ban, Judge Betty King, was a tough beak, prolific issuer of suppression orders, and self-dubbed 'queen of banning things'. Her hard-nosed outlook was likely the consequence of the nature of her work. She had sat through four trials in a row where the victims' bodies had been respectively electrocuted, chopped up and put in wombat holes, burnt, and dismembered and flushed down a toilet. King also kyboshed a televised debate between gangland matriarchs Judy Moran and Carl's mother, the late Barb Williams.

Judge King ruled *Underbelly* could not screen in Victoria while the murder trial of the men accused of shooting Lewis Moran was underway. The gangland drama had used real names and was based on real events. The ban was put in place in February 2008. Broadcasting network Channel Nine fought the screen gag in a series of legal actions but it was not until September that they were allowed to show just the first five episodes in edited form. But by then, true to their criminal roots, Victorians had simply obtained and watched bootleg copies of the show en masse. The court ban simply added an illicit thrill to the couch-potato activity of watching a DVD. But as Judge King herself later noted, it was not actually an offence to watch, only to broadcast.

Mooted restrictions placed on *Underbelly* only boosted Mokbel's mystique. They included pixilating the face of the actor playing Mokbel and overdubbing any references to 'Tony' or similar with 'Mr B'. Local papers were banned from even publishing the photo of the actor playing Mokbel. By the time Mokbel's murder trial for allegedly bankrolling the hit on Lewis Moran came around, even the lawyers in the bullet-riddled city were talking like Raymond Chandler.

Prosecutor Andrew Tinney launched the Crown case that Fat Tony paid the killers to execute Lewis Moran as a counterpunch against the Carlton Crew. 'In March 2004 there lived a man in Melbourne called Lewis Moran. Victoria was in the midst of a violent and long-running conflict,' Mr Tinney commenced. 'Carl Williams was at the centre of much of the violence ... Lewis Moran was in grave danger. Carl Williams hated Lewis Moran. Carl Williams hated the Moran family generally and wanted its members dead.'

The two gunmen and the driver involved in the death of the 58-year-old drug-dealing grandfather had been convicted over it. The hit organiser, Carl Williams, had also put his hand up to the murder. The Crown said Carl's friend Mokbel procured and funded the execution – but Tony denied any involvement. The getaway driver, who cannot be named but who we will call 'Bones', told police Mokbel was up to his neck in the Lewis Moran murder plot and had bankrolled the hit.

At Tony's trial Bones gave evidence that he met Tony in the carpark of Bridie O'Reilly's Irish pub in Brunswick three days after Lewis was killed. Mokbel popped the boot of a silver Mercedes-Benz and pointed to a large yellow envelope stuffed with $50 and $100 notes, saying the money was 'all there', Bones said. But Bones claimed Mokbel had shortchanged him on the kill payoff and the envelope contained $140,000, not the agreed $150,000.

A Purana detective gave evidence that Carl had offered Bones the kill contract when they were both at the Mokbel-connected Grove Cafe in Coburg. Bones said Mokbel had reassured him before the killing that Lewis Moran was not under police surveillance. Bones said when the job was done Mokbel asked him if he was interested in any more work.

'I expressed a bit of anger at that comment,' Bones said. 'Tony patted me on the back and said "no offence" and I said "no offence taken".'

But Mokbel's legal team accused Bones of lies, damned lies and calumny. And they made the most of his decidedly dodgy past. Bones had been convicted of killings going back to the 1970s and was a member of a notorious crime family. 'This case is about one individual and one individual only,' defence barrister Peter Morrissey told the jury. '[Bones] is the reason why we are all here. Apart from [Bones] no one puts Tony Mokbel into the crime at all.'

The defence painted Bones as a vicious, deceitful rough-around-the-edges gutter crim. It did not help that cross-examination revealed Bones had lied under oath at a coronial inquest during the eighties. 'We all lied in those days, including the police,' Bones said.

Bones argued that he had been getting square and doing only legitimate work like plastering before the Moran killing. But the defence pointed out that less than a year earlier he had killed Shane Chartres-Abbott in the bizarre 'vampire gigolo' case.

The accused had been shuttled from Barwon to the Supreme Court and sat in the dock at the back of the courtroom in an expensive navy pinstripe suit. In contrast to Bones, Tony was a mild-mannered dapper gentleman whose name had been dragged through the mud. Mokbel's barrister, Morrissey, told the jury not to be afraid of the notorious figure and to turn around and have a look at him. As the jurors gazed Tony did his best impression of beatific humility.

'Tony Mokbel is a well-known person,' Morrissey said. 'You know he left Australia, you know he was brought back here, you know he is facing other charges. If he is guilty, you find him guilty

… just don't start off with the sense that "Oh well, it is Mokbel, he must have done it."'

Bones had got a sentencing deal of life with a minimum of nineteen years for the three killings he had done in just twelve months, and his motives for testifying against Tony were questioned in court. In the end Morrissey told jurors it was they who could write the ending to the story. 'You as the jury now have the edge on the press and all those in the entertainment industry,' he said.

The jury deliberated for three and a half days. When they returned Mokbel stood in the dock, held his breath and clasped his hands tightly together. The judge asked if the jury had reached its verdict and the foreman replied: 'Not guilty.' A smile flickered over Mokbel's mouth and he closed his eyes before shaking his barrister's hand. When the judge thanked the jury before dismissing them Tony shouted from the dock: 'And I thank you too.'

All homicide claims against Mokbel had fallen by the wayside. In both the Michael Marshall and Lewis Moran murders an admitted member of the killing squad fingered Tony as the paymaster. But both witnesses were discounted because of their criminal pasts. Similarly imperfect witnesses had got Carl Williams to do a deal and get jailed for decades. But in Carl's case there were a choir of them singing. The Crown witnesses against Mokbel in both murder cases were soloists.

What would have helped prosecutors would have been Williams turning Crown witness and claiming that Mokbel was involved in the executions with him. Police said there was a reason that did not happen. 'Roberta Williams has still got her kids going out to

Penleigh private school in Essendon,' said former Purana chief Jim O'Brien. 'Who's funding that? That's still being paid for by Tony Mokbel, I can tell you. So there's money still sitting there.'

Other legal observers were bewildered that the Marshall murder charges were laid and the Moran murder trial was run at all on such scant evidence. 'I struggle to understand how those murder charges were run. They were probably only run because he is who he is,' one court source said. 'Good on them for running them but I never thought he was going to go down for them. It's a testament to the success of the jury system that even someone as notorious as Mokbel can receive a fair trial.'

For a brief beautiful moment the real world corresponded with Tony's reality. He could beat any charge and would be smart enough to get out of jail while he still had plenty of life to live. Mokbel would have felt like a big celebration after knocking out the most serious charge. But instead of wine, women and song he would be bundled back into a van and returned to the loneliness and ennui of his cell at Barwon.

Mokbel still had a swag of drug charges to face. Police and prosecutors predicted he would get a long stretch if only for his remote control of The Company's large-scale drug trafficking. Authorities had hoped Mokbel would go down for the Lewis Moran murder then get a decent whack from the judge. That, they believed, would have snapped Mokbel out of his delusional fugue and made him want to do a deal on all remaining charges – possibly, they hoped, even roll over on a few of his old crim and cop mates.

But the success of Mokbel's various lawyers slowly and surely cutting charges from the super-crim's lengthy docket has made it seem that reality is bending to Mokbel's sheer bloody-minded intransigence rather than the other way around. Like a twisted, sociopathic version of a Disney tale Mokbel has taken the if-you-believe-in-yourself-you-can-achieve-anything philosophy to disturbing lengths.

Mokbel lawyers told how the approximately twenty charges against their client were reduced to eighteen once back in Australia. With the Michael Marshall murder dropped and the Lewis Moran murder beaten it left sixteen. That was then whittled down further – due to overlap and as part of the usual pre-trial legal horse-trading – to a charge of drug trafficking, a charge of incitement to import, two charges of conspiracy to traffick and four charges of trafficking a large commercial quantity. A single 'large commercial quantity' charge can attract a life sentence and Tony faced four of them.

A source from the Mokbel camp, perhaps a tad optimistic, said if Tony went down it would be for a minimum of something more like twelve years than the police hope of twenty.

Next Mokbel appealed his cocaine conviction. Tony had hoped if he successfully overturned it he could apply for bail and be free and at large pending his other cases. A free Tony once more at large while awaiting his other hearings would have been a revival worthy of Lazarus. 'He is the most chirpy, positive person I've come across,' one of his lawyers said.

In the end Mokbel's appeal against the cocaine rap was unsuccessful and the court left the original decision and sentence in place. Mokbel had enjoyed a seemingly inexhaustible supply of lives and a feline ability to fall on his feet when all odds were against him. Only the future would tell whether beating the murder raps and the shedding of charges was just his dead cat bounce or yet another rallying comeback.

The state's two highest security units – Acacia and Melaleuca – sit like two small jails in the belly of the large stone prison that is Barwon. The jail's vicious inmates have included Christopher Wayne Hudson, the Hell's Angel behind a lethal rampage in Melbourne's CBD, and John Sharpe, the Mornington monster who killed his daughter and pregnant wife with a speargun.

Mokbel's jailbird existence has consisted of being locked up in complete isolation in a four-metre-by-three-metre shoebox cell in the Acacia unit for eighteen hours a day. The contents of his cell are a kettle, small television, toilet and shower. There are no hooks or pointy surfaces, only bevelled edges, bolted-down fixtures and taps designed so that nothing, including inmates, can be hung on them. A sign at the entrance to the Acacia unit reads 'Blood Spill Kit'.

The ultra high security units have a team of wardens behind a transparent wall watching over a spartan common area and a line of locked doors. There is a square head-high window in the door of Mokbel's cell but the view is only of the back of a curtain hung on the wardens' side. Another curtain blocks any view through ventilation slats in the bottom of the door. They are there to prevent visual communication between the unit's inmates and awareness of the wardens' movements.

In Tony's cell a small fortified window to the outside world provides a rare source of stimulation. Upward-pointing external slats mean there is no view across the prison grounds or the flat and barren Lara landscape beyond. To see anything at all through the window Mokbel would have to bend his knees and crane his neck up to gaze out wistfully. The view is what another one-time jailbird called 'that little tent of blue which prisoners call the sky'.

Mokbel's days of dapper dressing are for the moment a distant memory. His designer suits can only be brought out of the prison's property area for his video-link court appearances. If Danielle got them dry-cleaned they had to be scanned and checked again on re-entry. For now his uniform is the Barwon high-security baggy red, which he can mix and match with a white T-shirt and white sneakers. The puffy tracksuits tend to make even the most hardened criminals look like extras in a kids' play about the blood bank. When Carl Williams was once brought to court in his he looked like a big huggable Teletubby, not a quadruple killer.

Tony's children and Danielle have braved the arduous security regime to visit him. Acacia unit visitors can be subject to vehicle searches, drug tests, eyeball scans, walk-through metal detectors, guards with metal detecting wands, pat-down and pocket searches and sniffer-dog checks before getting to their loved ones. Some scans and checks are done several times over as they enter the prison within the prison.

Danielle was not, at least initially, approved for contact visits with Tony. Instead she would have had to talk in a confessional-style box through a glass screen to the lover she followed halfway around the globe. Their relationship was said to be on again, off again, then on the rocks, then finally in shards. McGuire got a new man in her life, another bad boy for love, this time a senior Bandido bikie. Milad and wife, Renate, had also reportedly split.

During the six hours a day Mokbel's cell is open he gets 'outdoor' time and a small chance to socialise. But it is not exactly the great outdoors. He is moved to a bigger concrete cell with a locked door that has four tall concrete walls, a concrete floor and a web of wires where the roof should be.

He is locked in there with a maximum of two other inmates from the high-security compound. The yard, where the men can smoke, contains a kettle and a bolted-down table with attached metal chairs. The sky can be seen through the wire overhead but there is next to no sign of life and it's rare for birds to fly overhead. One yard has a boxing bag, a sloping sit-up device bolted to the floor and a speed ball. There is a metal toilet sunk into the concrete in the yards. It allows for the fact that even when they are 'out' they are locked in.

Mokbel has been using the yard to work out. He did not lose twenty kilograms like fellow Barwonite Carl Williams did before his murder, but jail sources said Not-So-Fat Tony has dropped some weight. While prisoners get up to two inmates in the yard for company, Tony and Carl were banned from playing together. Police were hoping they might instead start talking to them about each other and a few other characters.

There was a Mokbel family reunion of sorts behind the bars at Barwon. Tony was reunited with Horty and Milad (as well as one of the gunmen from the Lewis Moran hit) in a four-prisoner compound within Acacia. But it was a brief catch-up. Horty and Milad were soon moved to Port Phillip prison where they swapped their red tracksuits for green ones and enjoyed greater freedom, like going outdoors and having their cells open between 8 am and 8 pm.

Deemed not as at risk or as dangerous, Kabalan was sent to the lower security Loddon prison farm in central Victoria where prisoners can wander freely within the grounds, live in communal cottages, cook their own meals, and are locked in overnight together. He was quietly released in late 2009 and went back to live with Ma and his family at Chez Mokbel in Brunswick.

There is a court sketch of Kabalan where he looks like a man mountain with a head the size of a watermelon. When he comes to the door at the family home he is rotund and muscular but quite short. He is dressed like he has been labouring, he is polite, occasionally prickly, but has the family confidence, authority and down-to-earth nature. But the brother most likely to get square refused to spill the beans on the family's story.

'Our kids suffer at school, mate, because of what you print in the paper,' he said. 'To you it's all about the dollar. To me it's blood and family. Do you understand? No disrespect to you. My kids go to school or my brothers' kids and what happens then? They get into trouble. Teachers go against them. You don't understand all that,' Kabalan said.

'My daughter goes to get a job somewhere, she'll never get a job. Not in a million years because probably people know about the surname – and if it wasn't for people like you guys there'd be none of that.'

He noted that Tony had 'beaten all the major ones' but like most Mokbel family and friends he says Tony's story has been writ too large. 'Even when frigging Saddam Hussein got caught and everything, you put my brother before him [in the newspaper],' Kabalan told me.

With his brothers moved on Tony was left to the eerie silence of the high-security units with no compadres to charm and no audience to impress. On reprobates' row, where Mokbel's cell sits alongside the cells of terror plotters and gangland figures, there is no shouting through walls between inmates. There is no hollering to guards. And from the wardens' side of the doors there is not even any audible noise from the small televisions within. There is just the mute, melancholy soundtrack to a very stark existence.

Many of Mokbel's mates on the outside have moved on. Others remain staunch and listen sympathetically as Tony complains over the phone, 'Mate, they're kidding, aren't they?' about his public image. 'He's been charged with two murder charges. One got dropped and the other one he beat,' a friend said. 'There's a lot of fabricated stories and I know for a fact it's been blown out of proportion. They've made him Mr Big for no reason.'

As for admissions Mokbel made on covert recordings, the friend claimed Tony was often just big-noting and playing at being Mr Big. 'He was a lovely bloke. But it gets to your head. You start believing yourself once you've said something a few times.'

Renate Mokbel was also released from prison early on a home-detention program wearing an anklet that monitors her movements. She was to be housebound in the yellow mansion which authorities were set to sell. Any rift with Tony and Danielle over getting banged up was not permanent. For a while Danielle still visited Renate with her daughters in tow.

One of Mokbel's more recent ploys was to lobby prison authorities for improved conditions. Perhaps hoping to be moved to a closer, more comfortable jail, he has complained about the tyranny of distance between Geelong and Melbourne. Mokbel had faced a regular prison van commute to the city courts and back for his cases. But instead of an upgrade the prison told him that since he tires of the travel he can appear in court by video-link from the jail. More and more Mokbel was finding his reputation preceded him and the old charm didn't work quite like it used to.

To their mother, the Mokbel men, as when they were boys, can do no wrong. Lora Mokbel dresses in black for mourning and has a lot to mourn. She has lost the homeland she loved to war. She lost the husband she loved to death. And she has lost the four sons she loved to three Victorian prisons. 'To tell you the truth, if you ask me, I'm burnt out and heartbroken. What can I tell you?' Ma Mokbel said.

The sole Mokbel home that police know about but that remains unseized is the one she still sits out the front of – the one Sajih paid for with clean, hard-earned money.

As mini-Mokbels run, scream and shout inside, some of their parents statistically bound to be in jail, she told how her boys had been framed by jealous cops. 'The police are against them. They love to hurt them. They are intentionally against them to harm them, to lock them up in jail,' she said. 'I have no idea why, but it might be because they [my sons] are more powerful than them.'

Speaking from the verandah of her home in Melbourne's north, a big speedboat in the front yard, Mrs Mokbel told the author Tony was no killer and had earnt his millions honestly. 'This one feeds others. He does not kill,' she said. 'Tony used to put deposits on houses that were for sale and then rent them out and let it pay for itself,' she said. 'If you have five [thousand dollars] he would put ten out of his own pocket. If you gave him a [horseracing] tip, he would put on hundreds.'

Mrs Mokbel has a tough face, dark eyes, ruddy cheeks and the mourning dress of black cardigan, black headscarf and long black frock. She said she did not regret moving her family to Australia, despite the turn of events that followed. 'That's what happened. That is God's will,' she said.

Mrs Mokbel still spoke with her sons on the phone, but no longer made the journey to visit her boys in jail. 'They won't let me see them together, but [only] individually and my legs are painful,' she said. She said her sons were well liked in their old stamping grounds and in jail. According to Ma Mokbel the guards say nice things about the boys and they're good to their mother. 'Ask all the people in the neighbourhood about my sons' reputations, different nationalities – including Greeks – all talk well of them,' she said.

'My sons are very much liked by the prison guards. The guards tell me we have never seen anybody as good as your children here. The prison guards are very pleased with all of them. Since they were young, if anybody can say one bad word about my children they would be liars and I would feel like spitting on them,' she said, making a spitting gesture.

She said 'of course' she still felt that way now. 'Every time I speak to them they keep asking me, "Mum are you all right? Are you sick? Is anything wrong?"' she said. 'I swear on the life of my children, I promise, none of them has ever said to me, "Shut up."' She made the sign of the cross as she spoke of her four boys.

Relatives come and go and friendly neighbours wave to the woman who still has the look of a rural villager. 'I don't feel up to seeing anyone. I don't go anywhere,' she said. Asked what went wrong with her sons, she cited a sarcastic Lebanese saying which roughly translates to 'the pure people are many'.

After he had spent nearly three years in Barwon a small shift occurred in Tony Mokbel that would grow larger.

His old mate and fellow resident Carl Williams had been bashed to death by another inmate inside the jail. Danielle had drifted away. And with every bland Barwon dawn his outstanding charges were marching relentlessly towards trial.

As he went through his paces on his umpteenth vigorous workout and his millionth Sudoku number puzzle, Tony, the ultra-gambler and epic legal obfuscator, thought about many things. Good times. Bad times. Blood brothers. Arch enemies. Wine. Pizza. Women. Cards. Characters. Crimes. And finally, inevitably, he thought about the cases against him and found himself warming to a bet against type.

Some of the trafficking charges were quite old and not too strong. Tony's barrister (his latest was Peter Faris) should be able to unpick them at the seams before a credulous jury. But the Operation Magnum case – the recorded phone conversations and turncoat witness evidence involving The Company and his time in Greece – that was not very weak at all. The police prosecution brief ran to twenty volumes. The case had been listed to be heard first and all his lawyers' attempts at staying and delaying it had failed. Tony was a gambler but he was not a fool. If he fought the Magnum case he would be punished more severely for failing to even feign remorse and costing the public purse the huge expense of that and his other trials. Mokbel's lawyers and the prosecution lawyers had talked about possible deals. But then Tony was always saying, 'Let's do a deal.' Years earlier he had aggressively cornered Agent Ragg at the Supreme Court saying, 'I'll do two years.' But whether Mokbel could agree to a deal on his current batch that would ever be palatable to the state was regarded as unlikely. And then in April 2011 Tony Mokbel proved he was still full of surprises.

By the time Mokbel came back to court to settle his cases he had been an invisible man in his home state for more than two years. A stroke of a judge's pen and a huge number of gag orders had effectively erased Mokbel's name, history and existence from Melbourne's newspapers, airwaves and conversations. The blackout had seen Tony compared in whispered tones to Voldemort – the unspeakable name of the villain in the Harry Potter books.

In the end Tony's legal team and the Office of Public Prosecutions came to the table and did a deal. Mokbel pleaded guilty to trafficking a large commercial quantity of methamphetamine, trafficking a large commercial quantity of MDMA, and inciting the undercover operative to import a commercial quantity of MDMA into Australia; and the prosecution agreed not to pursue the other trafficking charges.

Tony's pleas were expected to get him about another two decades inside. And almost certain to make him the last of the brothers to walk out the front gates to freedom. Very hard time indeed. But still a lot less than life, and then death, behind bars and then exile inert and horizontal in a box. If he serves out two decades Mokbel will be in his mid-sixties when released and still have some life to live. Any legitimate money he might earn upon release is likely to be instantly swallowed by the tax office, which reckons he owes them a mint. But he still has associates holding property and assets that can be turned into cash whenever he wants. And he still has, police believe, untraceable millions squirrelled away.

Tony's story is all but played out. Yet there remain any number of final twists to his already curly tale. In fact two additional twists have played out in the time since the above sentence was written. No sooner had the ink on Mokbel's sentence deal dried than it emerged in an unrelated case that Victoria Police officers were routinely signing but failing to swear – on a bible or by affirmation – affidavits which they would then use to get search warrants against suspects. Sniffing opportunity in this development, Mokbel promptly reneged on the plea deal and went back to court to reverse his guilty pleas. His legal team got a series of officers involved in the Mokbel investigation to admit on the stand that they also failed to swear their affidavits.

Prosecutors argued that their case against the jailbird was strong, even without the affidavit evidence. Then the state government rushed to pass a retrospective 'Tony's law' to stop Mokbel and potentially thousands of other incarcerated crims walking from jail due to the police bungles. Awaiting a result, Tony went back to the boredom of a Barwon existence unleavened by legal intrigue. He focused on his workouts, his flexes, curls and crunches, and – like celluloid jailbird Cool Hand Luke – gobbling up to a dozen eggs a day in a protein-enriched mission to get buff. His father's genes and the eggs took their toll. In February 2012 Mokbel had a mild heart attack and was rushed to hospital where he had a stent put in. Bad news, like some kind of dastardly double-yolker, comes in pairs. The next month, as Tony recovered, the Supreme Court came back with its decision: Mokbel could not revoke his earlier guilty pleas.

Mokbel could still die in jail of natural causes. He is less than a decade from the age Sajih was when he died of a heart attack. Or he could die in jail of unnatural causes like his friend Carl. Less likely but still possible, he could mount a jailbreak and another successful escape.

The latter would be quite an achievement. No one has escaped from Barwon prison. The units are surrounded by four-metre-high concrete walls, electric fences and sound, motion and infrared sensors. The jail's walls have microwave and microfibre technology.

But it would be betting against experience to suggest Mokbel has learnt his lesson and would not attempt something brazen once stuck with an imposing sentence.

Alternatively Mokbel could serve his time quietly and without incident and gradually fade from public interest and view until released as an older man to a generation that knows little about his exploits. 'I hope that he would serve a lengthy jail sentence as an example to the Australian community that this kind of organised crime, public notoriety, celebration of the criminal is unacceptable,' Agent Ragg said. 'I'd like to think his role in Victorian organised crime history is over. And I think Victoria Police have done an outstanding job in dismantling the Mokbel organised crime empire.'

That ending would also please ex-Purana inspector Jim O'Brien, who despises high-profile criminals getting second acts in the public eye. 'I think they should just go to jail and be forgotten about and rot where they are,' he said. But, like the Lebanese adage, manacled and tossed into the sea Mokbel is just as likely to emerge with a fish.

Another possibility – and one publicly derided by Mokbel's legal team – is he takes an already workable sentence (and an absolute bargain compared to his actual guilt) and whittles it down further by doing deals on what he knows about police corruption.

Anything seems possible for the closing chapter in the fast, infamous life and unprecedented saga of the nation's bigwig of crime. Maybe Tony Mokbel will be like Paleokostas, double down on his already brazen reputation and pull off something dangerous, dazzling and remarkable. Or perhaps he will emulate the demise of

Squizzy Taylor and do his time only to be released into a society that has forgotten him and a new criminal landscape in which there is no space for him. A world for which he once held the title but where he has become powerless and where there is no longer respect for or fear of him. A gangland where the one-time bigwig who crammed four lifetimes into one is left out, old-fashioned, obsolete. Where Fat Tony is finally all out of time.

Epilogue

At the time of writing:

Carl Williams was murdered in April 2010 by another inmate wielding a piece of exercise bike. Victoria Police merged the probe into the unsolved Hodsons' killing with that of Carl's death in prison. Prisoner Matthew Johnson pleaded self-defence but in September 2011 a jury convicted him of Williams's murder.

The gangland war had sputtered from outrageous to pathetic. At the time of writing, the most recent fatalities of gangland figures were Carl's jailhouse death, the sad, lonely suicide of his mum and George's estranged wife, Barbara Ann, and the shooting of peripheral figure Des 'Tuppence' Moran at the behest of his sister-in-law Judy.

Judy Moran was convicted of ordering the murder of her brother-in-law 'Tuppence'.

On Sydney Road two hundred yuppies were set to move into the bluestone jail that beat Ronald Ryan, Christopher Flannery and Chopper Read. The intimidating structure that breathes Melbourne criminal history was converted into an apartment precinct – 'Pentridge piazza', complete with cafe. Brunswick locals have so far kept Tony's former five shopfronts along Sydney Road as just that. They had not been turned into a giant 'Bent Penis' or even straight high-rise developments.

Renate Mokbel was released early on a home-detention scheme. She was living in the Downs Street mansion but it was expected to be auctioned as a proceed of crime. She and Danielle managed to patch up any hard feelings with Danielle visiting her at the Brunswick home.

Zarah Garde-Wilson kept Caine's sperm but it was a smaller-time crim's babies she ended up having – a daughter, then later, twins, to a defendant called Lansley Simon with a string of priors, the most recent of which, spray-painting handbags at Versace's Crown Casino store, seemed more like a political or artistic statement than a misdemeanour. She was caught at a jail with 100 needles and 125 syringes in her car boot after claiming they were for her boyfriend who used steroids; she was never charged.

Agent Jarrod Ragg, of the AFP, got an Australian Police Medal on Australia Day 2009.

Detective Jim Coghlan, of Purana, did not.

Victoria Police and the AFP remain the best of friends.

Kabalan Mokbel's outstanding charges were dropped in a nolle prosequi (application by the prosecution to withdraw charges) shortly after Tony did his deal.

Horty Mokbel was accused of assaulting another prisoner but the case had not run at the time of writing.

Danielle McGuire continued to be unlucky in love. Her latest beau, Bandido sergeant-at-arms Toby Mitchell, was gunned down, though not fatally, in broad daylight in Brunswick in 2012.

Pillar of Hercules, at the time of writing, was still racing, just under less colourful new owners.

Steve from the Bonnie Doon shop had replaced his *The Castle*-influenced 'Bonnie Doon – ahhh the serenity' T-shirts with a Mokbel-influenced 'Bonnie Doon – the perfect hideaway' line of apparel.

Acknowledgements

There are a hundred people to thank for this book. Their endless contributions make the final product that has just one name on the spine. They don't get a curtain call, group bow or orchestra claps. For credit, but not for blame, are the following: my parents, my siblings, my friends, my teachers, my family, my colleagues, my contacts, my bosses, my publisher.

Thank you to those whose availability, honesty and candour were priceless. In many instances their sense for the story extended beyond answers to valuable tips, like pointing me in the direction of the serial Greek escapees who could be a book in themselves. Some strange bedfellows follow. But for helping me tell the story you're all beautiful to me.

Bernie Edwards, reassuring proof in a world full of self-promoters that humble people can still get ahead. Jim Coghlan, Jim O'Brien and Jarrod Ragg for their availability, good humour and candour. The bad boys might have better cars but the good guys have better jokes. Thank you also for updating my police lingo. ('Back in the eighties, mate, it might have been a wire.') Thank you to Lora Mokbel for revealing her perspective on her family's remarkable tale and to the Mokbel family and friends, here and abroad, including Kabalan and Gawy, who, while often reluctant, were never rude. Also: Mick Gatto, Judy Moran, Brian Murphy, Christine Nixon, Simon Overland, Roberta Williams and Bert Wrout. And for sources who it's in nobody's interest to name but who are the most important and for whom I will always remember the favour. You have to be recognised here like dead heroes in black ops but know who you are: * * * * * * * * * * * * *

For outright help or keeping a secret: Queenie, Laurie Nowell, Nick Richardson and the Meerkat. (Squareheads don't usually get pseudonym, but I'm told it's necessary in this case.) Thank you to the Meerkat for casting your eye, introducing me to the Ice Man, reminding me that the anecdote – like the chopper – is key, and that the punter not the purist is king. Hopefully unlike the chopper the anecdotes got the job done. Thanks to dawn-patrolling racing writer Rod Nicholson for checking my horse talk.

For blunt inspiration: Filthy, who fearlessly faced cancer and came out the other side unchanged, untempered and inappropriate. I never realised how much I liked you until you nearly kicked the bucket. You're almost like a brother to me.

Also to two hardboiled paddies who gave me creepy inspirational advice during the hard grind of research and writing. One, after explaining why it is wise to do oral interviews with police instead of writing your own statement: 'You will not know the answer if the question has not been asked.' The other, on the sometimes sphincter-clenching nature of asking impolite, inappropriate and impertinent questions: 'If you want to eat chops you've got to cut the throats of lambs.' You both know who you are.

There is next to no attribution once the story starts because I did not want to break up what I hope is the potboiler flow of the story with constant references to newspaper mastheads or nods to friends and acquaintances. So thank you to the journalists and authors whose hard work I pillaged to try to tell the whole Tony story. In rough order of most pillaged in quasi-topical clusters: Ed O'Loughlin, Fiona Hudson, Bill Hayton, Peter Wilson, David Murray, James Button, Helena Smith and Charles Miranda (Lebanon and Greece), John Silvester (Howden and prison pizzas), Geoff Wilkinson, Adrian Dunn, Nick McKenzie, Rod Nicholson (the track), Sue Hewitt and Laurie Nowell (the Octopus). Thank you to others whose work I've drawn on: Kate Hagan, Milanda Rout, John Silvester and Andrew Rule, Lauren Wilson, Adam Shand, the various authors of *Brunswick: One History Many Voices*, Anthony Dowsley, Keith Moor, Paul Anderson, Chris Johnston, Natasha Robinson, Katie 'Miami' Bice, Daniel Breen, Padraic Murphy, Elissa Hunt, Peter Gregory, Ross Brundrett. I'm sure I've missed some.

Thank you to those whose help with information and arranging interviews was also vital: Anne Stanford, Christine Panayotou, Nicole McKechnie, Nat Webster, the State Library of Victoria, Marika Fengler, Adam West, John Ferguson, Ann Strunks. Again I'm sure I've forgotten some and apologise in advance. Thanks to Loreto Kelly for shorthand and Rosemary Smallwood for vitamin C tablets and coldsore cream.

For career help I'd like to thank in order of appearance: Simon Castles, Iain Shedden, Rosemary Neill, Peter Blunden, Simon

Pristel, Damon Johnston, Chris Tinkler, Laurie Nowell, the refreshingly relaxed Mel Cain, and Julian Gray.

Sometimes the story is good enough to carry the words but for when it's not and the roles have to be reversed thank you to my inspirational writing heroes Camus, Greene, Wolfe and Morrissey.

For general recognition of help, support or for just being stand-up people who don't fit easily into a particular category I'd like to thank: Queenie, Fritzy and Gerry for allowing a dodgy lodger and providing random Melbourne and sports facts, Bry for French tips, Ned, Reezie, Nikita, Segolene, Prince, Robbo, Paddy, Moses, Red, Stevie, the McGraths, Toj and Mick, and Harry Zein.

The author can be contacted at tip.the.hack@gmail.com

www.ingramcontent.com/pod-product-compliance
Lightning Source LLC
Chambersburg PA
CBHW022030290426
44109CB00014B/810